Like downhill racers Europe's ski resorts each have their own style. Some dare expert skiers looking for thrills, others coax stem-christies from uncertain beginners; some pulse with nightlife, others sooth with the crackle of a flickering fire; some resemble a space station forced onto a mountainside, others provide a cozy step back into time. *Ski Europe* pictures the different personalities of over sixty European ski resorts. It is the perfect tool for helping skiers choose the best resort for their abilities and dreams.

Franz Klammer

For our European readers

This holiday guide to skiing was first published to explain the benefits of skiing in Europe to Americans. Now, with distribution throughout the United Kingdom and Ireland, we hope that the guide will help you choose your resort.

Ski Europe provides detailed information on lift ticket prices, ski school prices, hotel prices, restaurant recommendations, the best nightlife, child care facilities and how to arrange lodging in holiday apartments in each resort.

All prices are quoted in the local currencies, telephone numbers for resort information offices are international, and the national tourist office addresses are included for the U.K. as well as for Canada and the U.S.A. Other than a few references to dealing with the journey from the Americas to Europe, the information in this guide is valuable to anyone planning to ski in Europe.

I hope you enjoy *Ski Europe* and that it serves you well. If you have any comments, please write to me. The address is: Charles Leocha, World Leisure Corporation, PO Box 160, Hampstead, NH 03841, U.S.A.

Good skiing!! I hope to meet you on the slopes this winter.

Charlie Leocha

CHARLES LEOCHA AND WILLIAM WALKER

SKI EUROPE

WINTER 1989

A comprehensive guide to skiing Europe's best resorts

World-Leisure Corporation

Boston, Ma   Hampstead, NH

Send mail to:
World-Leisure Corporation
P.O. Box 160
Hampstead, NH 03841

Cover design by Jackie Schuman, New York

Illustrated country maps by Charles Kaufman

Printed in the United States of America

Distributed to the trade in USA, Canada and Phillipines by
Kampmann and Company, Inc., New York
Tel. (800) KAMPMAN or (212) 685-2928

Distributed to the trade in Europe by
Roger Lascelles, 47 York Road, Brentford, Middlesex TW8 0QP
Tel. 01-847 0935.

Distributed to U.S. Military, Stars & Stripes Bookstores, Mail Order and Special Sales by
World Leisure Corporation, 177 Paris Street, Boston, MA 02128
Tel. (617) 569-1966.

Library of Congress Card Catalog Number: 87-050899

ISBN: 0-915009-09-9

CONTENTS

Ski Europe

New powder, a packed piste, moguls and bumps, a steep and narrow run, lunch at a tiny mountain restaurant amid the sun, the clouds, the sudden shadows . . .

Then, a soothing sauna, a dip in the pool, a leisurely meal with a fine wine, a moonlight sleigh ride, a fireside interlude in a cozy lodge, or dancing at a disco . . .

Or, a full day of strolling, shopping and sightseeing as you wander through Venice, Milan, Zurich, Munich or Salzburg . . .

This is not a dream. This is the reality of a ski vacation in Europe, one that can actually be less expensive than a similar vacation to U. S. resorts. That's because there are two major factors to be considered in the cost of a ski vacation: getting there and back, and staying alive in the manner to which you've become accustomed. More on this later.

Why Europe?

Until now, skiing in Europe has been considered a dream vacation—extremely expensive and difficult to arrange. That is all changing. Airfares, which have been dropping, are at their lowest during the winter months. European ski resorts have also benefited from the same tourist realities that make Italy and France great inexpensive summer vacation destinations, as well as some of the least expensive summer vacation destinations, as well as some of the least expensive winter destinations. Austria and Switzerland, which may seem like expensive destinations, have organized their respective skiing industries in order to transform their resorts into vacation bargains.

Time factors

One of the major obstacles to skiing in Europe you'll hear about during any discussion is time: "I don't want to spend all my vacation time traveling. I want to ski." In fact, though, it takes only slightly more time to reach a European ski resort than to reach many resorts closer to home.

Consider the average urban skier, who needs about seven hours or more to reach a major ski resort. If you take a closer look, the air and land transporation to a ski resort in the western United States from the East Coast can add up to seven hours. Even a drive from Philadelphia or New York to prime New England resorts can take seven hours or more. Traveling to Europe takes about the same time and, normally, it takes only another two hours or so to reach its skiing areas.

Cost factors

As was mentioned, there are two major factors that affect the overall cost of a ski vacation. The first is transportation, the cost of getting to the slopes from where you live. Second are the costs of getting onto the slopes and of keeping yourself alive in whatever manner you're used to. These include hotels, meals, lift tickets and other goodies.

Minor costs are those related to child-care services, buying ski fashions, evening entertainment and so on.

For a European ski vacation, the transportation cost factor will be the largest. And, while it normally costs more to travel to a European ski area than to a U. S. destination, once you have arrived at the European resort the second cost factor becomes much more important. The differences in hotel, meal and lift pass prices are phenomenal. Cheaper by far than U. S. prices, they more than make up for the increased transportation costs. Even the minor costs are much less in Europe than in the U. S.

A skier traveling to Europe from an East Coast city in the U. S. will actually save money on a one-week vacation. Similarly, a skier traveling to Europe from the West Coast will save money on any European ski vacation lasting two weeks or more.

Ski Europe

This book will help you get the best value for your money while skiing in Europe. Explained are the best times to ski in Europe, and which months guarantee the lowest hotel prices and smallest crowds on the slopes. Also provided are tips based on certain institutional facts that color the European skiing scene, which can be taken advantage of in order to get more for your money. What we mean by "more" is more time on the slopes, more time with instructors, a more spacious hotel room, better meals at restaurants and bargains in getting to Europe and getting around in the mountains.

What's new with this edition

This edition has been expanded to include the best hotels in each resort—or at least what we consider the best, middle of the road accommodations and the budget pensions. We also have listed the best restaurants—both high-priced and high-cuisine, as well as restaurants with those very affordable, traditional good-value meals. If you are going to ski in Europe and plan to shoot the works, take this book along. It will show you just where to aim your spending. Or, if you are traveling with a family and looking for ways to stretch your budget, this book will tell you when to travel for the maximum savings and includes information on apartments which allow real savings and on daycare facilities which allow real freedom to ski.

A disclaimer on pricing

The prices in this book were, to the best of our abilities, accurate as of press time; however, this means that, in most cases, the actual prices you will be reading are from the 1986/1987 ski season. The intention is to provide the best possible information for your planning purposes. At the beginning of each country section a price increase factor based on late reports from Europe will be included to let you know approximately how much the prices have increased during the past year. In general Switzerland and Austria's prices are expected to either remain the same or increase by only three to five percent. Italy

No hotel, restaurant or ski resort has paid to be included in this book. The recommendations have been made based on personal visits to each of the resorts mentioned and discussions with year-long residents in the resorts.

Help us do a better job

The research for this book has been ongoing for the past decade. We both spent every available weekend and vacation exploring new resorts or returned repeatedly to our favorites. Each ski season we return to update material, plus we visit new resorts in order to continue to expand the resort coverage.

If you find a new restaurant, hotel, bar, or disco, please write to us. Or if you find something in the book which is inaccurate, misleading, or has changed, please let us know. If we use your suggestion, we will include your name as the source and will send you a copy of the new Ski Europe. Send suggestions to: World-Leisure Corporation, Attn: Ski Europe, PO Box 160, Hampstead, NH 03841, U.S.A.

High versus low season

The ski season in Europe seems to follow the relatively institutionalized vacation cycles of the Europeans more closely than the cycle of snow conditions. There are normally three seasons in the lexicon of resort operators: the super-high season (holiday period) during Christmas, New Year and Easter; the normal high season, which falls between the first weekend in February and the end of March; and the low season, which includes December, until the weekend before Christmas, the period between the weekend after New Year and the first weekend of February, and April.

The reason for a category of super-high holiday prices is obvious. Increased rates for the February/March high season seem less-obviously justifiable. This "high season" was developed to coincide with the school spring vacation breaks, which normally take place in February. This is the month when families can take a vacation together. It also means that the slopes are covered with more children than usual, even changing in character to become open ski classrooms as thousands of budding downhill racers zip fearlessly down every run.

Skiers should do everything possible to avoid planning their ski vacations for the holiday and high-season periods.

Low season, on the other hand, teems with bargains. Low season means nearly empty slopes during midweek, short lift lines with almost no waiting, and hotel and restaurant services at their peak. And low season, especially high-altitude centers in January, offers some of the best snow conditions. In addition, in mid-March through April, beautiful, mild spring skiing is possible. Early December is often a period of good skiing and prices are normally their low-season lowest, but snow conditions can be spotty. Before going, skiers should check with the resorts for the latest snow conditions. High-altitude resorts, which offer summer skiing, are always guaranteed to have snow, especially those with glaciers.

How different are the prices?

Low-season discounts are not just promotional hype—prices really are different. In most areas, for example, ski school prices are 20 percent higher during high season. Lift ticket prices increase by almost 20 percent as well.

Hotels and pensions levy even more dramatic increases. For example, a hotel package that costs 420 Swiss francs (SFR) may cost SFR 469 in February and SFR 560 during the holiday season. That amounts to a 33 percent increase in price between low and super-high season. One Swiss hotel we looked at had prices that differed by 44 percent between low and high season. It's the same story in Italy, France, Austria and Germany, the bottom line being that you'll save a lot by planning your ski vacation during low season.

"White-week" packages

Every resort offers some form of "white week." This is a specially-priced ski package which includes full or half pension, based on a one-week stay. The costs of lift tickets and ski school are often included in the package price. If not, there are usually special prices in effect which can be combined with the hotel "white-week" package. At some resorts, these packages also include free entrance to a public pool, sauna and ice skating rink.

"White weeks" are *semaines blanches* in French; in German, they are called *Weisse Wochen*; and in Italy they are referred to as *settimani bianchi*.

We've used "white-week" prices throughout this book, since they represent the least expensive way to ski. In addition, we've outlined exactly what is included in the prices given for each resort.

An example of the savings available during a "white week" in Switzerland is a program offered by the Hotel Schweizerhof, a four-star hotel in St. Moritz. There, the normal weekly low-season rate is SFR 980 (about $650). That rate is for a room with half pension only. With ski lessons and lift tickets added, the week price is SFR 1332 ($888). The rate for the special white-week package—including a ski pass, lessons, races and torchlight skiing—is only SFR 885 (about $590) during December before Christmas; and only SFR 1070 (about $713) in January. This represents a bargain that is repeated regularly throughout the European ski resorts.

At France's famous resort, Val D'Isère, the "white week" is organized into a series of formulas based on the package desired, hotel classification and meal plan. These plans are only made available during the low seasons. Accommodations at a three-star hotel with bath, including half board, ski pass, pool entrance, plus a special ski insurance package, will cost only 2790 French francs (FFR) (about $490).

The same package, only with bed-and-breakfast, in the same hotel will cost FFR 2190 (about $385). A two-star hotel offers a similar package, including half board, for FFR 2415 ($423). The same three-star hotel arrangements if purchased separately could cost well over FFR 3575 ($628), meaning that he who takes advantage of the *semaines blanches* can save more than 20 percent.

Tignes, a resort just down the valley from Val D'Isère, shares the same lift system and slopes. One "white-week" package in Tignes requires staying in an apartment with no meals included, but a six-day ski pass is part of the package. The cost starts at FFR 1230 just before Christmas, which is about $215, or just $30 a day.

Thanks to the concept of low season and "white-week" packages, Europe can still be a skier's bargain paradise.

Getting to and around Europe

As we mentioned earlier, the most expensive part of a European ski vacation is transport. First, you have to cross the Atlantic, then you have to get to the resort. Simple enough, but doing your homework in order to get the best deal can be a bit complicated. A travel agent can help out with the specifics, but if you are a do-it-yourselfer, remember that there are tradeoffs between cost and convenience. In short, you want to go to Europe to ski and see as much as possible; you don't want to spend seemingly endless hours in bus and train stations waiting for connections to remote mountain valleys.

Obviously, the major cost to be borne is in getting yourself from the U. S. to Europe. While transport to Aspen, Colorado from New York City constitutes about thirty-seven percent of a week's ski vacation budget, the transport segment of a typical European ski vacation to Austria represents almost 60 percent of your total costs.

Trans-Atlantic air travel is also where a clever traveler can save the most money or end up spending far more than necessary. And the transfer from the airport to the resort can add up to significant costs in both time and money if you don't plan ahead.

Across the Atlantic

The airfares charged for crossing the Atlantic have been at all-time lows for several years. There is more capacity and more service from almost every area of the country, which makes getting to Europe more convenient, easier and less expensive than ever. And, of course, winter air travel works to a skier's advantage, since prices are often 40 to 50 percent lower than during the peak summer months.

A travel agent can be extremely helpful during this phase. Using one, however, should be supplemented by doing some investigating on your own. The airline fare structures are complicated, and seemingly changing on a daily basis—even with scheduled airlines. And when charters and group-tour flights are included, the options become phenomenally complex.

Tell the travel agent exactly what you are looking for and explain what you think you should have to pay based on ads in papers and brochures you have read. The agent will either confirm your opinions or will let you know what has changed since you last received information. Try to find an agent who will guarantee the lowest possible fare. These agents often will let you know exactly what is available and you can make a decision, even if it's to take a more expensive flight based on convenience or better connections. There is no additional cost for using a travel agent; you can only save both time and money by working through a good one.

Basically, you have three choices available for trans-Atlantic air travel:

Scheduled airlines—There are many advantages in taking a scheduled airline. The airline must adhere to its general schedule. If there is a problem with the aircraft, passengers are normally transferred to a flight on another airline. In emergencies, a scheduled airline offers flexibility with additional flights and interline connections.

Another aspect of the flexibility offered by scheduled airlines is the ability to land in one city and leave from another. Called "open jaw" in airlinespeak, this type of ticket allows you to land in Milan, ski the Italian side of the Matterhorn for a week, then head to Austria for the second week and fly home from Munich. You can also arrange limited stopovers for an additional charge, depending on your ticket, making it easy to squeeze in a few days in Paris or London on your way to the slopes or back home.

It helps to plan your trip as far in advance as possible. In order to get special airfares, which approach the lowest charter airline fares, many special tickets offered by scheduled airlines require advanced booking by as much as one month with advanced payment. Arrival and departure dates must be set in advance and any changes may result in additional charges.

Charter flights—These flights are money savers and in some cases offer excellent connections for skiers. Special flights organized for ski vacations often land at airports much closer to the slopes than any scheduled airline. For example, the charters for many of the French resorts land in Lyons or Geneva, both of which are much closer to the mountains than Paris. This eliminates a significant amount of transfer time. These special ski charters are often sold with transfers to the slopes, which can also help avoid delays and hassles.

There are some problems with charters. Often you are only guaranteed the flight date rather than a time. The charters also reserve the right to reschedule your flight, cancel it and add fuel charges. Your best protection is to fly with a charter airline that has been in business for some time, one that is familiar to your travel agent.

Try to get some form of flight cancellation insurance, in case you don't leave on the date requested, and also get additional medical insurance to cover the cost of an emergency trip home in case of an accident.

Package Tours—Package tours combine air travel, ground transfers and hotels. Make sure you understand exactly what you are getting in the package. The rates are normally very competitive; however, be sure to compare different programs. Seemingly identical packages, offering the same hotels, transfers, meals and dates can sometimes differ by as much as 44 percent in price. One tour we checked out cost $468, while an identical tour offered by another operator cost only $325.

Depending on currency fluctuations, package tours can either be big bargains or can end up costing you more than doing it yourself. Since many tour operators guarantee their rates for the entire season, they gamble on the currency-rate changes. If European currencies continue to drop against the U. S. dollar, the package tours, which are priced in the U. S. dollars, will be less of a bargain as the ski season progresses. In this case, you would do better flying to Europe and making your arrangements directly at the resort. However, if European currencies strengthen against the dollar, the package tour could become a better bargain for the skier. Since prices in this book are given in European currencies, it should be easy to compare whether the package is a better bargain than doing it yourself.

Dealing with jet lag

The most unwelcome traveling companion on an overseas ski vacation is jet lag. While there are no "cures," here are several suggestions that may help to ease you into the European time zone.

—Go to bed early and wake up earlier for three or four days before traveling to Europe. This will allow your body to get a gradual headstart in adjusting to European time. At 9 p.m. on the East Coast of the U. S., it is 3 a.m. in Western Europe. If you can go to bed between 9 and 10 p.m. for a few days before your trip, you will only have to overcome about three hours of jet lag rather than six all at once.

—Try to sleep as much as possible on the plane. Many people take sleeping pills and instruct stewardesses not to disturb them for meals or drinks. If you have a sleep mask, use it.

—Drink as little alcohol and eat as little as possible during the flight, but drink plenty of water since the air in the cabin is very dry.

—When you arrive at the resort, take about a two-hour nap during the afternoon or early evening. Make sure to get yourself up, then go out and explore the town, returning to sleep at about 11 p.m. or midnight.

Car rental

For the independent skier who wants to get the most out of a European ski vacation, a rental car offers the most flexibility and is a bargain—even when only two skiers share expenses. Rental cars can be picked up directly at the airport upon arrival in Europe. Aside from making getting to the ski resort a breeze, a rental car gives you freedom to explore the area around the resort or to take a short side trip if the weather isn't perfect or when you just want a break from skiing.

The driver of the car usually must be 21 years old and must have a valid driver's license which has been in effect for at least one year. It is not necessary to have an international driving license; your home state license is acceptable.

If you make reservations seven days in advance of your arrival with any of the major car rental companies, you will qualify for special European vacation rates. These rates normally are about $200 a week, excluding taxes. This means that two people sharing a car can expect to pay a little more than $100 apiece for transfers to the resort and more freedom during their stay.

Depending on where you pick up the car, you will have to pay additional value-added tax (VAT), which is significant. Current VATS are:

Germany	14 percent
Italy	18 percent
France	28 percent
Austria	21 percent
Spain	12 percent
Switzerland	none

As an example of how VAT can affect the total rental cost, consider a car that lists for $200 a week. Renting it will end up costing:

in Germany	$228
in Italy	$236
in France	$256
in Austria	$242
in Switzerland	$200

While the actual rental rates in all these countries are different, the point is that to rent your car in the most advantageous country, you must consider the value-added tax and drop-off charges if you plan on picking the car up in one country and dropping it off in another. Generally, there are no drop-off charges if the car is dropped off in the country where it was picked up. The best rental car deals in the Alps are in Germany.

We called Avis, which has locations near almost all the skiing areas of Europe. The prices for a category B car, including taxes and based on the exchange rate at the time of our conversation (May 25, 1988) were: in Germany—$207; in Italy— $250; in France—$278; in Austria—$251; in Switzerland—$239; and in Spain—$168.

When you make reservations, be sure to tell the reservation agent that you will require a ski rack and chains. Both are usually provided free of charge when ordered in advance. When you pick up the car the ski rack will be easy to see, but the chains must be scrutinized. Make sure that you have the correct size chains for your car. Check the number on the box carefully against the size of the tires. Since you are the one who will be putting the blasted things on your car, you should have a great interest in having the right size chains. There is nothing more disconcerting than finding out that you have chains one size too small when you are stuck only a few hundred meters from the top of a pass.

Taking the train

There are good train transfers from Munich to Garmisch and to Austrian resorts; from Zurich and Geneva to most of the Swiss resorts; and from Milan to some of the Italian resorts. The major problem with rail travel is the hassle of dragging equipment on and off the train, compounded by the usual need to change trains at least once during a trip to an out-of-the-way resort. The Swiss rail system is the only one which has established a workable luggage transportation system which relieves one of carrying heavy luggage. Baggage can be checked in at the train station at Geneva or Zurich airport and then delivered to your resort. The system works in reverse with the luggage actually checked through to your final destination— New York, London or anywhere. The cost for the service is SFR 9 per piece of luggage.

The recommendation is to avoid taking trains. Four people sharing a car always save money over taking a train and, in many cases, two people can save money, or they will find the difference to be so small that car rental is the way to go.

The Eurailpass and other national train passes are not much good for a ski vacation. It is better to merely purchase a second-class ticket to the resort, since if you are skiing, you will not be traveling by train enough to justify buying a long-term pass.

By bus

For many resorts, taking a bus is the only way to arrive if you choose not to rent a car. The bus system in the mountains is excellent. Most scheduled trans-Atlantic carriers offer connecting services with the major resorts as well. The carrier will inform you of the departure time and the travel time to reach the resort. Charter flights for ski tours are normally tied in with transportation to the resorts. Check before you go.

Accommodation and meals

Where you sleep, live and eat constitute the most expensive parts of your stay at a European ski resort. While the slopes are a common denominator, accommodation and meals vary widely, not only with the type of hotel or restaurant but with the season as well.

Choosing a hotel

If you arrive in a resort without reservations, plan ample time to select a hotel. This means arriving a little earlier and taking about a half hour to check out what the room situation is like.

The local tourist office will steer you in the right direction and will tell you which hotels have rooms available. Ask for three or four recommendations, then go check out the rooms. When traveling during low season—January or April—do not let yourself be pressured into taking a room you don't want, since, in most cases, there are plenty available.

Many times hotels and pensiones vary significantly even within the same categories. When you have decided where you want to stay, there are several other factors which will affect the price of your room. You'll have to decide whether to take full or half board or only breakfast (see below). Make sure to ask if any reductions are available. You may get a special rate by staying a full week or by staying through Friday night and leaving on Saturday, the day most ski weeks turn over.

Ask for half pension or breakfast only and compare prices; make sure that you understand exactly what the room rate includes. Are the listed prices for the room or are they per person? If you insist on getting clear information in the beginning, it will make your trip much more pleasant.

Country by country

Hotels in different European countries are organized and run by different standards. These standards affect how the hotels are listed and what amenities you can expect within their various categories.

Accommodation in Italy and France is controlled by a government rating system which is too difficult to explain and often seems to make no sense. Hotels that are grouped within the same category with similar room rates often vary greatly in reality. Some regulations produce confusion, such as a requirement in Italy that in order to be classified as first-class a hotel must have 40 rooms. Thus, some 36-room hotels with fabulous rooms and perfect service are listed as second-class.

Hotels and other accommodations in the mountains are usually far cleaner and the service far superior to what you normally find in the rest of France and Italy.

Switzerland, Austria and Germany are basically no-nonsense countries. The hotels are clean and neat. The visible rating system is based on stars, with the highest rating being a five-star hotel, which means luxury class. The hotels tend to be accurately rated based on price and category.

Yugoslavian and Bulgarian hotels are functional and uninspired, but provide mountains of food and are kept clean.

In general, almost any hotel room with bath is acceptable. Even the two- and three-star hotels are well maintained. Prices, however, are significantly higher in these three countries when compared category by category with Italy or France.

One fact of life in the mountains during the winter season is the requirement to take at least two meals, or half pension (see below), in the hotel where you are staying. During high season this requirement is firm, and some hotels may even insist on full pension. The price is worth it in most cases. In your hotel search, however, ask several locals which hotels or pensions have the best food. Their replies should also enter into your decision on where to spend your week in the resort. We will discuss alternatives below.

Season by season

The best season to stay in any resort hotel and to eat at any restaurant is low season. This is normally from December 1 through the weekend before Christmas, then again from the weekend after New Year's through the first weekend in February, and again from approximately mid-March through the month of April. The exact dates vary. Be sure to check with your destination resort to see when the low season starts and finishes.

Since low season is when the hotels and the resorts are not packed to capacity, the kitchen and hotel staff have time to provide exceptional service. In addition, the on-site facilities, such as sauna, steam room, pool or exercise room tend to be less crowded.

The realities of low season also allow you to bargain for the room you really want. Let's say you have visited four hotels and you have chosen one you feel offers the best services. You can speak discreetly with the manager and inform him that you would like to stay at his hotel but that the hotel down the road offers a room that is almost the same quality but costs less. Caution: This ploy does not work if you're not telling the truth! In many cases, the manager will offer a special rate on the spot which matches the rate of the other hotel, especially if you plan to stay for a week and he has an empty room.

You win in two ways: you get the hotel room you want and its price is a better bargain.

Such bargaining should only be attempted if you've arrived with no reservations. Be pleasant and smile—it's magic everywhere in the world. During the bargaining session you have a chance to get to know the manager a bit and he will not mind your haggling in the least.

If you have held the room for some time, you are committed to the agreed-upon price. Haggling over a reserved room is considered bad form and will not enhance your stay at the hotel.

You can, however, make your stay even more enjoyable by using the money you saved on the hotel rate to tip the hotel staff. In countries such as Italy this is considered a display of *bella figura*, or good image. You will be remembered and you will get preferential service. Unlike the sorry state of tipping in the United States, tipping in Italy really bears results.

Pensions

Pensions are usually smaller, family-run affairs that cost significantly less than hotels. The pension guest is in many casgs made to feel a part of the family during his stay.

Some pensions have bath and toilet in the room, others have the bath and toilet down the hall or just outside your door. The pensions recommended in this book have rooms available with private bath and toilet. If you do not mind a semi-private arrangement, you can request that type of room and save even more.

Many pensions, especially in the mountains, offer a full restaurant service and will include all three meals in the price during the ski season. Many require that you take at least half pension (see below) when you stay for a week. It usually is well worth the price.

Bed-and-breakfast (Garni)

These are what the name implies: accommodations that offer room with breakfast only. Normally, you cannot take lunch or dinner there. This means heading out to discover local restaurants.

The bed-and-breakfast arrangement is often the least expensive in a mountain town, other than staying in private homes or apartments. Do not let yourself be fooled by the low price, though. Remember, you will have to pay for your meals in restaurants, which will add significantly to your costs. Though pensions and hotels may appear to cost more, when meal prices are taken into consideration they may really be a bargain.

Garnis and bed-and-breakfasts do offer several advantages. First, you have a chance to try several different restaurants and different styles of cooking during your stay. Second, you can often save money by eating less. Hotel menus include a full meal with all the trimmings and each is priced expecting you to eat everything on the daily menu. You may only want to eat a plate of spaghetti and be on your way. In other words, you pay only for what you eat.

Full pension, half pension

What exactly do these terms mean?

Full pension means that your hotel will provide breakfast, lunch and dinner during every day of your stay. Many refer to it as full-board. For example, if you arrive Saturday at noon you will be able to eat lunch (perhaps served at 1 p.m.), then have dinner in the evening. On the last day of your stay you will be able to eat breakfast. Or, if you arrived later in the afternoon, say, around 5 p.m., you would have dinner and would be allowed both breakfast and lunch on the day of your departure.

The meals are served during set times in most hotels and pensiones. If you miss the mealtime, the establishment is not required to offer an alternative meal. Some of the better hotels will offer you a meal in a smaller grill restaurant.

When you agree to full pension, ask whether the hotel will offer either a box lunch to take to the slopes or whether they have a coupon arrangement with a restaurant on the slopes. If the hotel does not have such an arrangement, you will be required to return to the hotel for every meal. This can really cut into your skiing time. Or you will have to forgo the meal even though you are paying for it. This could be an important consideration when deciding between hotels.

Half pension means that the hotel will offer breakfast, plus one additional meal, normally dinner, every day of your stay. Often referred to as half-board, this is often the best arrangement. You are free to eat what you want and where you want during the day while on the slopes. If you plan to go out on the town to eat at a special restaurant, you will be able to arrange to have lunch at the hotel and leave yourself free to enjoy dinner elsewhere. Basically, you can easily eat every meal for which you are paying.

During high season many hotels require you to take full pension. But during low season you can often get the room at half pension only and, in many cases, with breakfast only.

The basic meal is all that is included in the full- or half-pension price. Any wine, water, extras, changes from the menu, coffee or liqueurs are billed as extra charges. Make sure that you ask about them and that you know for what you are paying.

If you ask only for a "wine from the region," you may be surprised when you see the price on your bill.

What is breakfast?

Since there is a big difference in what constitutes breakfast in Europe, here is a primer.

In Switzerland, Austria, Germany and Italy's Val Gardena region, breakfast means yogurt, cold cuts, cheese, jams and jellies, butter, rolls and endless coffee or tea. In some hotels, you get boiled eggs and juice all included in the breakfast with the room.

In France and in most of Italy, breakfast means a basket of rolls, sometimes a few sweetrolls, butter, jam and jelly with coffee and tea. Juice and eggs are almost always extras. Cold cuts, yogurt, cereal and cheese are rarely available.

Staying in apartments or chalets

An alternative to staying in a hotel, pension or bed-and-breakfast is choosing an apartment or chalet. These are often scattered through the town and offer reasonably priced accommodations.

Apartments are most popular in Switzerland and France. The Italians are now beginning to get their apartment rental arrangements organized, and some resorts, such as Courmayeur and Val Gardena, have several apartment choices.

Apartments come in all sizes. You can rent a studio apartment, which is perfect for a couple, or an apartment for four, five, six or eight persons. The price per person drops considerably as the size of the apartment increases. These are fantastic bargains. The daily price can be as low as $10 to $12 (£6-8) per person if two or more couples share an apartment.

The apartments are normally rented with a fully equipped kitchen, all utensils and a dishwasher. Sheets and pillowcases and a clean-up are sometimes included; other apartments may be rented with the bedding and cleaning services as extra charges. Check also for a utility fee. In some cases it is included; in others, you pay at the end of the stay based on the amount of oil or electricity used.

You can cook your own breakfast and as many meals as you

want, which will also save a lot of money. A supermarket is usually nearby or on the ground floor of the apartment building where you are staying. Grocery prices are just about the same as those in any large European city.

If you decide that you would like to stay in an apartment or chalet, contact the tourist office and ask for a listing of the apartments available during the period you plan to visit. The tourist office will send you a list of the apartments. Make your choice and return the material to the tourist office. Some tourist offices will send an apartment listing and you will be required to direct subsequent correspondence to the owners.

If you arrive with no arrangements, the procedure goes like this: the tourist office will make several calls and send you off to see several apartments and to speak with the owners.

As with hotels and pensions, you can bargain and you should look at a few places to get an idea of what is available. Note the distance to the nearest supermarket, sauna and swimming pool. Check out the distance to the lifts. It is a joy to be able to step outside your door in the morning and immediately start skiing.

The leading apartment/chalet rental firm in the world is Interhome. In some resorts this company virtually controls the apartment rentals. Interhome has offices in Britain as well as representatives in the United States. In U.K. contact: Interhome Ltd., 383 Richmond Road, Twickenham TW1-2EF, tel. 01-891 1294; telex: 928539. In the U.S. the representatives are: Mcguire Travel Marketing, PO Box 23, Glen Ellyn, IL 60138, tel. (312) 665-3337 and Villas International, 71 West 23rd Street, New York, NY 10010, Tel. (212) 929 7585. Both representatives have vacancy lists and can confirm availability immediately.

Staying in a private home

Private homes at many resorts will rent out rooms. These rooms are normally very inexpensive with prices ranging between those of a bed-and-breakfast and an apartment. If you are traveling alone, a private home is often the best bargain you can get.

Staying in a private home can give you a better feel for the local scene, you pick up hints on the best places to go on the slopes and in town and, in many cases, you will find yourself treated like a friend of the family.

Once again, start at the local tourist office. It has addresses and phone numbers of the families who will rent out rooms. The tourist office will call and make any arrangements necessary. Ask to see several rooms and then make your choice.

In some cases, the room price includes breakfast but the arrangements vary from house to house. Expect to pay between $10 and $20 (£7-14) a night, depending on the resort and time of the season.

Make sure that baths or showers are included in the price; if not, ask for the price and the best time of day to take a bath or shower. Hot water can be at a premium, especially just after the slopes close for the day.

The European ski scene

What should a skier expect when arriving at a European resort? Culture shock aside, there shouldn't be too many surprises since the U. S. ski industry has been modeled to a great extent on the long-established European resorts. But there are some notable differences and this chapter will deal with some of those European variances, as well as offering tips on getting more from your ski vacation in Europe.

The weather

A friend had just arrived in Switzerland from New England the week before Christmas and we were getting ready to go skiing. Her preparations for the day amazed me. She began by putting on lots of bulky clothing: sweaters, a jacket and other arctic-expedition-like paraphernalia.

"Whoa," I said. "What are you doing? You want to be able to move on the mountain, don't you?"

"I don't want to be cold," she replied.

"Well, you'll melt if you insist on dressing like that," I said.

After this argument she reluctantly agreed to take off half of the clothing (it wasn't enough) and risked taking my advice to wear only a turtleneck, a sweater and a jacket or windbreaker.

The point is this: skiing in Europe is not a freezing proposition. The weather is very mild in its mountain areas. Even in the coldest sections of the Alps, the winter daytime temperatures are in the twenty-degrees Fahrenheit range. Windy days, few and far between, usually herald a coming snowstorm.

What to wear

Try to dress in layers, and because temperatures are relatively mild, you will rarely need more than a ski jacket over a turtleneck shirt. On most days, a turtleneck worn under a light sweater and a windbreaker will be more than enough. Don't underestimate the temperatures, though; they seem to drop rapidly whenever you are sitting in the wind on a long chairlift. Europe's heavy use of T-bar and poma lifts will help keep you warmer, although American skiers may swear at having to stay on their feet during the trip up.

Protection from the sun

Europe's resorts are no different than any other skiing area when it comes to sun, especially during the Spring. Sunburn or snow blindness can ruin any vacation, so use sun screen, lip protection, and always wear glasses or goggles. The glasses do not have to be tinted; the glass itself stops harmful ultraviolet rays.

General snow conditions

Snow in Europe is not as dry as snow in Utah or Colorado, due to lower elevations and milder climate. Nor is it as icy as New England snow, thanks to more constant temperatures. Generally, the slopes are not as carefully groomed as those in the U. S. and relatively consistent snowfall obviates the need for extensive snowmaking equipment.

The best snowfall seems to take place in January, making both January and February good months in which to ski. Plan to go in January if you can, though, since February and March are also the most expensive time to ski, excepting the Christmas, New Year's and Easter holiday periods. The week before Christmas is normally a pretty good time to go, but chancy.

Spring skiing sees the Alps at their finest and prices are again at low-season levels. An instructor is invaluable during spring skiing, for in his company you will learn the best times to ski different areas as the day progresses and the sun warms the snow. The secret is to get onto the run just before you begin breaking through the crust and then move to the next section of the mountain.

Lift lines

One major difference between skiing in Europe and the United States can be seen in lift-line etiquette. In the U. S., lift lines are relatively orderly: a line for singles is maintained along the far right or left, and most everyone takes pains to avoid stepping on or skiing over another skier's equipment. The result is that you almost never end up jammed together during the move through the lift line.

Not so in Europe. Though the lift lines in various countries on the Continent differ as to the degree of aggressive behavior, in general, they are a free-for-all. Until you reach the point where barriers have been set up to funnel skiers into the lift, there are no controls. He who moves the fastest and shuffles forward the most aggressively is usually the first to get up the lift. While there is a general effort not to blatantly trample over each other's skis, be resigned to the fact that your equipment will be stepped on no matter what you do or how mad you look. Here are some tips to handling lift lines:

—Before you enter the line, see whether it turns to the right; if so, you should go to the far outside left of the line. If the line turns to the left, go to the extreme right. If you have ever tried to turn a sharp corner with skis on, you will begin to understand the wisdom of this suggestion. There is no mercy shown inside the lift line. Once you are stuck on the inside of a sharp right or left turn within the barriers you are in trouble.

—If the line is relatively straight, make sure to get on its outside edge. You will quickly see that the mass of skiers funnel down the narrow barriers on either side. Those who get caught in the middle get squeezed from both sides and move about half as fast as those on the outside edges of the crowd.

—When faced with a choice between a T-bar or poma lift versus a chair or cable car, you should normally pick the faster T-bar or poma. If the distance is great, however, the cable car or chairlift will get you to the top of the run more quickly, even if getting onto it may mean more waiting time.

—Maintain a sense of humor. You can be sure that it will be tested, especially on weekends.

—The best time to ski and avoid the crowds is during lunchtime. You'll experience clear slopes, shorter lift lines and fewer frustrations. In Italy and France, the lines all but disappear as everyone heads back to the hotels for a big lunch. In Switzerland and Austria the noon-hour difference is not as great.

Etiquette on the slopes

The Austrian Tourist Office lists ten rules for the slopes,which, though not especially profound, should generally be followed when skiing in Europe.

1. Keep equipment in good condition.
2. Do not endanger others or destroy property.
3. Ski in control, keeping weather and terrain in mind.
4. It's the uphill skier's responsibility to avoid the skier below him. Give other skiers a good safe margin.
5. After stopping, look around you before starting again.
6. Get up quickly after a fall and do not stop in blind spots on the trails.
7. If you must walk up a slope, keep to the edge of the run.
8. Obey all signs and markers.
9. You are obliged to help injured skiers. Protect them from further risk and get first aid.
10. If you are in a skiing accident, you are required to furnish identification.

Before you go

You really do not need to bring any special documents other than a passport for traveling in Europe. Before you go, you should take a close look at your health insurance to be certain that you will be covered in case of an accident. Most policies provide worldwide coverage, some are limited in the case of skiing accidents, while others group skiing accidents under the broad category of "accidental injury," which may mean that your deductible will be waived. Know what coverage you have. If you do not have coverage, arrange to buy special ski insurance. Your agent should be able to point you in the right direction.

Several companies, such as Europ Assistance, (tel. 800-821-2828) offer this insurance. In addition, you can purchase ski insurance once you arrive at the resort. Carte Neige in France is easy to purchase at most resorts. Check with the local tourist office for details.

Make a photocopy of your passport pages with your photo and personal information and write down your passport number. Also, have a photocopy made of your airline tickets and the credit cards you will be taking with you. Make two copies: Keep one with you, separate from your passport, tickets and credit cards, and leave the second copy with a friend or relative.

In case you somehow lose everything, these backup records will be invaluable. The passport copy will help in getting a replacement at an overseas consulate or embassy. The ticket copy may help in getting a replacement and alerts the airline to look for a stolen ticket with that number. The credit card numbers will make reporting stolen cards and limiting your liability much easier.

Credit cards and travelers checks

Most large resorts and full-fledged hotels accept major credit cards, but don't expect the smaller pensiones and hotels to accept them. The normally accepted cards are American Express, Diners Club, Carte Blanche, Visa and MasterCharge (called "Eurocard" in Europe). Some resorts even allow skiers to pay for lift tickets with credit cards but they are few and far between. It is best to come prepared with adequate cash or travelers checks to cover expenses during your trip. American Express are the best-known travelers checks, but in this area of Europe almost all are easily exchanged.

The basic rule of changing money at a bank applies at ski resorts—even more so than in most places. The hotels and restaurants that accept travelers checks almost never give you a rate of exchange equal to the one you can get from a bank just around the corner. Plan ahead and save yourself the difference. If you are changing a small amount of money it is often better to exchange at your hotel since they normally do not charge a minimum exchange fee.

Taking your own equipment

Most airlines will allow you to check your ski equipment onto your flight for no additional charge. However, upon your arrival in Europe, check with personnel in the baggage-arrival area to find out where your equipment can be picked up. Skis are often delivered to a separate area of the baggage section.

Renting equipment

You can also rent all the equipment you'll need at your destination resort. Ski rentals—depending on the quality ski you want—range from about $6 to $15, with discounts for periods of three days or more and weekly rentals running about $33 to $75. It's best to bring your own boots, however, since these are extremely important to your comfort, and rental boots that are consistently comfortable have yet to be found. If you do rent boots, expect to pay between $3 and $8 a day, or about $16 to $37 a week depending on quality of boot.

Buying equipment in Europe

One of the biggest bargains of your trip may be in investing in new equipment. Ski equipment in Europe often costs less than identical equipment in the U. S. Depending on what and where you buy, you can recover some of your trip's expenses. Most of the world's ski boots are manufactured in the northern Italian town of Montebelluna. Prices for them are higher in the U. S. to cover shipping and higher retail overhead. If you plan to ski in the Dolomites, near Cortina d'Ampezzo, Montebelluna is only a short drive away. The expert skier may want to go directly to the factory and have the boots custom fitted. Brands made in Montebelluna include Dolomite, San Marco, Nordica, Caber, Technica and Munari.

The roster of quality skis manufactured in Austria, Switzerland, Germany, Italy, Yugoslavia and France includes Rossignol, Atomic, Kneissel, Fischer, Vokl, Dynastar, Dynamic, Elan and Maxell.

Italy is a world leader in ski fashion, with designer labels such as Anzi Besson, Belfe and Fila, all available at prices well below those in the U. S.

One quirk worth noting is that unlike retailers in the United States, who place a high premium on equipment sold at ski resorts, European resort retailers often find themselves in competition with stores in the bigger cities and are often forced to limit their markups. If you plan to buy ski equipment and clothing in January, or in the spring, keep in mind that at those times much of the equipment is offered at sale prices.

It often pays to make a purchase, such as ski boots, at the resort where you will be skiing. The small premium you pay there is well worth it. The shop owner, for example, can mold the boot to your foot if there is a problem with the fit. This can be done overnight but if it is going to take longer, the owner will make sure that you have a rental boot for the next day.

Remember, whenever paying for your equipment, always ask what discount there is for payment by cash. Frequently the shop owner will discount merchandise by as much as ten percent. If you wave an American Express card around, the shop owner will almost always make a discount in order to get cash. This is because American Express requires a larger percentage from the retailers than other bank cards, which makes merchants very willing to deal.

Taking photos in the snow

The best souvenirs of any vacation are the pictures you take and bring home to share with friends. What's more, photos help you to remember the good times you had, the places you visited and the people you met.

Standard and automatic cameras, however, do not make it easy to take good photographs on ski slopes. The overall brightness of the snow and bright sky often confuses light meters and automatic exposure systems. Many travelers have returned home with pictures that are washed out and underexposed, or in which the snow looks like a dirty sheet rather than the sparkling whiteness they remembered and hoped to catch on film. Follow these tips in order to get the best results when shooting photographs in the snow.

—Always make sure that the sun is somewhere in front of

you when you take any picture in the snow. This allows you to capture the glistening sunlight and the texture of the snow.

—If shooting into the sun with a manual camera, close down the camera's f-stop to its smallest aperture (highest number). This will cause the sun to appear with a star-like effect.

—With a manual camera, remember that light is being reflected off the snow. In order to counter it, set the camera's f-stop down about two numbers. The best solution is to meter directly off the subject, then take the picture.

—With an automatic camera, either override the automatic feature or select a plus-two f-stop setting if your camera will permit.

—Snow heightens the effects of ultraviolet rays. A uv filter helps insure accurate colors. If you are taking black-and-white photos, use a yellow, orange or red filter to heighten contrast.

—Your camera gets cold and so does the film. This means slower speeds unless you keep the camera warm. Try to keep it inside your jacket until ready to shoot.

Meeting the Europeans

Take along a small notebook in which to jot down names and addresses of people you meet at the resorts, or special things that you enjoyed and want to pass on to other friends. Don't be afraid to follow up some of the contacts you make on the slopes or at the resorts. Europeans are usually sincere when they invite you to come and see them. They tend to make the invitation out of sincerity rather than an assumed obligation. If you plan to spend some time in Europe or plan to return there, the people you meet can add a special extra to any trip if you stay in touch. Remember, you add a difference to their lives and are as interesting to them as they are to you. Good friendships often result from such sharing.

Resort locals can also add to your knowledge of the country by recommending special ski runs, which may be obscure, by suggesting a good wine or hot drink to enjoy after a day of skiing, and by explaining which local specialties you should order in a restaurant or at your hotel.

If you remain open to everyone, you will enjoy your vacation and return far richer than when you left.

Cross-country

All European resorts are not equal as far as cross-country skiing is concerned. Though this book concentrates on the best-known downhill resorts, most have developed good cross-country facilities. Others are adjacent to some of the best cross-country skiing areas in the world.

In this section we have highlighted the cross-country possibilities for most of the resorts we cover in this book. We have also mentioned some other top cross-country areas not listed in the book and provided addresses and phone numbers for more information. Otherwise, use the resort section for hotel, restaurant and other information.

Switzerland

Arosa—The cross-country trails are modest (about 20 miles of prepared trails) but well maintained and from the beginning of December into April you can count on a variety of trails through the countryside.

Champery—Very limited.

Crans-Montana—There are three main trails with a total of about 24 miles. Your best cross-country adventures will probably be on the nearly seven-mile loop on Plaine-Morte glacier.

Davos—Excellent cross-country trails in classic Alpine scenery. Altogether there are nearly 45 miles of prepared trails with seven main loops kept in top condition. Good choice for the cross-country enthusiast.

Engelberg—Low rated for the cross-country enthusiast with less than 15 miles of prepared trails. Auto-free Melchsee-Frutt has an additional nine miles of trails.

Flims/Laax—Good cross-country area with a total of nearly 45 miles of double-tracked trails in Flims, Laax and Falera areas. Cross-country adventure treks with guides are offered in this region.

Gstaad—When considered with Saanen and other areas of the Weisse Hochland, cross-country is excellent with nearly 50 miles of trails, guided adventure treks and excellent instruction.

Jungfrau Region—Grindelwald, with about 20 miles of trails is the best in the area. Good instruction is available. Wengen and Mürren are both very limited. The most beautiful trail is a seven-mile circuit in the Lauterbach valley near Lauterbrunnen.

Klosters—Moderately interesting with nearly 40 miles of tracks split between four prepared trails. Combined with Davos the area is quite extensive and beautiful.

St. Moritz—One of Europe's greatest. A paradise for the true cross-country fan. No one talks long about cross-country skiing without bringing up St. Moritz. This elegant resort has a remarkable network of 75 miles of trails in the immediate area and, overall, there are about 200 miles of cross-country ciruits on the valley floor and frozen lakes in the region. St. Moritz also has a one-mile-long lighted trail for night-skiing fans. The course of the famed Engadiner Ski Marathon race is nearby.

A great place to vacation for the skier who seeks cross-country only and demands great variety.

Saas-Fee—Extremely limited!

Verbier—Has 42 miles of prepared trails, but the connecting network is not exceptional.

Villars—Limited.

Zermatt—Cross-country is only a side pursuit with limited trails totaling only 15 miles.

France

Chamonix—Moderately interesting trails total about 25 miles in the valley. Best if combined with downhill skiing but not a good cross-country resort on its own.

Megève—Surprisingly good network of trails totaling nearly 45 miles in the Megève-Combloux area. Good variety and some good challenges on endurance.

Flaine—Moderate to mediocre quality network totaling about 20 miles. Go elsewhere if cross-country is first on your mind.

Tignes/Val d'Isere—Poor choice for real cross-country skiers. Only short trails with a total of nine miles of prepared track.

Les 2 Alpes—Below-average offerings with only 12 miles of prepared loops split between ten trails.

Les Trois Vallées—Above-average network of trails by French resort standards. A total of nearly 50 miles of prepared loops spread over the rolling valley countryside.

The Jura—Europe's greatest cross-country ski adventure is a 120-mile trek across the highlands of the French Jura region, which stretches from Belfort along the Swiss border toward Geneva. Nearly 40 percent of this mountain region is wooded and the connecting trail, called the GTJ (Grand Traverse du Jura) is a superb run. The trail sections are difficult, ranging from three to 29 kilometers each, as you make your way from Maise, near Belfort, nearly 120 miles to La Pesse, south of St. Claude. There are inns all along the trail.

For details on the Jura trek, write GTJ: Office de Tourisme Regional, Place de la 1e. Armée Française, F-25000 Besancon, France.

For general information on cross-country all-in trips in the Jura, write Accueil Montagnard-Chapelle-de-Bois, F-25240 Mouthe, France; or A.G.A.D.-La Pesse, F-39370 Les Bouchoux, France.

Austria

The Arlberg—If you are only looking for occasional cross-country skiing this will provide limited alternatives to the downhill religion in this region. The St. Anton/St. Christoph side of the mountain offers the best cross-country. Lech and Zürs are extremely limited.

Badgastein—There's more than enough variety in the Gasteiner valley for cross-country enthusiasts. A total of 55 miles of trails are divided among the resorts. The six trails from Bad Hofgastein offer the most variety. There's an added incentive for cross-country here because anyone who completes 75 kilometers (45 miles) earns a bronze medal. The gold is awarded for 1000 kilometers (620 miles), but clearly is beyond the reach of one-time vacationers.

Innsbruck—Perhaps the second or third greatest cross-country area in all Europe with over 60 miles of trails in the immediate area of the city. Instruction is excellent. And as an added bonus, the marvelous resort of Seefeld is only a short bus ride away.

Seefeld—Our top choice for all of Europe is Seefeld, which hosted the 1964 and 1976 Olympic cross-country competitions. Nearly 100 miles of cross-country trails are maintained and most of the circuits lead from the Olympic Sport and Convention Center. Accommodation is outstanding and reasonably priced. In addition, an international atmosphere makes foreign visitors feel welcome.

There's a challenging 18-mile circuit, plus 15- and six-mile loops making up the heart of the trails here.

For more information contact—Verkehrsbüro, A-6100 Seefeld; tel. 05212-2313.

Ischgl—Less-than-average network totaling only 12 miles.

Kaiserwinkl—This is a cross-country skiers' paradise in the Austrian Tirol a few miles off the autobahn between Munich and Innsbruck. The towns of Schwedt, Kössen and Walchsee have combined their trails for nearly 85 miles of Nordic runs. Each town has its own cross-country center and the interconnected circuits branch out from the centers. For information—Fremdenverkehrsverband, Postfach 127, A-6345 Kössen; tel. 05375-6287.

Kitzbühel/Kirchberg—Some of the best cross-country trails in Austria. Great variety and many miles of trails.

Montafon—When all eleven main resorts in the Montafon valley are considered this is an excellent cross-country area. But, you need a car to drive to the various areas. No single resort has enough variety for a vacation. Over a dozen trails total about 45 miles.

Schladming—Excellent cross-country trails especially on the Ramsau side of the valley where a wide-open plateau just below the Dachstein glacier offer perfect terrain. Plan to stay in Ramsau since the other towns are a long trek away from the best cross-country areas.

St. Johann in Tirol—Excellent choice for cross-country vacation. Not as much variety as Innsbruck-Seefeld, but the nearly 74 miles of trails are maintained for the serious skier. Changing rooms, first aid and restaurant facilities are excellent on the loops. Also an excellent choice for the skier who want to mix downhill with cross-country.

Oetztal—Meager offerings. Less than ten miles of trails.

Kaprun/Zell am See—One of the best-kept secrets among cross-country devotees. A great network of nearly 72 miles of trails in the area plus a connection to an additional 40 miles of trails in the neighboring valley. The ski school also has good courses.

Zillertal—Good variety with over 40 miles of track.

Germany

Allgäu—The most challenging network of cross-country trails in Germany is found in this region. The trails branch off from the ski towns of Oberstaufen and Immenstadt. Part of the network includes a great marathon-length, 26.2 mile loop. This area is not covered in this book. Contact the German tourist office for further information.

Garmisch—You'll discover long, exceptionally scenic trails with nearly 37 miles of loops in the Garmisch-Partenkirchen area. Above Garmisch, in the Graswang Valley, there is beautiful cross-country skiing which takes you near Linderhof, perhaps the most beautiful of Ludwig's Bavarian castles.

The Black Forest—Germany's best-known cross-country area. The best circuits are around Titisee and up to the slopes of the Feldberg, the highest mountain in the region. Altogether there are about 600 miles of trails in the Black Forest with nearly 75 miles of loops near Feldberg. Perhaps the most challenging runs are from Neustadt where organized cross-country groups kick and glide for nearly 60 miles with planned stops at hotels and guest houses along the way. This region is not covered in detail in this book—contact the tourist board for more information.

Italy

Italy has not developed an extensive cross-country system except in the Madonna di Campiglio area and in parts of the Dolomites.

Pinzolo, only a few kilometers, about a 20-minute drive, from **Madonna di Campiglio** is the sight of one of cross-country's major 24-endurance races. The area near Campo Carlo Magno, in the Madonna di Campiglio area, has an expert cross-country course.

Cortina d'Ampezzo—Good cross-country area with over 45 miles of prepared trails. A good place to mix downhill with cross-country if you wish. This resort was once the site of the Olympics.

Kronplatz—Few resorts mix the pleasures of cross-country and downhill better than those in Italy's Pustertal. Here in the South Tyrolean region, Kronplatz resorts boast nearly 90 miles of cross-country trails branching out from the central town of Bruneck (*Brunico*, in Italian) below the Kronplatz plateau.

If you come in January, you can take part in the 35-mile-long cross-country race, which begins in Innichen (*San Candido*, in Italian) and ends in Antholz. The shorter 24-mile race course ends at Olang.

Downhill skiers can try out the slopes from the 2275-meter (7462-foot) Kronplatz summit.

Not in this book, for more information contact: Crontour, I-39031, Bruneck; tel. 0474-84544.

Gateways to the Alps

Amsterdam

Amsterdam. It makes a perfect hub from which to choose any alpine resort. KLM flights connect to all the ski resort areas of Europe, plus special programs such as cruises down the Rhine and rail passes through the Rhine Country offer alternative travel possibilities to the mountains.

Amsterdam itself with easy connections from the airport to the city offers sightseeing opportunities to travelers with as little as a four hour layover and for those with more time Amsterdam is rich with museums, nightlife and charm. Tourist Information is just outside the railway station and the city is easily explored by tram, bus, metro, tour boats, bicycles and foot.

The "Top 10" of Amsterdam for those on a quick swing through the city are: 1. A canal tour—it's full of great historical background and will provide a good orientation to the city. 2. The Rijksmuseum—packed with Rembrants and plenty more. 3. Van Gogh Museum—just down the road from the Rijksmuseum and full of, you guessed it, Van Goghs. 4. The Begijnhof—this tiny, hidden courtyard is how Amsterdam used to be! Calm in the center of the bustling city. 5. Anne Frank's House—the house with hidden rooms where Anne Frank lived with her family before being taken to the concentration camp. 6. The Red Light District—once upon a time a "must" for anyone in Amsterdam. Now, still interesting but stick to the main streets and don't do your wandering during the wee hours. 7. Leidseplein—the open-air café center of Amsterdam and the heart of the pulsing nightlife. 8. Kalverstraat—the main shopping street and one of the best people-museums in Amsterdam. 9.

The Albert Cuyp Market and the Flea Market—great street markets open every day except Sunday. 10. The Heineken Brewery—take a tour of the most popular brewery in Europe and stop for a sample of the brew after the tour.

Zurich, Switzerland

Skiers striking out for virtually any Swiss ski resort or for resorts in the western part of Austria may find themselves in Zurich for a night or two. This Swiss banking capital might be expected to present a stuffy commercial face to the world. But the real Zurich is a city that has managed to marry prosperity and progress with old-world tradition.

A good place to start is the **Bahnhofstrasse**, where you'll see a few of those famous Swiss banks and also some of the most exclusive shops—with some of the highest price tags in the country. This is the city's main street, often called the picture window of Switzerland.

If you walk the Bahnhofstrasse you'll eventually come to Bürkliplatz and Lake Zurich. Where the Limmat River flows out of the lake, boat tours offer the best views of the city.

On foot you'll find the most scenic sections of the old town between Bahnhofstrasse and the Limmat. One of the city's major attractions is the **Swiss National Museum**, on the shore of the Limmat adjacent to the main train station. The museum chronicles Swiss civilization from prehistoric time to the present. The collection from the Roman era is particularly good.

The most-visited churches are also within walking distance of the central area. Across the Limmat, the **Grossmünster** 11th-century cathedral is distinguished by its twin towers. The Münster bridge from the cathedral leads to the 12th-century **Frauenmünster Church** with the famed stained-glass windows created this century by Chagall.

A few minutes' walk from the cathedral is Zurich's **Lunsthaus,** a beautiful art museum with an excellent collection of Swiss masters as well as works by Van Gogh, Cézanne, Renoir, Manet, Degas and Picasso.

If you spend the night in Zurich, head for the **Niederdorf** section of town which stretches along the Limmat, across from the train station. This is where Zurich eases the stress of world financial responsibilities. Along crowded streets the oldtown section of Zurich pulsates with live jazz, smokey bars, packed discos and scores of restaurants. For a more traditional respite, plan to have an elegant dinner in an old guild house before plunging into Zurich's lively nightlife.

Geneva, Switzerland

If your skiing plans are in the area of the Valais in Switzerland, any of the French Alps or in the Val d'Aosta in Italy, Geneva is an excellent gateway to Europe.

Geneva is one of Europe's most beautiful lakeside cities, and any tour should begin first, with a few moments on the **Pont du Mont Blanc,** the Mont Blanc bridge, for a panoramic view of the Alps; with clear weather the outline of Mont Blanc crests on the horizon. Then a climb up the north tower of **St. Pierre Cathedral** offers a superb view of the city, which is built around the contours of a small section of Lac Leman (Lake Geneva). The interior of the cathedral, built over a period of 300 years beginning in the 10th century, offers a stained-glass illumination of Swiss religious art and architecture.

The attractions in Geneva are spread out, a bus tour may help to get an overall orientation of the city. Later, catch a city bus or a taxi to the places you want to revisit.

The ill-fated League of Nations, founded after World War I, had its headquarters here in the **Palais des Nations**. Today this building serves as the European headquarters for the United Nations. Tours of the building are offered throughout the year.

Geneva's greatest park runs along the lake and combines the Mon Repos, Perle du Lac and Villa Barton—all landscaped park areas that form a beautiful walking range.

The city's best-known museum is the **Art and History Museum,** which features distinguished collections in archeology and decorative arts.

For an offbeat fling, check the **flea market** held on the city's Plaine de Palais Wednesdays and Saturdays.

Frankfurt, Germany

Though Frankfurt, itself, is not in the heart of the Alps, skiers occasionally spend a night or two in this West German business capital while heading for or returning from an Alpine vacation.

That time need not be wasted, for this is a vibrant city with attractions enough to keep anyone entertained.

Frankfurt's accessibility is outstanding—only 15 minutes by train or taxi from the airport. Trains leave approximately every 20 minutes and whisk passengers to the central train station. From there, its only a short walk or quick taxi ride to any of the tourist attractions. If your time is very limited, take a cab; it allows you to save the waiting time for the train. Fare to any of the main tourist sites should be no more than $12-$15.

The **Hauptbahnhof**, or railway station, is an adventure in itself, a genuine slice of pre-war Europe with soaring girders supporting a massive skylight roof that towers above nearly two dozen tracks. Here, stop in and visit the tourist information center where hostesses will orient you to the city and will provide maps and other material to make your visit easier and more enjoyable.

From the train station the first destination is the **Römerberg**, a square near the Main (pronounced *mine*) River that has been the focus of extensive city renovation efforts in recent years. The gabled facades of the three burghers' houses on the Römer square have come to serve as the symbol of the city and mark the core of the old quarter. Here the Laisersall, or Imperial Hall, was site of many celebrations when Holy Roman Emperors were crowned in Frankfurt.

This is the district of the **Altstadt**, or old city; although the bombing in World War II destroyed nearly 80 percent of the city, many of the oldest buildings have been restored, including historic St. Bartholomew cathedral, the Nikolai church on the Römerberg and the unique, oval Paul's church across the street.

Close by, for a visitor who wants to do last minute (or first day) shopping, is the **Zeil**, Frankfurt's most fashionable pedestrian shopping street. The Hauptwache, a square where the main shopping streets Zeil and Rossmarkt meet, reigns as the commercial heart of Frankfurt. Further down the Zeil stands the recontructed **Alte Oper**, the old opera house, which rivals the beauty of pre-war Dresden buildings. In the same area is the **Goethe House** and museum honoring Germany's most famous writer.

For nightlife **Sachsenhausen** is lively and loud. The district across a footbridge on the opposite side of the Main River from the Römerberg area, bustles with pubs and restaurants, and all pour *Applewoi,* a distinctive apple cider.

Munich, Germany

The Bavarian capital is southern Germany's crown jewel, not only lovely but the country's greatest art center. Munich's greatest attraction, however, is that it rivals any other city in Europe for sheer merrymaking, much of it inspired by the formidable one-liter mugs of beer served morning, noon and night. Spend at least an evening in one of the city's great beer halls.

Every visitor should check out **Marienplatz,** the main square. At 11 a.m. daily the dancing figures in the town hall Glockenspiel perform. Nearby is the **Frauenkirche,** or Church of Our Lady. Its 450-year-old onion-shaped domes topping the church's towers have come to symbolize Munich. The best view of the city is from the 332-foot high north tower, where on clear days the Bavarian Alps nearly 50 miles away can be seen. For an even higher view, though a bit out of the center of the town, visit the 1972 **Olympic grounds** for an elevator trip up the television tower which is almost three times higher than the church viewing tower downtown.

Munich's collection of art museums is too extensive to list, but suffice to say whatever your interest—paintings, ceramics, sculpture, ethnology, etc.—there should be a collection for you. Of special interest, and a must-see, is the **Alte Pinakothek** which houses one of the world's greatest art collections, including rooms full of Rubens and excellent Dürer paintings.

The **Deutsches Museum** features a great technical collection rivaling the Smithsonian and shouldn't be missed. This museum is a fantasy world of pushbutton fun with machines to crawl through and explore including a WWII submarine. If you have children they will never want to leave.

One excursion you may want to take is to **Dachau,** site of the German concentration camp, now preserved as a memorial. It's approximately a 40-minute drive from the center of the city.

If you have an extra day or two in Munich, consider a bus tour to the castles of Ludwig II, the Dream King—some called him mad—of Bavaria. A particularly good tour is called the

"Royal Castles Tour," promoted by the Bavarian Tourist Board. The luxury bus trip visits **Neuschwanstein** (inspiration for Disneyland's castle), **Linderhof** and **Herrenchiemsee,** three great castles built by Ludwig, as well as some other residences of the Wittelsbachs, Ludwig's royal family.

Innsbruck, Austria

Innsbruck is the easiest arrival city to visit during a ski vacation because it's already in the Alps. Great skiing is only minutes away and that means you can take time at the end of a day or before you head out in the morning to tour.

Innsbruck—in German, the bridge over the Inn River—has twice hosted the Winter Olympics in the last 25 years (1964 and 1976). The city shares with Grenoble, France the distinction of being the only two cities within the Alps with more than 100,000 population.

A nice thing about visiting Innsbruck in winter is that skiers are welcome everywhere. In some museums and public buildings in Europe you might get a second glance or feel uncomfortable visiting in your ski outfit. Not in Innsbruck. Innsbruck residents know that many visitors like to ski half of the day and sightsee the rest.

First-time visitors should head for the heart of the old town along the Maria-Theresienstrasse for the most breathtaking view of the Larwendel Mountain range in the distance beyond the famed city street. A two-hour walk through the old town takes in the oldest buildings, including the **Goldenes Dachl,** a former royal 16th-century building with gold-plated copper shingles on the roof.

Visit also the **Hofburg,** or palace, and **St. Jakob's cathedral**. Popular among visitors is the **Tirolean Folklore museum,** which has an outstanding display of traditional costumes and exhibits from the entire Tirol region. It's open every day (except Sunday afternoon) from 9 a.m. until noon and from 2 until 5 p.m.

Milan, Italy

Most skiers heading for the Italian slopes will land in Milan, the commercial and fashion heart of Italy. The city is only about an hour-and-a-half drive from the main Val d'Aosta resorts of Courmayeur and Cervinia. This surprising city deserves exploration either upon arrival or departure from Italy.

One of the jewels of Milan is the majestic white-marble **Duomo,** or Cathedral. The facade, finished in the early 19th-century by order of Napoleon, is breathtaking and tours are organized to allow a walk on the roof where no less than 135 pinnacles and scores of marble statues adorn the cathedral.

Walk through the **Gallaria**, one of the first covered shopping malls to the **La Scala** the most famous opera house in the world. Here you can take a tour of the opera house and see the gilted splendor of one of the world's great theaters. If you are in Milan for an evening you might check into seeing an opera here. The season lasts most of the winter.

The **Sforzas castle**, built in the mid-1300's, and the park which surrounds it are both fun to explore. The **Bera Palace** houses an art collection with works by most of the Italian renaissance masters as well as El Greco, Rembrandt and Rubens. Perhaps the jewel of Milan's art treasures is the painting of **The Last Supper** by Leonardo da Vinci. It can be seen in the Church of Santa Maria delle Grazia.

If you have some additional time, a visit to the **Leonardo da Vinci museum** filled with models of Leonardo's wild inventions is facinating. The museum also houses Milan's science and technology collections.

Lyons, France

Recently, Lyons has become one of the air gateways for skiers heading to the French Alps. Though most French ski resorts can be reached by direct bus from the airport, Lyons deserves a visit of at least a day or two. This city is one of the commercial, artistic, and gastronomic capitals of France.

The city's **Fine Arts Museum** houses the most impressive French collection of art outside of the Louvre in Paris. Other museums packed into the city include the **Museum of Textiles** with one of the best tapestry collections in the world.

The major attraction for tourists is the **old town** which is the most extensive grouping of 15th-century and Renaissance buildings in France. A visit to the **St. Jean Cathedral** and a walk through the narrow streets past artisans' workshops in old gothic doorways and medieval courtyards yield a new discovery every few yards. This area is crisscrossed with covered passageways, called *traboules*, which give access from one street to another and pass through courtyards and old buildings. The old town has over 100 of these unique passages.

Take the cable cars to the top of the hill dominating the old town. Here enjoy the basilica, and a fabulous view over Lyons. The **Greco-Roman Museum** houses antiquities such as inscribed old Roman tablets, a Gaulish calender and beautiful mosaics. Outside, the former Roman theater is restored and new ruins of some of the most important Roman temples have been excavated.

The marionette, or string-controlled puppet, was created in Lyons. Today, *Guignol and Madelon*—the French equivilant to Punch and Judy—still perform and poke fun at national and local politics.

Lyons is one of the gourmet centers of France. A meal in one of the city's leading restaurants will be an experience you will savor for some time.

Annecy, France

This is the hub of the *Haute Savoie*. The lakeside city offers the old and the new in stark contrast to each other. Even along the lake, modernistic buildings around the Place de la Libèration tower over the hidden old town. But, down the Thiou canal, the city's most ancient waterway, the medieval town huddles between the modern buildings. The old town is built on a series of picturesque canals and is a sister to Venice and Bruges in that regard.

This is a tour to the Middle Ages. Visit the church of **Saint-Francois**, the **Palais de L'Isle** and **Old Prisons**. The **Castle of Annecy** dominating the town has been restored and offers a different view of the red roofs of old Annecy, the lake and the mountains in the distance.

If you have time a trip around the lake by car is a joy. Take either the shorter coast road, or take the *col de la Forclaz* road for more spectacular views.

Austria

Austria is a country where sincere hospitality is deemed as important as great skiing. Austrians seem to go out of their way in order to make visitors feel at home. From the ski instructors to the hotel managers to the restaurant owners, the Austrians seem to take genuine pleasure in knowing that you have enjoyed yourself in their country. Their word for this spirit, *Gemütlichkeit*, encompasses everything a good host should be.

This country is one of the skiing capitals of the world and it is very affordable—a factor which, when added to the warmth and hospitality you'll encounter, will engender one more fond memory to take home with you.

A note on prices

The prices in this section reflect 1987/1988 winter season rates and should be used as a guide only. They will increase approximately one to three percent during the 1988/1989 winter season.

All prices are given in Austrian schillings (Sch). The book was researched when the schilling was at an exchange rate of Sch. 12 to $1. Any subsequent change in the exchange rate will be the biggest factor affecting the prices.

Times for a season

High season—Christmas, New Years, 20 December to 6 January and 4 February through 31 March.

Low season—until 19 December, 7 January to 3 February, and after 1 April.

Use these dates for planning purposes. If you are planning to travel during the borderline weeks make sure to check with the individual resorts since their dates may vary by a week due to local school holidays.

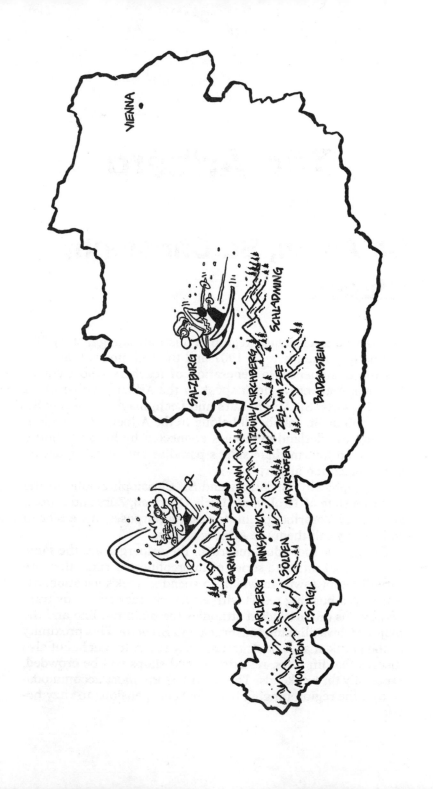

The Arlberg
Lech, Zürs, St. Anton, St. Christoph, Stuben

The Arlberg is a legendry region in Austrian skiing history. Ski instruction began here in 1907 and the techniques that were developed influenced a generation of teachers who went to America. And yet we don't speak of the Arlberg, rather of its famed resorts: St. Anton, Zürs and Lech, maybe even tiny St. Christoph or St. Jakob. All belong to the Arlberg Pass region, a skiing wonderland of resorts connected by lift and shuttle bus. It's an intermediate skier's paradise only three hours by car from Zurich airport.

Geographically, St. Anton and St. Christoph belong to the Austrian state of Tirol, while Lech, Oberlech, Zürs and Stuben are part of Vorarlberg. But, for skiing purposes, it's easier to collectively call them the Arlberg slopes.

Though the individual resorts of the Arlberg share the same snow and an intricate series of interconnected runs, they are very different towns in which to spend a week's vacation. **St. Anton** is a bustling resort with extremely easy access by train and by bus or car since it straddles the main rail line and the major highway linking Innsbruck and Bregenz. This proximity to the public makes St. Anton an easy resort to reach, but also insures that lift lines, restaurants and shops will be crowded, especially on weekends. The town has the most accommodation in the region ranging from low-cost pensions to ritzy hotels.

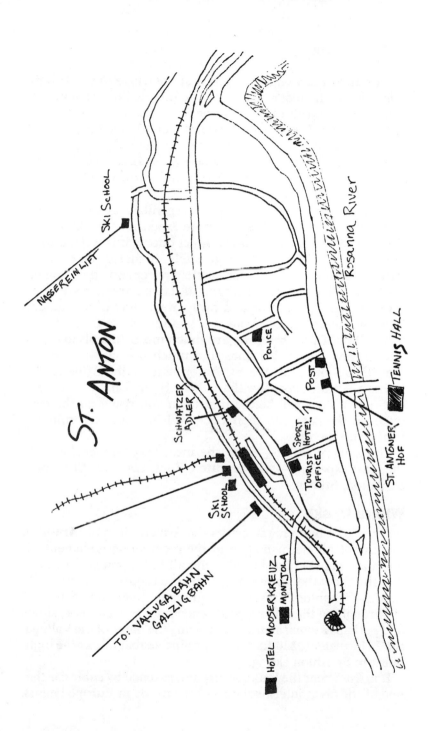

Stuben is a tiny village which is at the fringe of the Arlberg. It is small with moderate hotels. The Albona lift which rises in two stages connects easily with the St. Christoph/St. Anton side of the Arlberg. Due to its location it can be much colder than the other resorts in the winter, but has an advantage in the spring when its snow is still good after Lech and Zürs are winding down. This is an unpretentious town and the least expensive in the Arlberg.

St. Christoph is the highest Arlberg village at 1800 meters. It is small, more exclusive and more expensive than St. Anton. The lifts start almost from the hotel doors. It is a good town to get away from it all. Unfortunately, it shares the crowded conditions of St. Anton as far as lifts are concerned during the weekends. However the morning lift lines are much shorter.

Lech and Zürs are tucked away at the end of a dead-end (during winter) valley about a 20-minute drive from the St. Anton Pass. They, therefore, are much more difficult to reach. This means shorter lift lines and much less crowded slopes than those found on the St. Anton side of the Arlberg. The towns are more expensive than either St. Anton, St. Christoph or Stuben. Zürs will be the first town you reach on the road up from the pass and then Lech will be about ten minuted further up the valley.

The Arlberg resorts—from the most expensive/exclusive to the least expensive—may be rated: Zürs, Lech, St. Christoph, St. Anton, Stuben.

Where to ski

If any resort best characterizes the Arlberg, it is **St. Anton**, a mixture of Alpine rusticity and the most modern elements of international ski high life. Despite all its trappings, however, it is the snow that draws people by the thousands daily to St. Anton—""Stanton," in ski slang to many American visitors.

Throughout the Arlberg you'll encounter guest houses, shops and perhaps a *wurst* stand or two using the name of the Valluga, the 2811-meter (9220-foot) rocky pinnacle that marks the high-point in St. Anton skiing.

It is from near the Valluga summit, reached by cable car that one of the great intermediate skiing cruises in Europe begins.

The slope from the Vallugagrat (2650 meters—8692 feet) is filled with hundreds of turns as you work your way for at least a half hour to the valley floor.

Experts can take the final section of the cable to the top of the Valluga. After a difficult climb only accompanied by a guide, they can ski down to Zürs.

You'll find less nerve-rattling skiing farther down. We recommend the massive mogul field off the Tanzboden lift where you'll see the best skiers bouncing from mogul to mogul, occasionally adding a 360-degree turn for flair.

The village of **St. Christoph**, which sits along the crown of the Arlberg Pass at 1800 meters (5904 feet), is the other ground station for skiing this side of St. Anton.

The blue and red runs are cruises that offer great enjoyment. And there's good skiing for beginners from the base at St. Christoph.

The other ski area on this side of St. Anton is the Kampall, a 2326-meter (7629-foot) summit where you'll enjoy the two blue runs to the Gampen mid-station at 1850 meters (6068 feet). From Gampen, continue through the trees into town or drop over the ridge into the Steissbachtal and take the last half of the Valluga run. We prefer continuing along the blue run from the Gampen into town.

St. Anton's third ski area is the Rendl (2100 meters—6888 feet) on the opposite side of town. The best intermediate run is from the Gampberg summit (2400 meters—7872 feet) back into town.

Zürs and Lech can be skied together but there is no real connection between St. Anton and Zürs (as mentioned, guides take experienced skiers from the Valluga to the Zürs side) and between Stuben and Zürs. You have to depend on your car or a Post Bus, costing about Sch. 15.

In themselves, both Lech and Zürs qualify for resort status, even if their lift passes don't cover the entire Arlberg. In Lech, skiing centers on the Oberlech region which is reached by a T-bar and chairlift from the center of the town. A system of 16 lifts take skiers up to 2377 meters. This area will keep an intermediate busy for two days and off-piste possibilities will challange experts. Opposite Oberlech is the Rüfikopf area. From

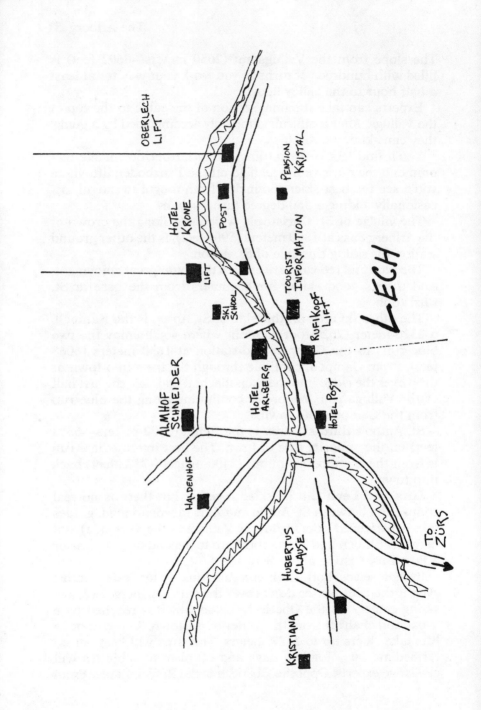

here experts, *real experts*, can drop down the face to Lech, or intermediates and beginners can comfortably cruise on to Zürs.

Zürs is a tougher area as far as marked trails go. All the runs from the top of the Trittkopf (2434 meters) are rated intermediate but would rate a black diamond in the U.S. Once again experts can make their own trails straight into the town. The Madloch side of the valley has six long intermediate runs and three long beginner runs. However, after the area has been well skied, skiers can venture almost anywhere on this side.

The run between Zürs and Lech is one you'll enjoy. Take the lifts to the 2438-meter (7997-foot) Madloch Joch and then ski the red Madloch run into Lech. To get back, take the cablecar to Rüfikopf above Lech and then ski down and across to the base of the Hexenboden lift and Zürs. For a variation you can ski into neighboring Zug from the Madloch and then come back up via the Zugerberg lifts. From there, it's a red-rated cruise back down into Oberlech.

Stuben was our favorite bargain village in the region, tiny with only a few lifts. The best run was intermediate—from the Albona Grat (2400 meters—7872 feet). Stuben is connected with St. Anton/St. Christoph by the blue-rated trail from the Albona mid-station to a crossover tow at Alpe Rauz. From there, take the chairlift to Pfannenkopf and work your way down into St. Christoph.

Mountain rating

Intermediates run the show in the Arlberg region. St. Anton is overwhelmingly red and blue on the ski map with some challenges that merit expert skills.

Lech and Zürs are beginner/intermediate areas by the color of the prepared runs. Experts can test their mettle by going off-piste. This area has some of the best off-track powder skiing in Europe.

Beginners are not forgotten, for there is always a cluster of easy slopes at the bottom of each mountain.

Ski school

St. Anton advertises the "largest ski school (tel. 05446-2306 or 3411) in the world." Whatever the validity of the claim, there are 300 teachers registered here and a total of nearly 700 in the area. The school classes form up in amazing numbers each morning at the base of the Kampall. Lech and Zürs also have 300 instructors with classes forming at the base of the Schlegelkopf lift. Ski school prices are approximately the same through the entire region.

1988/89 Ski school prices for St. Anton/St. Christoph:

Individual lessons

for one day (four hours)   Sch. 1600
for two days   Sch. 3000
Sch. 150 additional for each additional person.

Group lessons

for one day   Sch. 340
for three days   Sch. 740
for six days   Sch. 950

Prices are slightly higher during high season.
The cross-country ski school prices are the same as for alpine lessons.

Lift Tickets

These are 1988/89 prices. The best bargain is the Arlberg area pass. There are discounts of approximately 40 percent for children and 20 percent for seniors (men 65+ and women 60+). There is also approximately a 15 percent discount during the low season.

for one day   Sch. 325
for two days   Sch. 610
for six days   Sch. 1570
for seven days   Sch. 1770
for fourteen days   Sch. 2840

Accommodation

The local tourist offices maintain lists of area hotels, rental apartments and chalets (*see addresses below*). *Note: If you are planning to be in the resort during Christmas or New Year and are staying at a small hotel, plan on taking a jacket and tie. Guest houses and smaller hotels often organize a traditional dinner and small party. It is a beautiful tradition and makes the guests feel they are indeed there on a special day.*

The first price is for the special one week package offered during January, sometimes called the *Pulverschnee-wochen* which includes room, half board, lift tickets and ski instructor. The last price noted is the normal price during high season for a double room per person. Expect to pay 15 to 20 percent less during low season.

St. Anton

Hotel Schwarzer Adler (tel. 2244) Sch. 8490—A great hotel if you want to splurge. Considered the best hotel in town. Great atmosphere in a place doing business since 1570. Normal daily rate: Sch. 1150-2200 (half pension).

St. Antoner Hof (tel. 2910) Sch. 9120—Hotel is located away from the main downtown street but only about a three minute walk away from the action and about five minutes to the lifts. Normal daily rate: Sch. 1450-1700 (half pension).

Hotel Mooserkreuz (tel.2730) Sch. 7580—Sauna and indoor swimming pool plus at the end of the day ski back to the hotel. Normal daily rate: Sch. 980-1150 (half pension).

Montjola (tel. 2302) Sch. 7210—Small, cozy lodge of a hotel. About three minutes walk from the center of town. Normal daily rate: 860-880 (half pension).

Berghaus Maria (tel. 2005) Sch. 7930—Away from center of town and quiet. Excellent cooking; friendly service. Normal daily rate: Sch. 950-1290 (half pension).

Hotel Mössmer (tel. 2727) Sch. 4990—Normal daily rate: Sch. 450 (Bed-and-breakfast only).

Tannenhof (tel. 2364) No weekly package. Normal daily rates: Sch. 450-550 (B&B only).

St. Christoph

Arlberg-Hospiz (tel. 2611) Sch. 12,420. The most exclusive spot on this side of the Arlberg. The restaurant is perhaps one of the best in Austria. Normal daily rate: Sch. 2080 (half pension).

Maiensee (tel. 2804) Sch. 6360—Right next to the lift with all the amenities. Normal daily rates: Sch. 1030-1170 (half-pension).

Lech

Hotel Post (tel. 2206; telex: 39118) Sch. 13,000. Attracts a slightly older crowd with family money, but is a beautiful and very traditional and cozy hotel in the Alpine tradition. Normal daily rate: Sch. 1450-3200 (half-pension).

Almhof Schneider (tel. 3500; telex: 39115) Together with the Post considered the best in town. It is cozy, not as formal as the Post and more modern. Normal daily rate: Sch. 1550-3500 (full pension).

Arlberg (tel. 2134; telex: 39122) Sch. 14,765 (full pension). Old elegance, slightly worn. Normal daily rate: Sch. 1480-3280 (full pension).

Berghof (tel. 2635) Sch. 9550 (full pension). Top quality with sauna, whirlpool and tennis, but no pool. Normal daily rate: Sch. 1370-1780 (full pension).

Kristiania (tel. 2561) Sch. 9865. A bit out of the mainstream of the town but very nice. Normal daily rate: Sch. 1260-1995 (half pension).

Sonnenburg (tel. 2147; telex: 552) Sch. 8920 (half pension). Located in the Oberlech section of Lech. Normal daily rates: Sch. 990-1800 (half pension).

Haldenhof (tel. 2444) Sch. 8500 (half pension). A small family owned hotel where the owners bring all the guests together each week. It is the perfect Austrian experience. Normal daily rate: Sch. 950-1390 (half pension).

Hotel Lech (Tel.2289) Sch. 6750 (half pension). Normal daily rate: Sch. 850-1150 (half pension).

Kristall (tel. 2422) Sch. 6890 (half pension). Central location and friendly service. Normal daily rates: Sch.630-700.

Hubertushof (tel. 2701) Rustic building; especially good bargain. Located out of the center of town in Zug. Make sure you specify that you want a room with private bath. Normal daily rate: Sch. 460-520.

Pension Sursilva (tel.2431) Sch. 7030 (half pension). New pension in town. Good value and modern facilities. Normal daily rate: Sch. 790-830.

Zürs

Zürserhof (tel.2513; telex: 632488) Sch. 12,940-14,130 (full pension). This is one of the most luxurious hotels in the Alps in a class with the Palace in St. Moritz. Suites and mini-apartments are available for Sch. 18,010-19,130 during the ski weeks in low season. The normal room rates: Sch. 1930-2160 (full pension).

The other hotels in Zürs are all quite good. Try the **Arlberghaus** (tel. 2258) Sch. 7580-9680 for the ski week, or Sch. 870-1150 normal daily rate. The **Schweiserhaus** (tel. 2463) is one of the least expensive at Sch. 6030 for the ski week, and Sch. 600 for the normal daily rate.

Stuben

Post Hotel (tel. 761) Sch. 6450-6975—A good choice for uncomplicated skiing with on-site ski rental, ski school and a bank. Ask about its all-in plan. Normal daily rate: Sch. 695-820.

Haus Erzberg (tel. 729) Sch. 4560—Small (thirteen beds); includes breakfast only. Normal daily rate: Sch. 310-380

Hotel Mondschein (tel. 721) Sch. 6675-6975—Excellent hotel in historic building (built in 1739). Indoor pool; friendly atmosphere. Normal daily rate: Sch. 735-860.

Dining

Our tip in St. Anton is the dining room in the Hotel Berghaus Maria. If food plays a big part in your ski vacation plans, book a room here.

The Schwarzer Adler (tel. 2244) sets a table that brims with Austrian specialties. Menu and à la carte prices start at Sch. 140.

To demolish your budget, we recommend the Arlberg Hospiz at St. Christoph where $40 is gone as quickly as the sumptuous noodles, creamed mushrooms, roast duck, etc. Don't expect to see Prince Charles on the day you've reserved, but he's numbered among the star-studded clientele.

All the way down to earth, take a snack in the *Bahnhof* restaurant near St. Anton's famous Hotel Post. The food is good and inexpensive.

On the mountain, choose from several places, the most popular being the cafeteria at the Valluga cable car's second station.

In Lech try the restaurants in Hotel Montana (tel. 2460)—featuring the best wine celler in town,—and Hotel Salome (tel. 2306). Hotel Krone consistantly gets good recommendations. For nouvelle *Austrian* cuisine try the Goldener Berg (tel. 2205) or Brunnenhof (tel. 2349). The Hotel Post restaurant (tel. 2206) serves excellent traditional nouvelle cuisine and the Schneider (tel. 3500) has excellent traditional Austrian food. Just outside Lech, in Zug, the restaurants Alphorn and Rotewand offer excellent food in the best of Austrian tradition. For cheaper eats try Pizza Charlie for good Italian food and head up to Gasthof Omesberg for great traditional Austrian.

In Zürs the best restaurant is, naturally, in the Zürserhof. Try the Lorünser (tel. 2254), as well, for excellent meals.

Apartments

If you want to rent a vacation apartment, ask for the apartment listing brochure from each of the tourist offices in the Arlberg. They maintain a complete list of the several hundred apartments and chalets available in season.

In Lech, apartments can be rented with four beds for approximately Sch.1500 per day, during high season. In Zürs expect to pay around Sch. 1750 per day, during high season. In St. Anton a four-bed apartment can be rented for about Sch. 1200 per day. The prices are middle-of-the-price range prices.

Nightlife

In **St. Anton** for a one-stop nightspot, we recommend the Sporthotel near the center of town. Here you can do everything from arranging a week's lodging (half pension from Sch. 5950) to drinking at the bar, dancing in the nightclub and enjoying a good meal in the restaurant.

In St. Anton's central pedestrian zone you'll be able to find something that suits your night tastes by simply taking a stroll.

Our ski instructor recommended the Krazy Kanguruh, which has a reputation as the town's biggest après-ski watering hole, but we can't praise it wholeheartedly. Away from the center of town, it was crowded when we visited.

We preferred the cozy Valluga Bar in town, a subterranean club with music.

In **Lech**, we were partial to the disco in the Hotel Almhof-Schneider, perhaps only because friends have stayed at the hotel. A more chic after-hours address is the bar and disco at the Tannenbergerhof or head to the Hotel Krone where there is live music and a good local crowd! Expect to pay about Sch. 60-100 per drink.

For a great evening of singing, yodeling and dancing, good food, wine from hanging decanters or beer, try the Hubertus Clause tucked away in Lech. The zither player, who has been playing here for over ten years, does a fantastic job on old rock and roll numbers and polkas. If you've been waiting to dance to Hello Mary Lou played on a zither, here is your chance. Thursdays and Fridays are very crowded since the ski school classes descend *en masse*.

Child care

Ski courses for children are offered, as is a ski kindergarten for kids from age five, plus baby-sitting services (from three upwards). The ski school includes lunch with a drink and there are further reductions if the parents are also enrolled in the ski school.

Children's ski school

for one day	Sch. 470
for three days	Sch. 1110
for six days	Sch. 1520

The school is open from 9 a.m. until 4:30 p.m.
Kindergartens, for children two and older, are available in all the resorts. Prices in Lech and Oberlech are Sch. 310 per day and Sch. 940-1020 for six days. Lunch is Sch. 70 extra. Opening hours are normally from 9 a.m. to 4 p.m. Expect to pay similar rates in the other Arlberg resorts.

Getting there

You'll probably fly into Zurich, although the trip is not any more difficult from Munich or Innsbruck.

From Zurich, it is a little over three hours by car, or you can take the train—the Arlberg Express—directly to St. Anton.

Getting to Lech and Zürs is slightly more difficult. One can get off the train in Langen and then take a bus up the hill, or get off the train in St. Anton and take another bus up to the villages. Swissair runs a special skibus from Zurich airport direct to Lech at 12:30 p.m. On Saturdays the bus makes an additional run at 7 p.m. Fare is Sch. 400 one way, and Sch. 700 round trip. Reservations can be made at Tourist Office Lech (tel. 2161-15; telex: 052-39123).

Direct trains connect Langen with Cologne, Dortmund, Munich, Innsbruck, Salzburg, Zurich, Paris, Brussels and Calais.

Driving from Zurich, take the autobahn to St. Gallen and then to Feldkirche and to the Arlberg Pass. From Munich and Stuttgart it is easiest to travel to Bregenz, then head to Feldkirche and the Arlberg.

Other activities

Winter activities along the Arlberg Pass are centered around skiing and you'll have to choose swimming, tennis or sightseeing for alternatives.

Day outings are offered to Innsbruck and to Bregenz and the shores of Lake Constance.

Check with Heli Tyrol (tel. 2732) for information on express air trips to Innsbruck and Graz, Austria.

Tourist information

St. Anton: Fremdenverkehrsverband, A-6580 St. Anton a A.; tel. 05446-22690.

Stuben: Verkehrsverein, A-6752 Stuben; tel. 05582-761; telex: 52459.

Lech: Verkehrsamt, A-6764 Lech; tel. 05583-21610; telex: 05239123.

Zürs: Verkehrsamt, A-6763 Zürs; tel. 05583-2245; telex 052-39111.

Badgastein

Skiing may be the number-one pastime in the Gasteiner valley but the area's popularity as a meeting place for European vacationers keeps it lively year round. Austrians from all parts of the country head up the valley during the winter. The resort area is a grouping of four systems: Badgastein, Sportgastein, Bad Hofgastein and Dorfgastein.

Curiously skiing may not even be the major reason for the arrival of tourists. Badgastein first gained fame as a thermal spa resort. The resort attracted the upper crust of society and a rather etiquette-conscious clientel. That formality which developed over the years, especially in the grand hotels—many of which still have private thermal pools—continues today. The winter coat of preference will probably be fur and the lineup of shiney automobiles in front of the casino looks like a Mercedes dealership. Though the thermal spa visitors still cling to protocol, the modern skiing tourist has softened the formerly stiff rules of decorum.

Where to ski

The best skiing is from the top station on the Stubnerkogel at 2248 meters (7,373 feet) where an exceptional intermediate run streches nearly seven miles. This run, the Angertal piste, drops 1300 meters (4,264 feet). From the ground there is a lift connection to the Schlossalm area above Bad Hofgastein.

There's a challenging World Cup run from the Graukogel summit opposite the Stubner. The lift takes you up to 2000 meters (6,556 feet) and the black run takes you down; or a side trail accommodates intermediates.

Also try Sportgastein, about six miles away and easily accessible by bus. Best of the runs is from Schideck at 2165 meters (7,101 feet). From here an additional run—the piste from the 2686 meter (8,810 foot) Kreuzkogel—is worth trying.

At the top, a choice of four different trails awaits you. Best of them is the north trail which is left unprepared and provides great powder skiing with the right conditions. The nearly five-mile run covers a vertical drop of almost 1500 meters (4,950 feet).

Mountain rating

The valley, particularly Badgastein, is intermediate country with the most notable exception the World Cup course. It is a good place to tune up your ski legs and leave some spring in them for partying later. If you are strictly expert, you'll enjoy approximately a dozen runs but once finished with them you'll be ready to move on. Experts should check out an off-piste group or a guide for a morning. Both will offer little-known runs down unprepared sections of the resort and will provide most of the challenge you crave.

Ski school

Three ski schools with a total of 100 instructors provide courses in the valley. In Dorfgastein call 06433-538, in Bad Hofgastein telephone 06432-6339, and in Badgastein call 06434-2260. Average instruction prices for one hour of **private lessons** are: Sch. 360 per hour. **Group lessons** will cost: One day—Sch. 420; three days—Sch. 930; and six days—Sch. 1150. Three day cross-country lessons are Sch. 450.

Lift tickets

The best choice is the Gastein *Super Ski Schein*, a combined ticket for the area resorts, linking 60 lifts and a network of buses and trains. These are 88/89 prices.

for one day	Sch. 290
for two days	Sch. 560
for three days	Sch. 790
for six days	Sch. 1400
for seven days	Sch. 1580

Low season prices are appproximately 14 percent lower

Accommodation

Choose from a great selection of hotels in Badgastein and Bad Hofgastein. there is less variety in Dorfgastein nearer the entrance to the valley. Of the three, Badgastein probably offers the most European ski atmosphere, including a healthy helping of nightlife.

There are four five-star hotels in Badgastein. Our favorite in town is the expensive **Bellevue** (tel. 06434-2571) and **Elisabethpark** (tel. 2551) while the four-star **Hoteldorf Grüner Baum** (tel. 06434-25160; telex: 067516), remains an excellent choice for resort accommodations outside the center of town. Rooms from Sch. 550 daily; with full pension from Sch. 710. The restaurant is one of the finest in the Gastein valley.

In town consider **Das Weismayr** in the center of things. This 135-bed hotel (tel. 06434-2594; telex: 067531) offers traditional accommodation with sturdy old-style European furniture, thick carpets and tapestries. Rooms per day start at Sch. 650 with half-pension.

Check out the 116-bed **Hotel Mozart** (tel. 06434-2686) with rooms from Sch. 215 per day; or Sch. 380 per day for half-pension. Another budget choice is the **Hotel Stubnerhof** (tel. 06434-29910) with half-pension from Sch. 360 per day or just the room for Sch. 320.

Apartments

Most visitors stay in hotels and pensions or a few private homes in the Gastein valley. Also available are vacation chalets with the largest number in Bad Hofgastein. Details on chalet and apartment rentals are available through the tourist offices in any one of the three resorts.

Dining

We found a restaurant in Badgastein that is far above average. It's **Vinothek**, a palace of eating pleasure with prices to match. The menu runs from Sch. 300 to Sch. 880, but the dishes are outstanding. Fresh vegetables, perfectly prepared meat and, as might be expected from the name, a superior selection of wines. A great place to splurge. Most evenings reservations (tel. 06434-

32118) are advised. For a traditional inexpensive Austrian meal try the Orania Stuben.

Nightlife

After a day on the slopes, the elite choose the tables at the Casino in Badgastein or retire immediately to the bar near the playing tables. After 11 p.m. the evening grows progressively wilder in Mühlhäusl disco club in Badgastein. The Glocknerkeller in Bad Hofgastein is a typical Austrian pub with live music and dancing each night.

Child care

Child care facilities are offered for children three years and above in Badgastein and Bad Hofgastein. The minimum age in Dorfgastein is four. Individual baby-sitting service is also offered with information available from the tourist ofice.

Getting there

The best international airport connections are through Salzburg. The best way to get to the resorts is by car, driving south, along the magnificant Tauernautobahn to Bischofshofen and on to the Gastein valley. Expect about an hour's drive.

Other activities

The three towns offer a wide variety of outdoor recreation. A day trip to Salzburg with a tour down the salt mines is one of the preferred outings. Badgstein and Bad Hofgastein are famed thermal spring resorts. Make sure to take time to enjoy the hot springs during your visit.

For the non-skier the view from the Schlossalm at the 7,000 foot level is worth the lift ride up from Bad Hofgastein. In Badgastein visit the Nikolauskirche and the local museum.

Tourist information

Kurverwaltung, A-5640 Badgastein, tel. 06434-25310; telex: 67520

Kurverwaltung, A-5630 Bad Hofgastein, tel. 06432-4290; telex: 67796

Kurverwaltung, A-5632 Dorfgastein, tel. 06433-277; telex: 67737

Innsbruck

Innsbruck, Austria's most famous ski resort, has twice hosted the Winter Olympic Games (1964 and 1976). This is the capital of Austrian Tyrol. Don't make the mistake of believing that if you sign up for a trip to Innsbruck you will be stepping into a quaint ski resort. Innsbruck is a bustling city which happens to be surrounded by a group of small resorts providing good skiing.

The city of 120,000 residents in the valley of the emerald-green Inn River has such a collection of cultural attractions that skiing is not the dominant factor here, as it is in most other resort towns and cities.

Fortunately the skiers, though they will have to put up with the inconvenience of a relatively long bus ride to the lifts, will have a chance to ski up to five different areas in the immediate vicinity of Innsbruck, plus the opportunity to strike out for a day in St. Anton, Ischgl, Kitzbühel or the Stubaital. Europe's best cross country resort, Seefeld, is also right next door. It is a good way to test a lot of Austria's skiing and have a better idea of where you may plan to spend more time next season.

Where to ski

There are five major ski areas ringing Innsbruck. They are—in descending order of difficulty—Hungerburg-Seegrube, Axamer-Lizum, Tulfes, Igls and Mutters. Altogether, nearly 65 miles of trails are prepared for downhill specialists and an equal length in cross-country circuits.

Experts should strike out for Hungerburg, across the Inn from the other slopes. This is the gateway to the great black trails of the Hafelkar. We recommend the mogul-studded, steep black run from the 2334-meter (7657-foot) summit as one of

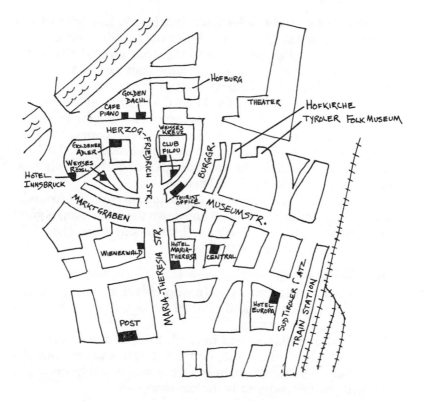

the most challenging we've skied in Austria. If you can't ski this one well, you're not an expert.

Of the Olympic slopes, the Axamer-Lizum is best known. The slopes of Axams, a village about six miles outside Innsbruck, start at the 1600-meter (5249-foot) level. There is nothing here but a parking lot and plenty of skiing for a day.

Heresy to say, but we liked three other runs better than the famous Olympic course, the Hoadl (2340 meters—7677 feet). The first two, from the nearby 2236-meter (7336-foot) Pleisen and slightly lower Kögele, take you all the way back to the valley floor. The Kögele is best of the two with a great four miles of skiing. Hardest was the demanding run down the Birgitzköpfl on the opposite side of the valley. The moguls pound your thighs and the steep slopes test an intermediate's courage.

Tulfes, nearly eight miles from Innsbruck, has skiing from the 2677-meter (8783-foot) level. For the powder and off-trail specialist, we highly recommend the area around the Glungezer summit. But you've got to climb half an hour or more on your own to enjoy the best off-trail variations.

Igls, at 900 meters (2952 feet) is in the shadow of the Patscherkofel, the 2247-meter (7372-foot) summit station for the men's downhill run. You can ski the same 2.4-mile course traveled by Austrian Franz Klammer to win a gold medal at the 1976 Games. The bobsleigh run is also at Igls and guests are allowed on the course. (Price: Sch.350/person).

The Mutters ski area, around the mountain from the Axamer-Lizum (or over the Birgitzköpfl and down the mountain) is good intermediate territory. The runs branch out from the Pfriemesköpfl (1800 meters—5904 feet).

Mountain rating

As a two-time Olympic city, Innsbruck offers much for the expert skier. Each of the major ski areas will give the intermediate countless tests.

And beginner skiers need have no fear: all those Austrians had to learn how to ski, too, and the starter and training lifts are usually right at the bottom of the longer cableways. The moment you're ready, so is the mountain.

Ski school

Each area has organized instruction with a total of approximately 200 teachers working in the region daily. Private and group lessons for downhill and cross-country are given. Call the Innsbruck ski school (tel. 05222-25715) for details.

Individual lessons

one hour	Sch. 320

Group lessons

for one day	Sch. 340
for three days	Sch. 740
for five days	Sch. 900
for six days	Sch. 950
for six half days	Sch. 790

School courses meet on the slopes, but you can take a shuttle-bus to the area you're skiing.

Lift tickets

Day tickets for the individual areas of the Innsbruck region cost from Sch. 150–220. The best bargain is the regional pass, which is good for a minimum of three days.

for three days	Sch. 655
for six days	Sch. 1060
six of eight days	Sch. 1170

Buses run daily from Innsbruck to the main slopes. For information, call 23176. In addition, buses also take skiers to the best cross-country circuits in the area.

Accommodation

While it may be more romantic to stay in one of the neighboring villages, the attraction of skiing Innsbruck is that you can enjoy the benefits of a major city—one of Europe's cultural capitals, in fact.

The city tourist office advertises accommodation ranging from a sleeping bag to a king's bed.

The best budget accommodations are offered through the tourist office-sponsored Club Innsbruck plan. Check with the tourist office for the plan's winter price list of accommodation, half-pension included unless noted, for a minimum of three nights. The half-pension, daily rate is given below unless otherwise noted.

Europa-Tyrol (tel. 05222-35571; telex: 53424) Sch. 780—On Sudtiroler Platz, this is a quality choice for Innsbruck. It is only a short distance from the old city and near the top attractions.

Hotel Alpinpark (tel. 48600; telex: 53509) Sch. 520.

Hotel Maria-Theresia (tel. 35615; telex: 53300) Sch. 650 with breakfast only—a quality hotel in the center of town. A Best Western property.

Hotel Goldener Adler (tel. 26334; telex: 53415) Sch. 650—One of the old traditional and beautiful hotels in town.

Hotel Grauer Bär (tel. 34531; telex: 53387) Sch. 520.

Hotel Weisses Kreuz (tel. 21890) Sch. 410—In the center of town; good location for city sightseeing.

Hotel-Pension Binder (tel. 42236) Sch. 300.

Gasthof Weisses Rössl (tel. 23057) Sch. 440 with breakfast—central location.

Gasthof Engl (tel. 83112) Sch. 250.

In Igls—The town of Igls adjacent to Innsbruck is the closest town to a mountain resort in the immediate vicinity. In fact, it could make a very pleasant destination in itself with Innsbruck nearby for occasional forays.

The two best hotels in town are the Schlosshotel (tel. 5222-77217; telex: 53314) and the Sporthotel (tel. 5222-77241; telex: 53314). The first is formal and quiet, the second is right in the middle of the town and a bit bouncier. For middle-of-the-road hotels try the Astoria or the Bon-Alpina. Pension Gruberhof and Pension Oswald are good low-priced establishments where you can get good half-board for about Sch.350/person/day. Two very nice bed and breakfast places to try are Hotel-Garni Lettgebhof and Pension Tyrol.

Apartments

Lodging in Innsbruck is primarily in hotels and pensions. For information on chalet and apartment rentals nearer the slopes, contact the Innsbruck tourist office.

There are more apartments in Igls. Send your particulars to the tourist office and they will send a list of available apartments.

Private rooms in Igls will end up costing, with bed and breakfast, about Sch.150-160 per person per night.

Dining

Restaurants listed below are in the heart of the city, where you'll also find the best lodging opportunities. In the individual towns there are countless dining establishments and mountain restaurants.

An excellent combination for eating and overnight lodging is Weisses Rössl (tel. 23057) at Liebachgasse 8 in the old city. The menu ranges from Sch. 60 to Sch. 125. They prepare some of the best typical Tyrolean dishes.

Visit the Goldener Adler (tel. 26334) in the old city if you have a craving for good beef, especially grilled T-bone. The menu begins at Sch. 100. An excellent traditional restaurant. Expect to pay $40 for two. Another great Austrian restaurant is the K & K Restaurant in the Hotel Schwarzer Adler (tel. 27109).

We agree with a Tyrolean friend who took us to the Altstadtstüberl (tel. 22347), promising it was one of the most reasonably priced restaurants in the old city. The menu begins at Sch. 70.

Considered the best restaurant in town by many is the Restaurant Kapeller (tel.43106). The Belle Epoque (tel. 28361) in the Clima Hotel also continues to hold its reputation for great food at high prices. The menu begins at Sch. 615.

Nightlife

We recommend you walk the Maria-Theresienstrasse and the central old city for just about all the nightlife atmosphere you could ever desire. The view is beautiful and small pubs and bars are hidden in alleys and under archways. Head to the "Cafe Piano" across from the Goldener Adler and then try out the bustling "Club Filou" with a great disco and bar on Stiftsgasse.

If you want to find the section of town with students and more local discos head for Riffi on Schöpfstrasse.

Check with the tourist office for a list of concerts taking place around town—they also sell tickets at the information office. I had the chance to enjoy a great "boogie woogie" concert at the Kongresshaus during my last visit. You never know who's touring Europe while you're on vacation.

Child care

Child care and ski kindergarten courses (age four and up) are available in Innsbruck's ski areas. Contact the ski kindergarten (tel. 22310) for details.

In Igls, the kindergarten is in the Kurpark, tel. 777482. One hour costs Sch. 30, five hours is Sch. 130, and ten hours costs Sch. 240.

Getting there

Innsbruck has its own airport with daily jet service from throughout Europe. Munich is the most frequently used international airport for travelers from the United States, but that is changing somewhat with the increased use of the Innsbruck airport. Tyrolean Airways, Innsbruck's hometown airline, is now flying scheduled service from Amsterdam, Frankfurt, Zurich, Vienna and Paris. Tyrolean Airways offers a perfect alternative to trains or a long drive by car or bus.

By car, the trip is from Munich via autobahn to the Inntal autobahn crossing, and then to Innsbruck—no more than three hours.

A more scenic auto trip is from Munich to Garmisch-Partenkirchen, scene of the 1932 and 1936 Winter Olympic Games, and then about a seventy-minute drive over the mountains to Innsbruck. Add at least two hours for sightseeing in Garmisch.

Other activities

Innsbruck shares with Grenoble the distinction of being a town within the Alps which has more than 100,000 residents. Innsbruck is the capital of the Austrian state of Tyrol and has a wealth of art and historical treasures. It is also on the way to the Brenner Pass, lowest route through the Alps to Italy.

Innsbruck is accustomed to visitors in ski outfits, whether inside a museum or at a fine restaurant. Visitors always head for the heart of town along the Maria-Theresienstrasse for the outstanding view of the Karwendel mountain range behind the classic old-city street.

The best way to see Innsbruck is to walk through the old town. Allow about two hours. The most photographed house in the old city is Goldenes Dachl, a former royal building from the sixteenth century with gold-plated copper shingles on the roof.

Visit the Hofburg, or palace, and St. Jakob's cathedral, plus the Tyrolean folklore museum. The city boasts dozens of other attractions listed for you by the tourist office.

Tourist information

Fremdenverkehrsverband Innsbruck-Igls and Umgebung, A-6021 Innsbruck; tel. 05222-25715; telex: 53423.

Ischgl and the Paznaun Valley

Ischgl, hard to pronounce (say Ish'-gull) but easy to ski, became in a few short days one of our favorite Austrian resorts. High in the Alps (1400 meters-m4592 feet), hard on the border with Switzerland, this ski center in the Paznaun Valley, is something of a secret to non-European skiers.

Ischgl is a resort with it all, wide open pistes, cross-border skiing, extensive off-piste areas, small alpine village atmosphere and excellent après ski and nightlife.

Further up the valley is Galtür, a much smaller and quieter resort with a correspondingly smaller ski area.

Where to ski

Ischgl's slopes are the best in the valley. In addition, neighboring See, Kappl and Galtür all have lifts. Across the range of mountains, in Switzerland, Samnaun is connected by lift with Ischgl.

Three gondola lifts connect Ischgl with the main skiing area 1000 meters above the town. The Silvrettabahn and the Fimbabahn bring skiers from opposite ends of town to the Idalp area (2311 meters). The Pardatschgratbahn takes skiers from the eastern section of town to Pardatschgrat at 2624 meters. Though the lift lines at the Silvrettabahn look daunting, the wait, even on the busiest days is not excessive due to a capacity of 2400 skiers per hour.

From the Idalp sector, lifts fan out to all corners of the resort. In fact, even skiers choosing to go directly to the higher Pardatschgrat will have to pass through the Idalp area to reach the other sections of Ischgl's slopes. The immediate Idalp area

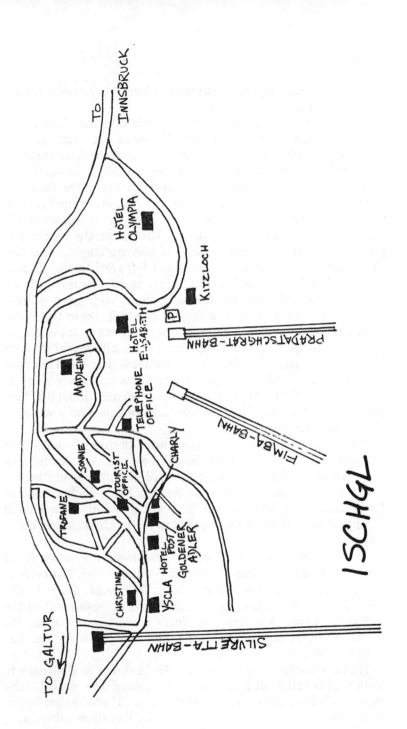

ISCHGL

TO INNSBRUCK

HOTEL OLYMPIA

KITZLOCH

HOTEL ELISABETH

TELEPHONE OFFICE

MADLEIN

PRÄDATSCHGRAT-BAHN

FIMBA-BAHN

SONNE

TOURIST OFFICE

CHARLY

TROFANE

CHRISTINE

YSCLA HOTEL POST

GOLDENER ADLER

SILVRETTA-BAHN

TO GALTÜR

serves as the nursery runs, offering a long, very easy with excellent lift support.

From Idalp, intermediates and experts take the chairlift up to Idjoch. Here, drop down into the Swiss Alp Trida section for long intermediate runs, or continue up to the Greitspitz for more challanging skiing in the Austrian section beneath the Palinkopf into the Hölltal or over another ridge to the Taja Alp.

At the end of the day take one of the runs from the Idalp or down the Velilltal for beautiful wide-open intermediate cruising. For another way to end the day, drop from the Pardatschgrat for a more challanging piste. If you are staying near the Silvrettabahn, you will want to head leftward to the middle station, then follow the No. 1 trail into town. For those closer to the Fimba or Pardatschgratbahn stations, keep going straight down into town. If there is a fork in the trail, ski to the right.

Determined off-piste skiers can arrange for a snow cat to take them to the Piz Val Gronda or the Heidelbergerhütte with a guide for a day of skiing across untracked snow. This area is scheduled for lift development but it's a few years away at this time. The Swiss must first construct an additional lift from Samnaun before the Austrian lift builders can raise a wrench.

Down to Samnaun

The Swiss town of Samnaun is the target of many Ischgl skiers because either they are determined to ski over the border to a Swiss town, or they are hot on the trail of duty-free cigarettes, perfume or whisky. In any case the run from the backside of the Palinkopf is relatively uninteresting and the town itself hardly of more interest than a visit to the nearest airport duty-free store.

Duty-free here is big business. If one smokes or wants to fill up the hot toddy cabinet, Samnaun is wonderful, but once is more than enough for the run from Palinkopf. Once in the town you must catch a post bus from the opposite end of the village to Ravaisch where a cablecar carries skiers up to Alp Trida. There is normally about a half-hour wait for the Ravaisch cablecar.

There is another trail from Alp Trida down to Compatsch. This trail is rather difficult and often closed due to avalanche (too much snow) or rocks (too little snow). If you do get down, a post bus will carry you back up to the Ravaisch cablecar.

Galtür

A shuttlebus runs from the village center to the skiing area. Skiing here is mellow. One day should be more than enough to explore every run. It is perhaps a better area for beginners than Ischgl.

A single chair and a drag lift take skiers up from the base to Birkhahnkopf. From there take the Ballunspitzlift to a choice of three easy expert runs or a good intermediate run. Skiers can head for a newly-opened section called Innere Kopsalpe which offers the toughest runs. On a sunny day this back bowl offers an advanced intermediate great fun for an entire morning or afternoon.

Mountain rating

Ischgl is not recommended for absolute beginners. The English of the ski school is limited to technical ski jargon and the nursery slopes are far above the town. Galtür would make more sense for an absolute beginner. The populace of Galtür also speaks more English than that of Ischgl.

Intermediates and experts will have a wonderful time in Ischgl. The area offers wide-ranging, well-prepared pistes and 50 miles of off-piste opportunities. Experts looking for only super-steep terrain will be disappointed. The resort is perfect for a mixed intermediate/expert group.

Ski school

Ischgl has the largest ski school but probably only as many good English-speakers as Galtür. Though the instructors can teach in English, it is nice to have an instructor who can converse in English as well. Ask for a good English-speaker, especially if you are heading out for individual lessons.

Group lessons are aproximately 10% less expensive in middle season. For participants in the week-long January ski program there is an additional 10% discount.

Individual lessons (88/89 prices)

for two hours	Sch. 700
for each additional person	Sch. 100
for one day	Sch. 1400

Group lessons

for one day	Sch. 340
for three days	Sch. 740
for five days	Sch .900
for six days	Sch. 950
for six half days	Sch. 790

Lift tickets

All skiers except beginners should purchase the Silvretta ski pass, which is good for all area lifts (Ischgl, Galtür, Samnaun and the entire valley), plus shuttle-bus transport. These are 1988/89 prices.

	high season	low season
for three days	Sch. 855	Sch. 735
for six days	Sch. 1570	Sch. 1325
for seven days	Sch. 1775	Sch. 1500
for thirteen days	Sch. 2745	Sch. 2330
for fourteen days	Sch. 2855	Sch. 2440

Individual area day-tickets in Ischgl cost Sch. 320 during high season and Sch. 285 during middle season. In Galtür: Sch. 245 (high season) and Sch. 230 (low season).

Seniors over 60 and children from 6-15 years get approximately a 40% discount on lift tickets.

Accommodation

Prices noted are for half-board. HS-High Season LS-Low Season. Special weekly package prices are listed at the end of each hotel description.

Ischgl

For the best in town head for **Hotel Elisabeth** Tel. 5411, Telex 58143 (Sch. 1500 HS, Sch. 1180 LS) Located at the base stations of the Fimbabahn and the Pardatschgratbahn. A perfect location. Good English, pool, sauna, solarium. Special weekly prices in early December and April/early May-Sch. 6760 including 6 day skipass and 7 days half-board. In January, Sch.9460.

Madlein tel. 5226, telex 58143. Daily price-Sch. 1200 HS, Sch.

990 LS. Centrally located. Features one of the best discos in town. Pool, sauna, solarium. Special weekly prices early December and late April/May Sch. 6295 including six-day skipass and seven days half-board. In January, Sch. 8130.

The ageing **Post** has all amenities including pool. (tel. 5233, telex 58140), the **Sonne** (tel. 5302, telex 58258) and **Trofana** (tel. 5387) have good English with prices ranging between Sch. 900-1050 HS and Sch. 650-850 LS. The Sonne is also an excellent après ski location.

Gasthöfe Goldener Adler (tel. 5217) boasts one of the best kitchens in town plus a sauna and steambath. Sch. 850-1120 HS, Sch. 710-970 LS. Special weekly prices including skipass and seven days half-board in early December and late April/May are Sch.4825. In January, Sch.6170.

Moderate

Olympia (tel. 5432, telex 58243) Sch.880 HS, Sch.620 LS. Located near the Fimba and Pardatschgrat lifts. Special weeks-Sch.5540.

Yscla (tel.5275, telex 58261) Sch.850 HS, Sch.650 LS. Near the Silvretta lift. Convenient to everything with one of the best restaurants in town. Special week-5610.

Charley (tel. 5434) Sch.650 HS, Sch.550 LS.. Special weeks-Sch.5050.

Bed and Breakfast

The best in town is **Christine** (tel.5346) Sch.600 HS, Sch.400 LS. Special weeks not available in January.

A moderate B&B is **Edi** (tel.5351) Sch.420 HS, Sch.340-360 LS. A bit out of the way, but good English and reasonable rates. Special weeks-Sch.3580.

The recommended lower-priced B&B are

Winkler (tel.5350) Sch.340 HS, Sch.280 LS. Located across from the Silvrettabahn.

Palin (tel.5268) Sch. 460-480 HS, Sch.350-370 LS. Special weeks-Sch.3650.

Engadin (tel.5358) Sch.390 HS, Sch.300-330 LS. No special January weeks.

Galtür

Prices in Galtür are considerably lower than those in Ischgl. Make sure to ask about the guest card when you arrive which allows considerable discounts in the town. The hotel prices noted here are the HS-LS range for half-board with bath. Telephone prefix is 05443.

For the best head to **Alpenhotel Tirol** (tel.206, telex 58262) near the center of town. Sch.650-900.

Fluchthorn (tel.202, telex 58271) Central village location with good disco. Sch.630-740.

Post (tel.422) In the village center with good disco. Sch.670-725.

Zum Silbertaler (tel.256) Near the tennis center and town pool. Sch.570.

Postgasthöfe Rossle (tel.232) Sch.540.

Bergfried (tel.208) Sch.400-450.

Galtürhof (tel.406) Sch.450-550.

Luggl (tel.386) Sch.370-480.

Bed and Breakfast

Berta Lorenz (tel.252) Sch.250-260.

Dr. Köck (tel.226) Sch.270-290.

Garni Kurz (tel. 307) Sch.250-300.

Hubertus (tel.243) Sch.250-260.

Apartments

The rental apartment business is well organized and bookings can be arranged through the tourist information office. Write to the office and provide details about when you plan to arrive, how many people will be sharing the apartment and what facilities you desire. It will respond quickly with several apartment choices.

Make your selection and notify the tourist office or the individual owner, depending on the instructions you get from the tourist office.

Normally, linens and kitchen utensils are included in every apartment. Heat, taxes, electricity and cleaning services may be extra. Expect to pay between Sch.100 and Sch.200 per person a night, depending on how many are sharing the apartment, where it's located and its relative position on the luxury scale.

Dining

In Ischgl perhaps the best restaurant is the traditional kitchen of the Goldener Adler. Locals also highly recommend the Trofana for good international cooking. Try the Kitzloch for fondue and barbequed steaks. Yscla has a good French and local menu.

In Galtür make sure to eat once at the Landle and at Zum Silbertaler. The Fluchthorn also serves hearty fare at reasonable prices.

In Samnaun try a meal at the Hotel Post. It's pricey but one of the best in town.

Nightlife

Here Ischgl shines. It has one of the best après ski scenes from 3 p.m. until 7 p.m. then excellent nightlife from around 10 p.m. until about 2 a.m.

The best après ski spots are Christine, just up from the Silvrettabahn and across the street from the Post and Goldener Adler; and the Kitzloch at the opposite end of town near Hotel Elisabeth and the Fimba and Pardatschgratbahn. Both spots rock from about 4 to 7 p.m. with a disc jockey spinning music, the bar serving half liter beers and the crowds singing and dancing in ski suits and ski boots.

The Sonne also has a lively crowd, but no dancing.

The three major discos begin to crank between 10 and 11 p.m. The **Tenne** in the basement of Hotel Trofana offers the most crowded venue with dancing alternating with wild contests. There is some type of cover charge but I never figured it out. The **Club Madlein** in Hotel Madlein and **La Not** in the basement of Hotel Post are the best dancing with the crowd shifting, based on which has the best live band. Club Madlein has a Sch.50 cover charge.

Galtür

With no first-hand experience of Galtür's nightlife, I pass on locals' suggestions. Certainly the atmosphere is quieter than Ischgl.

Try **Almhof, Alpkogel** and **Wirlerhof** for après ski at the bottom of the lifts. After dinner the action shifts into the village

to discos in the **Fluchthorn** and at the **Post**. The Wirlerhof
has a quiet disco if you are staying near the lifts. You might
also enjoy the traditional zither evenings at Zum Silbertaler
on Tuesdays and Thursdays and at the Hotel Almhof on Friday
nights.

Child care

Child-care services are available. Contact the Ischgl Tourist
Office (tel. 05444-5266) for assistance in arranging care. Frau
Gertude Ladner (tel. 5613) offers baby-sitting as well.

There is a guest kindergarten without ski school at Idalp.
Price with lunch is Sch.120/day and without lunch, Sch. 60/
day.

The Ischgl ski school (tel. 5257 or 5404) runs a children's
program. Starting age is four. Prices include a lunchtime snack.
These are 88/89 parice.

for one day	Sch. 400
for three days	Sch. 920
for five days	Sch. 1200
for six days	Sch. 1310
for twelve days	Sch. 2400

In Galtür the ski school is open for children of at least three
years. It is located near the Birkhahn chairlift. Children in ski
school can be fed lunch and supervised for an additional charge
of Sch.60 per day. Non-skiing kindergarten children must be
picked up by their parents between 12 noon and 1:45 p.m.
Ski school prices in Galtür are one day-Sch.330, three days-
Sch.720; five days-Sch.880; six days-Sch.930. Non-skiing kindergarten costs Sch.50 per day and Sch.30 per half-day for
guests staying in Galtúr with a guest card. for others the cost
is Sch.60/day and Sch.35/half-day.

Getting there

The nearest international airport is in Munich. From there, the
easiest highway route is Garmisch, Fern Pass to Landeck or
Innsbruck and on to Ischgl. The train stops in Landeck, where
there is regular bus service to Ischgl.

Other activities

Even in winter the beauty of Galtür cannot be disguised. A beautiful mountain village (1584 meters-m5197 feet high), Galtür is the gateway to the Silvretta Alpine Highway, which is open during warm-weather months. Photographing beautiful buildings is one of our hobbies and the parish church Maria Geburt in Galtür has delightful lines.

Landeck, an Alpine crossroads, around the corner from the valley opening, is a regional shopping center and is distinguished by the towering outline of Fortress Landeck.

As additional excursions from the Paznaun valley, you can travel to Innsbruck and München.

Tourist information

Fremdenverkehrsverband, A-6563 Galtür/Tirol; tel. 05443-204; telex: 58160 TIRGAL.

Fremdenverkehrsverband, Postfach 24, A-6561 Ischgl; tel. 05444-5266; telex: 58148 FVVSVRA.

Kitzbühel/Kirchberg

This Austrian resort of Kitzbühel has long held a reputation as one of the most beautiful Alpine towns. It also is reputed to be one of the hot-spots for apres-ski and excellent intermediate skiing. In all cases it lives up to its reputation.

In January, when excitement is building for the famed Hahnenkamm World Cup competition, Kitzbühel vibrates with action. The streets are filled with people at midnight and the sound music and laughter ripple over the cobblestones and along the narrow alleyways of the scenic town center.

If possible, arrive before nightfall in Kitzbühel, when the wrought iron entranceway lamps and flickering candles in the restaurant windows lend a special charm to the streets. You'll hear the jingle of bells on a horsedrawn sleigh and somewhere in the distance, someone in a gasthaus will let out a hearty laugh rising above the sounds of a piano or a zither. The exterior of Kitzbühel is old and lovely, quite romantic: the atmosphere inside is uniquely Kitz—light and bright, often boisterous and never dull. In Kitzbühel the skiing day is long enough to get you tired, followed by a night which seems to last forever.

The resort, which shares much of the same mountain, **Kirchberg**, has become a major factor in the area. Kirchberg is filled with a younger crowd and attracts more dedicated skiers and families. The smaller resort has a more limited nightlife and significantly lower prices than its glitzy neighbor. We will deal with Kirchberg in each section where the descriptions are not common.

Where to ski

The Ski Safari is a ski circuit through the Kitzbühel area which uses interconnecting lifts for more than 20 miles of runs. You can work your way from Kitzbühel to Pass Thurn, or reverse the direction and on the way tackle slopes that have about 19,000 feet in total vertical drop. For intermediates, it's quite an outing.

Kitzbühel (""Kitz" to insiders) centers on the famed Hahnenkamm, the primary slope above town where the World-Cup circuit aces race each January.

Relatively low-lying slopes go from Kitzbühel, situated at 780 meters (2560 feet), up to approximately 2000 meters (6561 feet). This means that before Christmas and after late February the slopes may not be completely covered.

To avoid long lift lines, a chronic problem, drive toward neighboring Kirchberg and take the new (opened last year) Fleckalmbahn to the Ehrenbachhöhe above the Hahnenkamm race circuit. On the way down, ski the "Streif run," site of next year's World-Cup race, then begin working your way around the ski safari. It's marked by circular signs depicting an elephant on skis pointing the way. Don't pass up the red runs on either side of Pengelstein. The trail to Kirchberg off the top is the better of the two.

For runs in the sun, we preferred the gentle, seldom challenging slopes of the 1996-meter (6549-foot) Kitzbüheler Horn across town. We skied in January and several local residents told us that the snow would melt in March. The best run is from the top station of the Hornköpfl lift all the way through the trees and into Kitzbühel.

The slopes on Pass Thurn, reached directly from lifts at the pass or by working your way up from nearby Jochberg, are more challenging. The runs are higher, up to 2000 meters.

Mountain rating

Kitzbühel/Kirchberg's skiing is strictly intermediate. There are enough blue runs available for the lower intermediate and beginner to keep harmony in any mixed-skill group of skiers vacationing here.

Experts, except those concentrating on their times along the Hahnenkamm run or the Gaiberg course above Kirchberg, should wedel on something more challenging than the prepared runs. Guides can take serious skiers on off-track explo-

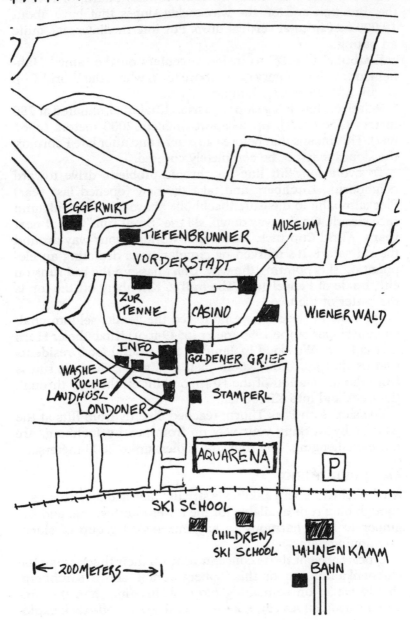

rations from Kitzbühel or from Kirchberg which will delight even the most hardened experts.

For cross-country enthusiasts, there are eleven circuits with nearly 70 miles of prepared trails. Neighboring Jochberg sponsors evening skiing for cross-country fans.

Ski school

In Kitzbühel the "Rote Teufel" (Red Devil) ski school (tel. 2500) is under the leadership of Olympic triple-gold medalist Toni Sailer. Classes are also conducted in off-trail skiing. The Kirchberg ski school is located in the center of town (tel. 05357-2209).

Ski lesson prices are regulated throughout Tirol. Full day group lesson—Sch. 340. Three days of group lessons—Sch. 740. Six days of group lessons—Sch.950.

Private lessons are Sch. 1750 for a full day per person and an additional Sch. 150 per extra person. The half day private instructor costs Sch. 1050 per person with Sch. 150 added for each extra person.

Cross-country lessons are available: One half-day—Sch. 300; three half-days—Sch. 550; six half-days—Sch. 770. Private instruction is Sch. 1050 for a half day plus Sch. 150 for each additional person.

Check out the special ski weeks offered before Christmas and in March. For example, during the last three weeks in March there is an all-in plan that includes six days' accommodations, six days of instruction in classes with a maximum of nine skiers, plus a seven-day lift pass. The cost for this package starts at Sch. 3245. Packages with breakfast only start at Sch. 2780 in smaller pensions.

Lift tickets

The best ticket is the Kitzbühel/Kirchberg area lift pass, which includes ski shuttle buses and swimming in Kitzbühel's Aquarena (even if you are staying in Kirchberg). These prices are for high season. Before Christmas, during January and from March 10 onward prices are approximately 15 percent less. These are 88/89 prices.

one day	Sch. 290
for two days	Sch. 550
for three days	Sch. 770
for six days	Sch. 1390
for seven days	Sch. 1510
for fourteen days	Sch. 2500

Accommodation

Kitzbühel

An excellent variety of lodging can be found in the main part of Kitzbühel, close to the slopes and nightlife. The city's tourist information office in the center of town (look for the big "I"), will provide assistance in making reservations.

We also recommend that you ask the tourist office about reservations for rooms in private homes and farms in the area.

Because of the large number of restaurants, you may want to choose bed-and-breakfast accommodation and try different restaurants during the week. Unless noted, prices are per person for double occupancy, high season, half-pension.

Tiefenbrunner (tel. 2141) Sch. 1080-1300. One of the best hotels in town.

Zur Tenne (tel.4444) Sch. 950 (bed and breakfast only). A top hotel in center of town with one of the best night clubs on the second floor. This is also a Best Western Hotel.

Schloss Lebenberg (tel.4301) Sch. 1100-1650. A converted castle just on the outskirts of the town. All the amenities for which a guest could ask.

Am Lutzenberg (tel. 3279) Sch. 660-700. An excellent middle of the road hotel.

Montana (tel. 2526) Sch. 800-900. Next to the Hahnenkamm lifts. Has swimming pool, sauna, and good kindergarten.

Bellevue (tel. 2766) Sch. 650-750. Middle budget hotel.

Klausner (tel. 2136) Sch. 740-820. Middle budget hotel.

Eggerwirt (tel. 2455) Sch. 600-680. A find. My favorite with a great restaurant. You'll love it.

Pension Foidl (tel. 2189) Sch. 400—Small pension, 31 beds.

Kirchberg

The accommodations here are not as luxurious as those found in Kitzbühel. There are no four-star hotels, but these hotels are excellent with good service and a fun-loving younger crowd than in Kitzbühel. If traveling with your family this is a perfect place to stay.

Hotel Sonnalp (tel. 2741) Sch. 800-950 (half-pension). With sauna and pool. Great for families.

Parkhotel Kirchberg (tel. 2383) Sch. 700-850 (half-pension). No pool.

Happy Kirchberg (tel. 2842) Sch. 700-840 (half-pension). Excellent hotel with heated outdoor pool, sauna and good kindergarten. Very good with children.

Hotel Seehof (tel. 2228) Sch. 520-590 (half-pension). Beautifully redone rooms, great location with ice skating on the lake by the hotel. A real bargain which everyone will enjoy.

Gasthof Kirchenwirt (tel. 2852) Sch. 400-500 (half-pension). Newly renovated with good food in the center of town.

Apartments

Lodging in the Kitzbühel area is primarily in hotels, pensions and private homes. The tourist office has a list of apartments but notes that the prices are the responsibility of the owners themselves. Expect to pay Sch. 225-275 per person per night for a two- to four-bed apartment. For information on chalet and apartment rentals, consult the local tourist office.

In Kirchberg expect to pay Sch. 200-230 per person per day for a two- to four-bed apartment. The tourist office will send information on available apartments.

Dining

In Kitzbühel, we were in the mood for a quiet meal and the Schloss Lebenberg (tel. 4301) outside town was a good choice, with a menu from Sch. 200. Try Unterberg Stuben for what may be one of the best meals of your vacation. The Tennerhof offers a delicious meal starting from Sch. 200, and if you win big at the Kitzbühel casino, take your friends to eat at La Cave (tel. 2555, for reservations). The menu there starts at Sch. 580. Restaurant Reisch and Gasthof Eggerwirt also have excellent kitchens.

In Kirchberg most arrangements are for full-pension. If you want to go out on the town the best restaurant is the restaurant attached to the Sporthotel Alexander. For excellent game try the Kirchenwirt. On the slopes try to head towards the Gasthof Schroll for *Kaiser Schmarren aus der pfanne*.

Nightlife

In Kitzbühel, Zur Tenne hotel (tel. 4444) has some of the brightest live evening entertainment. The jet-set crowd often gathers here following après-ski tea at Praxmair's (tel. 2646), the café that you should visit at least once during your stay.

Other good nightlife spots in Kitzbühel are the Take Five (after 10 p.m.), Stamperl (5-7 p.m.), Washe Kuche, and the Drop-in. There is also a Londoner Pub in Kitzbühel which is much tamer than the Londoner in Kirchberg.

Kirchberg is quieter than its glitzy neighbor, but it lays claim to perhaps the wildest après-ski bar in Europe, The Londoner. The bar has been so succesful that it has been copied in other towns but none are as exciting as the original in Kirchberg. The action starts as skiers come off the slopes. It's "dance-'till-you-melt" time from about 4 p.m. to 8 p.m. when most head off to eat in their hotels. And all through the madness everyone's smiles shine through their sweat. This is the wild after-skiing party every skier has dreamed of.

Later in the evening head to the Pferdestalle, Fuchslöchl or Rauchkichl for dancing. The party seems to shift each night, but Kirchberg is not too big to give you a chance to check out the action and then head back to where everyone's hanging out.

Child care

Information on child-care services is available through the local tourist office.

In Kitzbühel the kindergarten for children from one to three years of age is called Krabbelstubbe Max and Moritz (tel.2786). It costs Sch. 350 per day.

In addition, the local ski school (tel. 2500) offers ski kindergarten for children from age two-and-a-half to five.

In Kirchberg there is a kindergarten (tel. 2406) open Monday through Friday 8 a.m. to 4 p.m. (Wed. closes at noon); and Happy Kinderland in Hotel Happy Kirchberg (tel.2842) open daily from, 8:30 a.m. to 5 p.m. except Saturdays. Daily costs are Sch. 150 and includes lunch.

The ski school in Kirchberg also has special children's programs, with identical rates to the normal ski school plus Sch.75 for lunch.

Getting there

The best international airport connections are into Munich (although flights into Salzburg and Innsbruck bring you to the same area); from there, travel to Kitzbühel or Kirchberg by train.

By car, the trip is on the Inntal autobahn; take the Kufstein-Sud exit and then continue via St. Johann.

Other activities

Kitzbühel and Kirchberg, with good train connections, are ideally suited for excursion trips to Munich, Innsbruck and Salzburg. Day-trips by automobile are also not difficult because travel in and out is rarely hindered by icy roads.

Kitzbühel has two very beautiful churches. The centuries-old Pfarrkirche (parish church) and the adjacent Liebfrauenkirche (Church of Our Lady) give Kitzbühel a distinctive old-world feel.

In Kitzbühel, also visit the Jochbergtor, the only remaining gate of the old fortified city.

The Traidkasten at Hinterstadt 32 was once a mill but now houses the local folk museum and a ski museum.

Kitzbühel is lively at Christmas, although expensive. The annual Christmas market, religious observances and holiday festivities attract thousands.

The last half of January usually includes the World-Cup race and in early February there's an international cross-country race.

Kirchberg has one of the best organized horse-drawn sleigh ride programs. Costs for a sleigh for up to five people is Sch 300-600 depending on the time of day and the operator.

Tourist information

Fremdenverkehrsverband, Hinterstadt 18, A-6370 Kitzbühel; tel. 05356-2155; telex: 51-18413 FVVLA.

Fremdenverkehrsverband, Postfach 28, A-6365 Kirchberg; tel. 05357-2309; telex: 51-371.

Fremdenverkehrsverband, A-6370 Aurach; tel. 05356-4622.

Fremdenverkehrsverband Jochberg, A-6373 Jochberg; tel. 05355-5229.

Montafon Valley

The Montafon Valley, like neighboring Paznaun, offers good skiing and glorious scenery in the high country above the shores of Lake Constance. The two valleys are connected from June through November by one of the most beautiful Alpine roadways, the Silvretta highway.

The Montafon Valley, which branches off from the road to the Arlberg Pass at Bludenz, is made up of eleven resorts running along the valley: St. Anton i. Montafon, Bartholomäberg, Vandans, Silbertal, Schruns, Tschagguns, St. Gallenkirch, Gargellen, Gortipohl and Gaschurn with Partenen, at the other end, the gateway to the Silvretta highway. The major towns are Schruns, Tschagguns and Gaschurn.

Where to ski

With nearly a dozen places to ski, it was difficult to do more than take a few runs along the best slopes in each area. However, settling on a favorite was easy. That is the six-mile run from the Sennigrat summit (2300 meters—7544 feet) above Bartholomäberg, a few miles up the valley. You'll sing the praises of this intermediate cruise after skiing the valley's shorter runs. One piece of advice: everyone wants to get up the mountain in the morning, so avoid the lines in Schruns and take the Lapellbahn chair from neighboring Silbertal. You can easily work your way up the mountain from that side.

For ski variety, we had two favorites. The Golm, at 1900 meters (6232 feet) above Tschagguns, offered moguls, trails through the trees on the lower slopes and even deep powder. The run from the top is nearly five miles long.

Secondly, we enjoyed the Silvretta Nova area, which is actually a circuit of lifts connecting nearly 50 miles of trails above

the towns of Gaschurn, St. Gallenkirch, Gortipohl and Partenen.

We liked one other slightly isolated resort area. It is Gargellen, a 1423-meter (4667-foot) high village, tucked into a side
valley above St. Gallenkirch. Try the black run directly down
the lift on the Schafberg.

For cross-country, the best circuit is the 12-mile loop connecting St. Gallenkirch, Gortipohl, Gaschurn and Partenen.
There is also a nine-mile trail prepared on the snow-packed
surface of the lake at The Bielerhoehe above Partenen.

Mountain rating

The runs here are intermediate for the most part with a few
black trails to challenge the expert skier.

Beginner lifts abound at the foot of the mountains. The region is particularly good for advanced beginners just starting
to perfect their skills on the red runs.

While the Montafon is not known as a cross-country region,
the circuits are good and the mountain panorama is remarkable.

For those who like ski touring, there is a marvelous area with
many trails along the Montafon's highest ridges and slopes.
Even experienced skiers travel with a guide on these touring
excursions.

Ski school

There are eight ski schools in the valley. The most popular and
expensive are those of Schruns and Gaschern. The school in
Tschagguns has 40 teachers, several of them English-speaking,
and in neighboring Schruns about 30 instructors are available.
Lessons are offered, from beginner to advanced, with races for
the guests each week.

Cross-country skiers can choose from several trails, including a new one on the Schrunser Feld. It's called the "Zelfen"
circuit. Check with the ski school for information on cross-
country lessons.

Individual lessons

for one hour (noon–2 p.m.)	Sch. 260-320
for one day	Sch. 1100
for each additional person	Sch. 170-200

Group lessons

for one day (four hours)	Sch. 270
for three days (four hours)	Sch. 750
for five days	Sch. 950
for six days	Sch. 1000

Lift tickets

If you plan a variety of skiing, only the Montafon area ski pass should be considered. (1988/89 prices)

	adults	children
for three days	Sch. 790	Sch. 490
for six days	Sch. 1410	Sch. 870
for seven days	Sch. 1590	Sch. 990

Accommodation

We recommend the all-in weeks sponsored by the Tschagguns Tourist Office. Different packages cater to the beginner and intermediate skier, the advanced skier who wants to improve his technique, and the experienced skier who wants to ski hard. All three packages include seven days at half pension. The beginner package includes five days of lessons, four hours a day. Prices begin at Sch. 2050 a week (breakfast only with bath) and run to Sch. 5700 for the nicest accommodations.

We recommend signing up for one of the plans because, with eleven different towns offering hotels, choosing a place may take too much of your time. Fill out the accommodation card from the Tschagguns tourist office and it will find a hotel which fits your price and room needs. Specify whether you prefer to be in the center of town, have extra-quiet accommodations, get a room with a balcony or one near the lifts, and so on.

If you choose to make your own arrangements, we found three hotels that offered special comfort, value and the extras most vacationers expect.

Hotel Cresta (tel. 2557) Good service with a heated pool and sauna.

Sporthotel Sonne (tel. 2333) Good food, plus traditional mountain music and singing during folklore evenings.

Alpenparkhotel (tel. 2557) One of the best hotels in town.

Apartments

Check with the tourist office for information on apartment and chalet rentals in the area. Tschagguns, with about 2500 year-round residents, has some 3000 beds for tourists. Most are in hotels, guesthouses and private homes. An apartment for four will cost between Sch. 350-600 per night depending on the luxury.

Child care

The St. Gallenkirch ski school offers a ski kindergarten for children from age four. The school runs Monday through Friday, from 9:30 a.m. until 4 p.m. Prices include a lunchtime snack.

for five days	Sch. 1190
for six days	Sch. 1290

The ski school accepts children from three years for its baby sitting service. A lunchtime snack is provided and the service is offered Monday through Saturday, from 9:30 a.m. until 4 p.m. Cost per day is Sch. 340.

Dining

The best restaurants in the valley are the Romantik Hotel Heimspitze in Gargellan, the Löwen Hotel in Schruns and the Montanella Stuble in St. Gallenkirch.

For a good traditional meal head out for the Gasthof Löwe in Tschagguns, the Gasthof Krone in Schruns and the Gasthof Adler in St. Gallenkirch. We have also had good reports on the Alt-Montafon restaurant (tel. 05558-232) at Gaschurn.

Nightlife

The nightlife in this valley is very limited. The main center is in Schruns which has four pubs and four discos. For some après ski activity head to Otto's Kuhstall in St. Gallenkirch.

Getting there

The Montafon Valley is about 90 miles from Zurich airport, where most international arrivals enter Switzerland for this Austrian excursion.

From Bregenz on Lake Constance, it's about one hour by automobile, or take the train to Bludenz near the entrance to the valley where there's regular bus service.

Other activities

The center of adjacent, larger Schruns is only a 15-minute walk away. Both towns are set in the great natural beauty of the Montafon at the 2000-foot level, with the surrounding peaks reaching nearly 10,000 feet.

Day excursions to Lake Constance, about an hour away, and Zurich are popular.

Until the snow closes the Silvretta highway (normally in November), the drive from Partenen over the Bielerhoehe to Galtür in the Paznaun valley is superb.

Tourist information

Verkehrsamt A-6780 Schruns; tel. 05556-2166
Verkehrsamt A-6774 Tschagguns; tel. 05556-2457.

Schladming
with Dachstein-Tauern-Region

If you are up to the challenge of the fastest World Cup downhill run, if you are looking for wide and long beginner/intermediate runs through thick pine forests; if you seek the excitement of a glacier skiing experience on the Dachstein Galcier, or the peacefulness of one of the most extensive cross-country areas in Austria, the area around Schladming awaits.

Though relatively unknown to Americans Schladming, located in the center of Austria, hosts thousands of Austrian, German, Swedish, Danish, British and Dutch tourists. Already one of the leading vacation centers for the Austrians, the region has completed an extensive series of developments which have turned the valley into a world-class resort.

Schladming, the main hub of the area is nestled around a traditional town center which offers good shopping, nightlife and restaurants—all within a five-minute walk from the main lift system.

Rohrmoos about a five minute drive up the mountain from Schladming features more hotel rooms than Schladming and offers guests the possiblity of stepping out their door, putting on their skis and setting off down the mountain. But, Rohrmoos is spread out and a long walk from the Schladming town center.

Ramsau lies on the opposite side of the valley settled on a

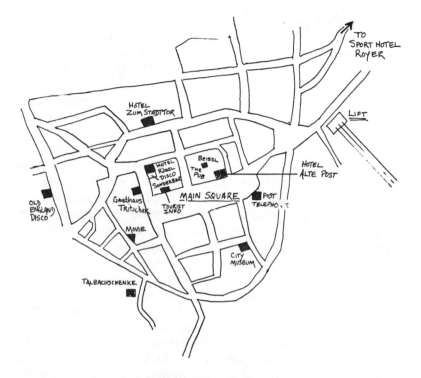

long plateau which features some of the most interesting cross-country skiing in Austria. Once again, accommodation is extensive but spread out.

Haus im Ennstal, a short drive along the valley from Schladming, still appears to be a typical small mountain village. Perhaps the most picturesque of the main villages in the region, Haus has not succumbed to square, concrete, modern hotels, nor a pulsating tourist trade. It remains traditional, anchoring the Hauser Kaibling ski area, scene of one of the most exciting women's downhill courses. The town is interconnected with the other villages by a frequent ski bus system.

Where to ski

The *Skiparadies ski pass* opens more than 75 miles of prepared runs on seven mountains along the Dachstein-Tauern valley. The major areas are Planai (1894 meters), above Schladming;

Hauser Kaibling (2015 meters) above Haus; Hochwurzen (1850 meters) above Rohrmoos; and the Reiteralm (1860 meters) above Pichl. Currently, only the Planai and Hochwurzen areas are interconnected by lifts, though plans which will eventually connect the entire series of valleys are in the works. All other areas are connected by frequent ski buses which ply the valley route continuously during the day. Each area mentioned above offers plenty of skiing for a day. That means only one bus to an outlying area in the morning and one back home in the evening.

The Planai is served by one of the fastest cablecar systems in existence—waiting time in the valley is minimal even on Sundays. T-bars open the back bowls of the Planai area; the valley-face of the mountain is crisscrossed by beginning and intermediate runs. The No. 1 run from the top of the Planai cable car to the bottom station is the longest on the mountain and an absolutely joyful experience. Intermediates have a chance to cruise and beginners can handle the entire run—the short steep sections sections are wide for an easy traverse.

The **Hochwurzen** area is reached through a series of T-bars and chairlifts. The lifts can take almost an hour if starting from the connecting chair with the Planai area. For people staying in Rohrmoos or skiers coming by ski bus, a single chairlift takes skiers to the top of the mountain. The upper areas are intermediate and the lower areas around Rohrmoos are a beginner's paradise.

Hauser Kaibling rising above Haus is normally not as crowded as Schladming. At times you are alone on a beautiful mountain with some of the best intermediate slopes you've skied under your feet. The mountain offers a mix of intermediate/beginner trails with intermediate the main focus. Even the Knapplhof Descent, marked beginner, is borderline intermediate. But, the trails are wide enough for easy traversing. Take the bus or park at the base of the Hauser Kaibling cable car just outside the town. The other cable car rising directly from the upper reaches of the town looks great on the ski map but should be avoided unless your hotel happens to be located nearby. It only carries eight skiers about every 15 minutes.

Reiteralm above the towns of Pichl and Gleiming, is a good day's worth of skiing for intermediates. Beginners have too limited an area to make the half-hour series of lifts worthwhile unless they are staying in one of the base towns.

Overall, the area uses up a week of skiing without repeating a section twice. Even good skiers will be hard pressed to cover every trail, on only the four main mountains, in six days of hard skiing.

Mountain rating

The area is an intermediate skier's paradise. Beginners should center their efforts on the Rohrmoos area though each section has beginner runs. Ski instructors bring even beginners, after three days of lessons, all the way down each of the mountains. Experts should keep their eye out for good powder and test themselves high up on Hauser Kaibling, or on the lower sections of the World-Cup downhill runs both in Haus and Schladming. The *real* experts should look into hiring a guide to take them off-piste for a great day or week of skiing.

Ski school

Individual lessons (88/89 prices)

one day (five hours)	Sch. 1300
one hour	Sch. 350
additional person	Sch. 100

Group lessons
Note: one lesson equals two hours of instruction

three days	Sch. 700
five days	Sch. 880

Rather than sign up for a ski course you may want to be part of a more informal group of skiers and get a chance to explore the valleys with expert mountain guides. Sepp Schweiger and Herbert Thaller have organized a **Ski Safari** program in Schladming. They will take experts in small groups to find powder, moguls and hidden tracks; intermediate skiers will have a chance to really explore the mountain with someone who knows every trail and mountain watering hole. The groups allow skiers to easily meet others of the same level and provide picnics and evening ventures into the bars and discos in town. Your guide will be a fully certified mountain guide and/or ski instructor. This is a perfect way for good skiers arriving alone to hook up with a new group of friends. Contact them through the tourist office or call direct Sepp—03687-22537; Herbert—03687-61148. Prices will range from Sch.420 per day to Sch. 1050 for five days. If you want more information in advance, write to the tourist office.

Lift tickets

The regional lift tickets cover four cable cars and 53 chairlifts and T-bars over seven mountains. Although I can't imagine why anyone would want a two-and-a-half hour "try out ticket," the region offers adults a ticket which costs Sch. 170 plus a Sch. 250 deposit, and children get a pass for Sch. 105 plus a Sch. 195 deposit. If the tickets are returned within the two-and-a-half-hour time limit, the deposit plus Sch. 100 per adult and Sch. 70 per child are refunded. It could be a good way to ride the gondola up for lunch.

The other one-day and half-day fares offer the opportunity to limit the areas but the differences are minimal. The following fares are for the entire seven-mountain area (children get approximately a 35 percent discount):

one day	Sch. 260
two days	Sch. 500
three days	Sch. 710
six days	Sch. 1300
fourteen days	Sch. 2350

Accommodation

These are our selections for the best the resort has to offer.

Sporthotel Royer(tel. 03687-23240; telex: 38227) Located in Schladming. The only five-star hotel in the area. This is a modern hotel with pool, indoor tennis and squash courts, sauna, jacuzzi, pony rides plus more. Room rates per day including half pension: Sch. 1200.

Romantik-Hotel Alte Post(tel. 03687-22571; telex: 38282) In Schladming. The oldest, most traditional hotel in town located on the main square. Rates per day, half pension: Sch. 750.

Hotel Zum Stadttor(tel. 03687-24525; telex: 38287) In Schladming. Has whirlpool and sauna. Rates per day, half pension: Sch. 750

Hotel Pichlmayrgut(tel. 06454-305) Located in Pichl. If you want to stay in an old Austrian estate, this fits the bill with pool, sauna and steambath. Pichl lifts start about a five minute walk from the hotel or catch the ski bus to Haus or Schladming. Rates per day, half pension: Sch. 640

Moderate to Budget
There are many hotels and pensions in the range of Sch. 430-500 per day including half pension. One recommendation in the center of Schladming is **Gasthof Tritscher** (tel. 03687-22435).

In the center of Haus, the **Hotel Hauser Kaibling** (tel. 03686-2378) offers pool and sauna, plus a location in the center of the charming town for Sch. 580 per day, half pension.

The adventurous can stay near the top of the Hauser Kaibling in the **Krummholzhütte**, where you have to share a bathroom and shower, for Sch. 280 per day, half pension. What you get is a room at the top of the mountain and about a ten-minute schuss down the mountain as your first step out the door.

Contact the tourist office and tell them what you want and what price you will pay. They maintain a centralized computer system which tracks all bookings in the Schladming area.

Dining
The best restaurants in town are the Alte Post, the Sporthotel Royer and the restaurant in the Stadttor Hotel.

Restaurant Tritscher is recommended as the best place to spend the least money and still eat well.

The Kalkschmiede has perhaps the best local traditional meals. It is located on the northern side of the valley on the road to Ramsau.

For great ski slope meals on the Planai, stop in at "Onkel Willi's Hütte" (yes, that's Uncle Willi's Hut) only a few ski glides from the top of the main Planai lift. On the Hauser Kaibling, the Krummholzhütte at the top and the Stöklhütte where the three lifts meet both have good skiers' food.

The Bürgerstube at the Hotel Hauserkaibling in Haus/Ennstal has also been recommended.

Nightlife

For a quiet wine and a talk try the **Talbachschenke** in three small rooms, each built around a toasty ceramic stove. The best dancing is at the **Sonderbar** under the Hotel Rössl. For the younger disco dancers try the **Old England Disco**. Other cozy meeting places include **The Pub** and **The Beissl** both just off the main square. The Beissl is in the passageway at 12 Main Square and is a good place to meet people. Stop in and check out La Porta, a newly opened bar near the town's old gateway.

The two main discos outside town, and also the two best spots for meeting tourists such as Swedes, Finns, Dutch, Danes and Germans, are the **Sport Alm** in Ramsau and the **Taverna** in Rohrmoos. If you are in Haus/Ennstal stop into the new Pub in the old castle.

Child care

Nothing is organized for children under four years. Those four and over can sign up for ski school at the same prices as adults. The ski school will take the children for the entire day. Add Sch. 70 per day for lunches.

Getting there

There are good train connections from Munich and Salzburg, both of which have international airports. If driving, the autobahn going south from Salzburg passes within 20 minutes of Schladming. Take the Ennstal exit.

Other activities

There are the obvious such as a visit to Salzburg, or to the salt mines near Salzburg.

The Loden fabric factory gives tours if arranged in advance by calling 06454-203. The factory and a factory outlet are located in Mandling, only about ten minutes from Schladming.

Some of the most famous caves in Austria are in the Dachstein region. The Ice Cave, Mammoth Cave and the Kappenbrullenhöhle are open for visits. Call 06134-362 for information.

Horse-drawn sliegh rides are available, ice-skating rinks are open in Rohrmoos and Haus/Ennstal, and there are public swimming pools in Schladming and Ramsau.

Tourist information

The central tourist information for the region is Gebietsverband Dachstein-Tauern, Coburgstr. 52, A-8970 Schladming, Telephone: 03687-23310; telex: 38286. They handle reservation requests for any town in the area. There are additional local tourist offices in Schladming, Pichl, Haus, Rohrmoos and Ramsau.

St. Johann in Tirol

St. Johann in winter is a Tyrolean resort town just far enough from the lifts to keep locals aware of the need to welcome visitors with a smile. In winter the town is afloat in a sea of snow, lending a special atmosphere to a place which can't decide if it is a resort village or a valley town.

Although St. Johann is only 700 meters (2,297 ft.) above sea level, the snowfall here is certain and heavy from Christmas until March. that one fact is music to the ears of serious skiers. The setting is picturesque with the familiar outline of the Kitzbühlerhorn part of the valley panorama. Kitzbühel, which also shares the mountain, is about 12 miles away.

The old Tyrolean hotels are large and have a deserved reputation for hospitality sometimes missing in bigger, better-known resorts. At night you'll know immediately from the lower decibel level this is not Kitzbühel. The streets don't fold up at 8 pm but the nightlife is quieter. During the cross country races in February the tempo pick up a bit.

Where to ski

The trails run along the flanks of the Kitzbüheler Horn. You can reach them from neighboring Oberndorf by chairlift or by cable car from St. Johann. The top station is Harschbichl at 1700 meters (5577 feet). At the top you have a choice of blue and red runs and one black trail.

We liked the black run, which really begins from Penzing at 1463 meters (4799 feet) and swings down through mogul fields to the parking lot above Oberndorf.

Intermediates take the run to the Eichenhof lift on the far side of St. Johann for a good downhill cruise. From the Jodlalm, just below the Harschbichl, you can follow the lines of a dozen different trails cut into the mountain.

There are easier slopes with beginners' lifts at the bottom of the mountain.

One of the year's biggest events is the Koasalauf, an international cross-country championship staged each February which begins at the Koasa Stadium and cross-country center on the edge of town. St. Johann offers more than 40 miles of cross-country runs and is one of the best locations in the country for combining Alpine and Nordic skiing.

Mountain rating

St. Johann is for intermediates and primarily for lower intermediates. The slopes are rarely challenging and only beginners and advanced beginners will find the skiing interesting enough for a week. However, with the regional ski pass you can try a number of challenging slopes in the area, in particular those on the Steinplatte, above Waidring about 15 miles from St. Johann.

Ski school

St. Johann and its neighbor towns have approximately 130 instructors available for the winter season. Many instructors are unable to teach in English and the number of courses for English-speaking students is limited, so inquire beforehand.

A price reduction is offered on six-day group lesson cards for early- and late-season instruction. Call the ski school at 2515.

Individual lessons

for one half-day	Sch. 850
for one day	Sch. 1400
(each additional person is Sch. 200-300)	

Group lessons

for one day	Sch. 340
for three days	Sch. 740
for six days	Sch. 950
for twelve days	Sch. 1800

Cross-country lessons

for three half-days	Sch. 570

Lift tickets

The St. Johann pass includes 19 lifts serving about 27 miles of prepared trails. These are high-season prices. There is a small discount during low season and children pay approximately 30% less. These are 1988/89 prices.

for a half day	Sch. 170
for one day	Sch. 250
for two days	Sch. 470
for three days	Sch. 650
for four days	Sch. 830
for five days	Sch. 990
for six days	Sch. 1150
for seven days	Sch. 1280
for thirteen days	Sch. 1980

A combination ski pass and pool pass during high-season costs for seven days—Sch. 1330 and for 14 days—Sch. 2200.

Accommodation

St. Johann has one of the best organized accommodation services in Austria. In fact, using the St. Johann hotel-apartment list with an accompanying reservation form, available free from the tourist office, you can arrange for any type of accommodation from simple bed-and-breakfast to apartment rentals.

We recommend that you come in early March when the snow is still good and the maximum price reductions are offered. The all-in package is outstanding: for seven days at half pension, a six-day ski pass for St. Johann, six days free swimming and six days of ski school, the price for a top-grade hotel is Sch. 5290—our favorite delux hotels are the Hotel Crystal (tel. 05362-2630) and Gasthof Dorfschmiede (tel. 05362-2323). The price for a middle-class hotel or guesthouse is Sch. 4450, about the price you'd pay for accommodations only at some resorts.

If you want the lowest-cost accommodations, you might consider the budget all-in bed-and-breakfast plan, which includes the other extras mentioned above for only Sch. 3155.

Eleven hotels and guesthouses offer the mid-range all-in package for Sch. 4220. Of the eleven, we recommend four:

Hotel Kaiserhof (tel. 2545)—On the edge of town. Good for cross-country with a six-kilometer loop near the hotel and other trails close by.

Hotel Martina (tel. 3540)—On the edge of central St. Johann, close to the Hochfeld chairlift.

Hotel Schöne Aussicht (tel. 2270)—Excellent location on the slopes near the Angereralm lift ground station.

Gasthof Hinterkaiser (tel. 3325)—A cross-country skier's paradise in the heart of the trail circuit, but isolated for alpine skiing.

Apartments

Apartment rental is as easy as finding hotel or pension lodging in St. Johann. Five hotels—the Fischer, Crystal, Brückenwirt, Europa and Sporthotel Austria—also offer rental apartments. Apartments which sleep four range in price from Sch. 500-700 per night.

Dining

Our favorite restaurant in town is in the Hotel Europa (tel. 2285). It is very traditional and has only recently been open for other than hotel guests. Also try out the Fischer restaurant with Austrian specialties and the Speckbacher Stuben.

Nightlife

We liked the Café Rainer where the après-ski atmosphere was excellent from tea at five onwards.

For a change of pace, visit the Café Klausner's traditional Tyrolean evenings with dancers and music. For a basic funtime bar try the Londoner.

Child care

Ski instruction for children and a ski kindergarten are offered (tel. 2515). The ski instruction prices are the same as for adults.

For details on baby-sitting services, call the St. Johann Tourist Office (tel. 2218).

Getting there

St. Johann is about 55 miles from Munich and Innsbruck; most people arrive from Munich. Take the Inntal autobahn and exit at Kufstein. Regular train service connects St. Johann with Innsbruck.

Other activities

In recent years St. Johann has pushed hard to expand its leisure-time recreational activities. Bowling (tel. 3377), horseback riding (tel. 2484) and tennis (tel. 3377) are now popular activities. Horse drawn sleigh rides are Sch. 135 per ride (tel. 38333 or 2207).

The town is beautiful in winter with one Tyrolean house after another offering traditional Austrian scenes painted on their exterior walls.

For outings, visitors travel most often to Munich, Innsbruck or Salzburg.

Tourist information

Fremdenverkehrsverband St. Johann, A-6380 St. Johann in Tirol; tel. 05352-2218/3335; telex: 5124117; snow info: 05362-4358.

Oetztal Arena
Sölden, Hochsölden, Obergurgl, Hochgurgl

An excursion to Austria's Oetztal is part skiing and part sight-seeing adventure. Good slopes and the glaciers guarantee year-round skiing. But it's the beauty of the Alpine backdrop that will leave a lasting impression. the valley follows the line of the Oetztaler Alpen, a range with ninety peaks over 3000 meters (9843 feet) high and 86 different glaciers coming down from the summits.

The main resorts in the valley are Sölden and Obergurgl. Hochsölden is a suburb of Sölden huddled above the larger town, and Hochgurgl is merly a cluster of six hotels up the mountain from Obergurgl. Sölden is stretched along the main road which traverses the valley. If only the road had a way to go around the town, this would be a beautiful resort. As it is, Sölden is still beautiful but with constant traffic. Hochsölden, at the end of a mountain road does not have the same traffic problem. Obergurgl and Hochgurgl are both a further half-hour drive back into the mountains from Sölden. Obergurgl is as picture-perfect as any alpine town tucked onto the mountains on three sides, complete with old church steeple and picturesque hotels.

Where to ski

The top ski areas of the inner Oetztal are Sölden, Obergurgl, Hochsölden and Hochgurgl. In addition, Zwieselstein and Vent, plus Untergurgl have skiing areas. Unfortunately the areas are not interconnected, nor do they share a common ski pass. It seems that geography makes the lift interconnections difficult and lift-operator politics complicate the shared ski pass. A ski pass acceptable in the entire valley would be better for tourism.

We look first at the interconnected area above Sölden. It is split into two areas—the Haimbachjoch/Rotkoglhütte sector and the Gaislachkogl. The skiing overall is wide-open. Though there are pistes marked on the map, with good snow skiers can ski virtually anywhere which makes Sölden a favorite of powder hounds and means plenty of skiing for a week above the treeline. The skiing is basically intermediate and beginner with some expert off-piste runs thrown in for good measure. In fact an adverturous expert will have no trouble keeping busy above Sölden and in the Obergurgl/Hochgurgl areas.

Access to the slopes is either by cable car starting from the upper end of Sölden or by gondola from the lower section of the town. I suggest the gondola since it moves many more skiers per hour. The gondola drops skiers in the middle of the Haimbachjoch/Rotkoglhütte sector. Either take the chair or drag lift up to Rotkoglhütte, or traverse over to the restaurant and take the chair up to Haimbachjoch. The Haimbachjoch side of the mountain is by far the more difficult of these two sectors.

Connection with the Gaislachkogl sector requires skiing down to the bottom of the Langegg I lift and taking the Stabelebahn and then crossing the mountain to the middle station of the Gletscherbahn which will bring you to Gaislachkogl. From here real experts can drop off to the right and take a steep unmarked Wasserkar trail. Tamer skiers (most of us) can head left and take the steep-enough red run back to the middle station. The Wasserkar triple-chair just below the cable car mid-station opens a group of expert runs. To end the day, lower intermediates can head to the bottom of the Heidebahn lift and then take the trail back into town. Better skiers can drop down the lower sections of the Wasserkar and end up in Innerwald.

The skiing above Obergurgl and Hochgurgl is even more extensive but served by fewer lifts. That combination means plenty of off-piste action. There are no interconnecting lifts between Obergurgl and Hochgurgl. The slopes are not particularly difficult, but more challanging than those in Sölden. Above Obergurgl the Festkogl lift opens a wide face with unlimited intermediate skiing. Experts can drop to the right hand side of the lift and take the unprepared run through the Ferwaltal back to the lower lift station. This area is high (1930 to

3035 meters) with good crisp snow. For a change traverse over to the Hohe Mut area which has a good unprepared run from the Hohe Mut restaurant and a group of shorter lifts and runs. Hochgurgl is reached by bus, if you aren't staying there. This town has developed into a relatively upscale community anchored by one of the best luxury alpine hotels in Europe, the Hotel Hochgurgl. Lifts peak out at 3082 meters where a mountain restaurant provides spectacular views. The skiing for experts is down the Königstal, for beginners in the center of the area and for intermediates under the Kirchenkarlift. Again, like Obergurgl, this area is perfect for continuous off-piste cruising.

Hochgurgl, Obergurgl and Vent, all above 1900 meters, have some of Austria's best summer skiing. We have not skied the glaciers when flowers were blooming in the valley, but fellow skiers assure us it's an adventure not be be missed.

If you want to concentrate on cross-country skiing, choose another area. There are trails, but not the network you'll need to ensure variety.

Mountain rating

With a few exceptions, particularly from the Gaislachkogl, the area's runs are for intermediates.

There are enough training areas at the bottom for ski schools. The beginner has plenty of terrain, especially in the center of the Haimbachjoch/Rotkoglhütte sector on which to keep busy practicing.

Experts looking for wild steeps will find the Oetztal only moderately interesting. Those searching unlimited off-piste will find a dream come true. In summer, when skiing is a real luxury, this is one of Europe's finest areas.

Ski school

The Sölden and Hochsölden ski schools have a total of 150 instructors. Obergurgl and Hochgurgl ski schools have more English-speaking instructors. Lessons are given daily, Monday to Saturday from 10 a.m. until noon and from 1:30 until 3:30 p.m. Private lessons are available through the local ski school (tel. 2364 or 2546) for about Sch. 300 per hour.

Group lessons

for one day	Sch. 340
for two days	Sch. 600
for three days	Sch. 740
for five days	Sch. 900
for six days	Sch. 950

Lift tickets

Tickets are good for all lifts in the **Sölden, Hochsölden, Gaislachkogel** area and for the ski shuttle bus. 1988/89 prices.

	adults	children (6-14)
for a half day	Sch. 240	Sch. 150
for one day	Sch. 320	Sch. 210
for two days	Sch. 620	Sch. 390
for three days	Sch. 880	Sch. 550
for four days	Sch. 1150	Sch. 710
for five days	Sch. 1360	Sch. 830
for six days	Sch. 1570	Sch. 950
for seven days	Sch. 1750	Sch. 1020

Lift tickets for the Obergurgl/Hochgurgl area are slightly higher

Accommodation

Sölden lives from its summer and winter tourist trade and has a complete range of accommodations. Unless indicated, prices are for half pension.

Hotel Central (tel. 05254-2260, tlx. 0533353) Sch. 1200-1500 HS, Sch. 1000-1300 LS. Includes whirlpool, sauna and Turkish bath.

Hotel Alphof (tel. 05254-2559) Sch. 720 HS. Sch. 550 LS. Includes many extras such as pool, solarium and steam bath.

Hotel Hubertus (tel. 05254-2489) Sch. 730 HS, Sch. 590 LS. One of the best hotels in Sölden with great food mid-distance from both main lifts and very close to the final lift back from Fillip's and après-ski.

Hotel Regina (tel. 05254-2486) Sch. 840-1050 HS, Sch. 580-690 LS. Near the main lift. Also offers apartments. The Austrian women's ski team usually stays here when training. Write early since this hotel is normally fully bookcd!

Hotel Sonne (tel. 2203) Sch. 500 HS, Sch. 650 LS. Near the lifts. Friendly, competent service.

Hotel Tyrol (and Tyrolerhof) (tel. 05254-2288) Sch. 590-650 HS, Sch. 470-520 LS. In center of town within walking distance to chairlift.

Hotel Edelweiss (tel. 05254-2298) Sch. 900. Good hotel in Hochsölden.

Obergurgl and Hochgurgl
The first price is the January package price which includes seven days half-pension and six days of lifts.

Hotel Edelweis and Gurgl (tel. 05256-223) Special week: Sch.6150. Perhaps the most convenient hotel to the lifts. A bit pretentious. Normal daily rates (full pension): Sch.850-900.

Hotel Romantik (tel. 05256-354) Special week: Sch.5660. Normal rates: Sch.810-910.

Pension Wiesental (tel. 05256-263) Very convenient to the lifts in the old town. Special week: Sch.4330. Normal daily rate: Sch.620-650.

Pension Gamper (tel. 05256-238) In the center of the old town with an excellent kitchen. Weekly rate: Sch.3900-4500. Normal daily rate: Sch.650-690.

Hotel Hochgurgl (tel. 05256-265) Perhaps one of the best hotels in the Alps by any measure. This hotel is in the same company as the Zürserhof in Zürs and The Palace in St. Moritz. No special week. Normal daily rate: Sch.1190-1590.

Hotel Ideal (tel. 05256-290) The bargain of Hochgurgl with all the right ammenities-msauna, fitness room, TV's and garage. No special week. Normal daily rate: Sch.600-750.
The Hotel and Wurmkogel and the Hotel Laurin in Hochgurgl are also recommended.

If you want a less expensive private home or apartment try the following names: Carmen, Kristiana, Mina, Sepp Santer, Andre Arnold and Hans Seppl.

Apartments

The tourist office in Sölden maintains a list of rental apartments and chalets in the area. The Inner Oetztal Travel Office (tel. 2366) will arrange booking for you. Also check with the Hotel Alphof for their apartment prices.

Dining

Like its room prices, the Hotel Central restaurant (for reservations, call 2260) is expensive with a menu from Sch. 195, but it offers the best meal in town. The kitchen in the Hubertushof is considered exceptional for local fare.

The Regina offers traditional cooking at considerably lower prices. Try the Alpenhof for fondue and grill evenings, the Sunny for fish, and Tyrolerhof and Sonne for fondue. The Nudeltopf is the best Italian restaurant in town. Höfle has a traditional Öztal buffet once a week.

In Hochsölden, we recommend taking a room and meals at the Edelweiss.

On Obergurgl head to the Romantik for Italian food. Try the Hochfirst and then the Grüner for good Tyrolean cooking. The Josl is known for its wild animal dishes.

Nightlife

Sölden is one of Austria's après-ski capitals. That is more due to the clientele than the variety of bars. In fact, there are only two spots for après ski from 3-7 p.m. Most skiers stop at Filip's (I'm not even sure it's spelled that way) across from the ski school. The dancing then continues at the "Après Ski" on the main street of town. These bars are packed shoulder-to-shoulder with skiers in ski suits and ski boots singing and dancing up a storm. This goes on until about 8 p.m. when most head back to hotels to change for dinner.

The late-night disco and party action takes place again in the "Après Ski" but also in the Almbar in the basement of Hotel Tyrol.

In Obergurgl try the Skihaserlkeller, the Rendevous Bar in the Hochfirst, the Josl and Edelweissbar. The town is small enough that with a little scouting the best spots can be easily found.

Child care

Child-care services are offered. For information, contact the Sölden tourist office (tel. 2212).

In Obergurgl the ski school runs a special course and a special non-skiing course for children but parents must fetch children for lunch.

The ski kindergarten in Sölden (tel. 2364) accepts children from three to eight years and is open Monday through Saturday from 9 a.m. until 4:30 p.m.

for a half day (without meal)	Sch. 220
for one day (with meal)	Sch. 330
for three days (with meal)	Sch. 800
for six days (with meal)	Sch. 1300

Getting there

Sölden and Hochsölden are in the Oetz Valley, a side valley of the Inn. The easiest route is from Munich via Innsbruck and then up the Oetztal. More scenic is via Garmisch and over the Fernpass to the valley entrance. There is regular bus service from the train station at Landeck.

Other activities

The Oetztal is another of those destinations you choose primarily for skiing. Innsbruck is the closest large city and day tours are offered. Call the Oetztaler Tourist Office (tel. 05254-8105) for details on excursions.

There are horsedrawn sleighrides for about Sch 400 per hour per group of four or five.

A new leisure center has opened this winter with two indoor tennis courts, swimming pool, bowling, fitness room, sauna, steam bath and massage. (tel. 05254-2514).

There are also regular Rodelparties or tobogganing parties where a bus takes a group to a mountain hut where there is beer and schnapps and dozens of tobogans. After drinking, eating and dancing everyone slides home on a long tobogan course. This is especially enjoyable during full moon.

Tourist information

Fremdenverkehrsverband Inneroetztal, A-6450 Sölden, tel. 05254-2212; telex: 533247.
Fremdenverkehrsverband, A-6456 Obergurgl; tel. 05256-258; telex: 534557; and
Fremdenverkehrsverband, A-6458 Vent; tel. 05254-8193.

Söll

The village of Söll in the Skigrosssraum/Wilderkaiser area of Austria is a tremendous favorite with English skiers and young people in general. The wide expanse of slopes with the backdrop of the rocky Wild Kaiser boasts 86 lifts spread above 7 villages, earning the title of the largest connected ski area in Austria.

The entire ski area is perhaps the most accessible in Austria to skiers coming in from Germany, situated as it is only 20 minutes from the Kufstein border crossing about an hour from Munich.

Söll carefully cultivates its small town image with little shops and stores whose operators are overwhelmingly friendly and usually strike up a conversation in English at the first opportunity. The main street, which leads past several hotels and most of the shops, is full of visitors at almost any hour of the day or night. While traffic is heavy, pedestrians have taken priority, causing motorists to wait, sometimes impatiently, as they crisscross the roadway to browse in shops.

It's quite clear from the heavy shopping in the local grocery stores that not everyone takes full pension. Full shopping bags mean a lot of picnic lunches and homemade breakfasts are prepared back in the room. Everywhere you encounter young couples strolling hand in hand, quite a change from the more elegant and expensive European resorts where the crowd is older and not always so affectionate.

Where to ski

The best skiing is concentrated in the valley headed by Soll, pronounced Zull. Up the valley is Sheffau, Ellmau and finally Going. Around the mountains in another valley are Itter. Hopfgarten, Westendorf and Brixen i Thale. Each has lifts. And all but Westendorf are on an interconnected circuit. Free bus service is provided from Westerndorf, providing skiers with a two-valley network of about 80 lifts and more trails than you'll be able to manage in one week.

The most convenient access is from Söll where a new six-passenger gondola went into service for winter 1988-89 replacing the antiquated single chair which has been a bottlenect in years past.

From the top of the Hohe Salve (1829 meters) at Söll you can appreciate the massive dimensions of the Wild Kaiser area which the English and Austrians know better as the Ski-Grossraum, literally the Big Ski area. You view includes the 1650-meter Brandstadl summit at Sheffau, the 1555-meter Hartkaiser at Ellmau-Going and further to your right the town of Kirchberg, gateway to Kitzbuehel.

On the skyline you can see ski slopes as far as Pass Thurn and the famed Grossglockner is on the distant skyline.

Good parallel skiers should do the Grossraum tour which begins and ends in Söll. Skiers work their way up and down the ridges, visiting Itter, Hopfgarten, the outskirts of Brixen, then back up to Zinsberg, down and finally back to Brandstadl and over to Hartkaiser, stopping along the way in Sheffau, Ellmau and perhaps Going although it's a short hike all the way into Going from the lifts at the bottom.

The black run from the summit of Hohe Salve above Söll will challenge a good skier. It's a 4,000 meter-long trail with a vertical drop of about 700 meters. The best intermediate run is the Rigi along the backside and then around the Hohe Salve, all the way down to the Gasthof Kraftalm where they serve a Jagertee (Hunter's Tea) which will blast your ski boots off. The recipe, according to the gasthof owner is tea, some rum, some more red wine, plenty of schnapps, a goodly amount of sugar and some herbs for aroma. He adds, don't light a match near the mixture while hot.

Mountain rating

The Wilder Kaiser is intermediate country with a capital I. You can head down any slope without hesitation and enjoy moderately challenging, well-groomed runs. A fine place to hone your skiing skills. Not recommended for the demanding skier craving black trails and thrills.

Ski school

Each town has a ski school. The largest of them, Schischule Söll, run by Sepp Embacher, has 90 instructors. Both valleys are noted for the high percentage of English-speaking instructors, a definite strong point for the Wilderkaiser region.

Lessons are offered daily beginning on Sunday and Monday. Instruction is from 10-12 and 2-4 p.m. Private lessons are also offered through the ski school office for approximately 320 schillings per hour with another 110 schillings for each additional student. The telephone information number is 05333-5454 or 5484. Beginners lessons are given directly across from the ski center on the beginner slope. Advanced and experts are taken up the mountain immediately. Even beginners go up after a couple of days at the bottom.

Group lessons

for one day	Sch. 340
for two days	Sch. 680
for three days	Sch. 740
for five days	Sch. 900
for six days	Sch. 950
for ten days	Sch. 1450
5 half day course 2-4 p.m.	Sch. 690

Lift tickets

The individual towns sell tickets good only for the local lifts, but the regional ticket is a better bargain and makes sense for the active skier. For those who anticipate limited skiing the point cards are best.

	Adults	Children
For half day (noon)	Sch 180	115
For one day	Sch 240	150
For two days	Sch 460	280
For three days	Sch 660	410

For four days	Sch 820	480
For five days	Sch 1000	585
For six days	Sch 1140	665
For seven days	Sch 1280	750

Check also the special ticket which allows some variation on ski days. A choice of 5 ski days in 7 days is 1140 schillings for adults and 665 for children. A choice of 7 ski days in 10 days is 1400 for adults and 830 for children. A choice of 10 ski days in 14 days is 1750 for adults and 1030 for children.

Note: A photo is required for all ski passes of 8 days or longer.

Accommodation

Söll is the most convenient because it's the first of the seven towns you come to in the Wilder Kaiser and the one we liked best. Especially quiet is Gasthof Greil, a ten-minute walk from the center of town. The hotel is quiet, the food tasty and filling and the staff friendly. About 400 schillings per person daily half pension. This hotel has a cooperating arrangement with larger British tour agencies and there are substantial room savings when guests use the tour agency rather than booking privately. Telephone 5333-5289.

The best hotel in town is Postwirt, a renovated, beautiful building right in the center of action, near the local tourist office. A room and breakfast is 590 schillings daily, half pension stay is 790 schillings. Low season rates are slightly reduced. The local phone is 5333-5221.

Equally attractive and historic is Feldwebel, just down the street. This 85-bed hotel has rooms from 340 schillings in high season (420 half pension). Telephone 5333-5224. Hotel Tyrol, about halfway between the Greil and the center of town, is Sch. 480 daily in high season with breakfast and about Sch. 580 half pension. Telephone 5333-5273.

On the mountain we liked the Salvenmoos where bed and breakfast was 250 schillings and half pension was Sch. 350. This is for skiers who want to hit the slopes immediately and those who don't need to go into town every few hours. Telephone 5333-5351.

There are over two dozen hotels in the Söll area proper. And private room and bed and breakfast houses are numerous. The local tourist office, beside the Postwirt Hotel, will find you a room in almost any price range almost immediately. For reservation information call 5333-5216.

Dining

The best meal we had was in the Greil, but we dined there several times so the chances were better that one would suit us. Good Austrian specialties.

The Stube of the Postwirt has the most atmosphere, given the group of old timers at the big front table who puff on their pipes and argue loudly about everything from Austrian politics to the merits of retired Formula One driver Niki Lauda and current ace Gerhard Berger (both Austrian, naturally). The food is good and filling. The Stube came in second for best apple strudel in town. It was good but not quite as fine as cafe Meribel, up the street past the local office for Thomson Tours.

Nightlife

The ski instructors and longtime visitors gather after skiing in the small bar of the Postbierstuhe. Just keep going past the Stube and you'll find the bar tucked away on the left. For laughter, some sing along action and live entertainment the Pub 15, an Italian place despite the name, is the place to visit. When we dropped in, the singer was American and the songs were English and American favorites. A good place to meet new friends is the Dorfstadl in the cellar of the Hotel Tyrol. There's a younger crowd and louder music at the Whiskey Muhle and at Disco Klaus.

Even though Söll is realtively small, with about 2,000 residents, the town has considerable experience with hosting visitors and there's a wide variety of entertainment to suit the taste of nearly all age groups.

Child care

The ski kindergarten is across the street from the ski school building. There is a price reduction for children from 5 to 15 who have at least one parent in the adult ski school.

| Five day kindergarten | Sch 765 |
| Six day | Sch 810 |

For an additional 80 schillings daily the ski kindergarten includes care and instruction for the whole day from 9:30 a.m. until 4:15 p.m. For information telephone the ski school at 5333-5454.

Getting there

The main arrival airport is Munich, about 70 minutes by bus from Söll and other towns in the area. If you're driving you take the Salzburg autobahn out of Munich and then the Rosenheim cutoff (called Inntal autobahn). You cross the border near Kufstein and take the second exit, Kufstein Sud. Söll will be marked on the autobahn exit sign. From the turnoff, it's about 15 minutes on a two-lane highway over one slight uphill grade to Söll. Altogether, the trip is one of the most convenient for the motorist or bus driver.

Other activities

Söll has a well-developed recreation complex with an extensive network of cross country trails. The recreation center had a beautiful indoor pool with a heated outdoor extension.

One advantage Söll has is its nearness to the Inntal autobahn. You are only about an hour's drive from either Salzburg or Innsbruck. Both cities are superb visiting points at any season of the year with a wide range of museums and scenic outdoor attractions. In addition, it is not unusual for the visitor with a car to visit Innsbruck and then venture down the Brenner motorway for a short excursion into Italy. The same is true for a visit to Munich when visitors arrive via Innsbruck or Milan without first visiting Germany.

Tourist Information

You'll find the tourist office in all the villages of the Wilder Kaiser helpful, particularly so in Söll where the staff of Christian Becker puts out the welcome mat for thousands yearly. For assistance and free brochures call 0043-5333-5216.

Zell am See-Kaprun

Once you've seen beautiful Zell am See and skied its runs, as well as those on the neighboring Kaprun glacier, the area will number among your favorite European winter resorts. The "Europa-Sportregion," as the area calls itself, is a popular destination for travelers from across Europe and the U.S.

Where to ski

There are two major areas: Zell am See's Schmittenhöhe lifts take skiers to the 2000-meter level, while Kaprun is famed as a year-round ski area with runs on the glacier beneath the summit of the 3203-meter (10,506-foot) Kitzsteinhorn.

To ski the Schmittenhöhe, avoid the main cablecar from town and opt instead for either the Sonnenalmbahn or, better still, the Areit chairlift from neighboring Schüttdorf and work your way up the mountain with the series of lifts.

The runs are good for intermediates and there are some expert challenges, too, particularly the two runs used in World Cup and regional downhill races. Our favorite is the trail from the Kapellenlift summit to Breiteckalm and then down a wonderful turning slope parallel to the woods. From there, it's black to the bottom. Locals call this run the "Trass." A trail intermediates may enjoy more is called the "Standard"; it drops from the top to Breiteck but then breaks back to the right over the Hirschkögel trail.

Kaprun is about six miles from Zell am See and it's another three and a half miles to the base of the area's lifts. Take the older cable car up to the glacier, or take the *Standseilbahn* that climbs the mountain inside a tunnel. Both go to the Alpin center, while the aerial cable continues on up to the top station at 3029 meters (9935 feet).

The skiing is intermediate with a couple of notable exceptions. One is the final part of the run from the top to the Breitriesenalpe cable car mid-station, and the other, if you have a guide and if you really are an expert, is through the rocks from the Salzburger Hütte.

Mountain rating

Zell am See is outstanding for intermediates; its network of trails and connecting lifts make skiing interesting.

For the beginner there are training slopes and plenty of room to take a fall or two without serious suffering.

Experts will head for the glacier at Kaprun where there are also plenty of challenging intermediate runs.

Ski school

Instruction in the Zell am See-Kaprun classes is conducted by approximately 150 teachers. Courses ranging from beginning through competition racing techniques are offered. Beginners classes start at 9:30 a.m. and advanced classes begin at 10 a.m. Information is available through the ski school office in the valley station of the Sonnenalmbahn (tel. 3207). Private instruction costs Sch. 1520 for one day (four hours) or Shc. 380 per hour.

Group lessons

for one day (four hours)	Sch. 340
for three days	Sch. 750
for six days	Sch. 950
for twelve days	Sch. 1700

Lift tickets

Tickets for the Europa Sports Region Pass (88/89 rates):

	high season	middle season
for three days	Sch. 790	Sch. 660
for four days	Sch. 1000	Sch. 840
for five days	Sch. 1240	Sch. 1010
for six days	Sch. 1400	Sch. 1180
for seven days	Sch. 1570	Sch. 1300

Daily rates at the separate sections of the Europe Sports Region are approximately Sch. 290.

Accommodation

Many of Zell's hotels and pensions are located near the lifts. In addition, for those who want to be nearer the Kaprun glacier there is accommodation in town and there's also a mountain hotel on the glacier.

Thumersbach, across the lake, is separated from the best skiing, but quite scenic. Check with the tourist office in Zell or in Kaprun for further information.

Zell also offers 24-hour service to individuals who come without reservations. Visitors can check an information board similar to those used at many U.S. airports at Zell and at the ground station of the Kaprun glacier cable car. By pushing a button next to the hotel's name, its location is illuminated on the map. You can then telephone the hotel directly and check on room availability.

The all-in package is good here. It's called "Schnee-Okay" and is available in low and middle season. First-class half-pension accommodation is available from about Sch. 4550 a week. Schnee-Okay includes seven days accommodations, a six-day regional pass, unlimited use of the ski shuttle bus and six days' admittance to swimming pools in Zell and Kaprun. At the other end of the price scale is simple bed and breakfast accommodation with all the other extras starting at Sch. 2535 a week.

The following hotels will arrange for the all-in plan for low budget accommodations:

Pension Bergkristall (tel. 8476)
Gasthaus Fischer (tel. 7114)
Pension Griesser (tel. 8403)
Pension Holzmeister (tel. 8513)
Pension Steiner (tel. 8415)
Hotel Tirolerhof (tel. 3721)
Hotel Waldhof (tel. 2853)

At the top end of the hotel scale, nine establishments in Zell and seven in Kaprun participate in the Winter Package Plan. Our top choices of the top category hotels were the Sporthotel Falkenstein (tel.7122), Hotel Sonnblick (tel. 8301) and the Sporthotel Kaprun (tel.8625). A top rated hotel is the Hotel St. Georg (tel. 3533 or through Best Western).

Apartments

The tourist office will provide a list of available apartments and chalets in the area. In addition, you can book directly through agencies in the area. For more information, call the Prodinger travel agency (tel. 2170), 6AMTC travel office (tel. 2208), Schüttdorf (tel. 7216) and Apartmentservice (tel. 7539). Apartments large enough to sleep four will range in price from Sch. 500-600 per night.

Dining

We can highly recommend the Erlhof (tel. 3173) overlooking Zell as a good place to eat with traditional Salzburgerland atmosphere and typical Austrian dishes. The wild deer venison is excellent. We also liked the homemade specialties in the Hotel St. Georg restaurant (tel. 3533).

Nightlife

We fell behind in our nightlife outings in Zell after trying to squeeze both skiing on the Schmittenhöhe and the glacier into the same day. We did venture out to meet a lively early-evening crowd at Disco No. 1 Taverne in the Café Feinschmeck. Later, we settled into the quieter, beautiful panorama bar on the roof of the Grand Hotel by the lake. Have at least one drink there during your stay.

Another alternative is to make the evening a sporting evening at the Kaprun Optimum, an indoor swimming pool and fitness center which is crowded through the evening with fitness-minded Europeans and is a great place to meet other skiers. Nightlife takes on a new meaning here.

Child care

The guest kindergarten in Zell is open Monday through Friday from 8 a.m. until 4 p.m. All-day care costs Sch. 80; until noon, Sch. 60.

The children's ski school is open daily from 10 a.m. until 4 p.m., except Sunday. A lunchtime snack is included and children from four to ten are accepted.

In Kaprun, call 8644 for information, and in Zell the number is 2600.

Getting there

Zell is about fifty miles from Salzburg, which has jet service from other European airports. The usual airport for international arrivals is Munich, about 115 miles away. Vienna is about 240 miles distant.

Zell has regular train service and offers a bus service to Laprun.

By automobile from Munich, drive to Salzburg by autobahn, and head toward Bischofshofen. Rental cars are available in Salzburg or Munich.

Other activities

A visit to nearby Salzburg, made famous a generation ago by the movie, "The Sound of Music," attracts millions each year.

In Salzburg, visit Mozart's birthplace and the Hohensalzburg fortress; take time to shop in the old city.

Both Zell am See and Kaprun deserve exploration. The Zell skyline is distinguished by the outlines of the St. Hippolyt church and the Vogtturm, (city tower).

Even non-skiers will enjoy the Schmittenhöhe on a clear day when you can see at least thirty 3000-meter (9843-foot) or higher peaks in the region.

At Kaprun, visit the Gothic Pfarrkirche and the castle ruin. If you're skiing the Kaprun glacier in summer or early autumn, visit the Tauernkraftwerk, a massive power plant on the outskirts of Kaprun. It's open daily from 8 a.m. until 5 p.m., April to October. Roads to the dams and lakes built for the power project may not be open after the first snow.

Tourist information

Check with the Kurverwaltung, A-5700 Zell am See; tel. 06542-2600; and Verkehrsverein Kaprun, A-5710 Kaprun; tel. 06547-8643; telex: 66763.

Mayrhofen Zillertal and Tuxertal

The Ziller Valley has somehow avoided great fanfare as a skiing region despite being one of the best and most accessible places to ski in all Austria. The chief resort of this region and most-visited by English-speaking skiers is Mayrhofen. It is typically Austrian with narrow streets, beautiful old buildings and cozy, timbered restaurants, cafés and hotels. Life revolves around the large square and the long, narrow main street. The cable car station in the center of town is almost always crowded and the spillover of skiers and shoppers combines to keep the main street alive with visitors during the day.

Mayrhofen reminds us a bit of Söll, another small Austrian resort, although the former is larger and has more interesting skiing.

A smaller town which makes resort noises is Zell am Ziller and at the head of the Tuxertal, Hintertux is at the base of one of the best glaciers for summer skiing. Hintertux makes no pretensions about being anything other than a glacier ski resort. If it sidewalks, they would fold up at lift closing time.

Where to ski

Mayrhofen and Zillertal

Wherever you look in the Zillertal there are lifts and most of them open up good intermediate skiing.

The best skiing is at Mayrhofen. Here, from the 2095-meter (6872-foot) Penkenjoch, a network of trails for all levels of skiers branches out. Avoid the older cable car from town and instead take the gondola from nearby Schwendau or the chairlift from Finkenberg on the other side of town.

At the top of the gondola from Schwendau, a chair takes you to the Horberg summit (2540 meters—8331 feet). The two mountains are connected and the runs here offer challenges for all levels, including expert.

Mayrhofen's second area, on the opposite side of the valley, is the Filzenalm. Take the long Ahornbahn cable car to the Filzenalm at 1905 meters (6284 feet). There were too many T-bar lifts and too little good skiing to hold us there for long.

In the Mayrhofen area, nine cross-country trails with a total of about twelve miles are prepared daily. Two of the trails are lighted for night skiing. Overall, cross-country opportunities are not interesting for the Nordic enthusiast.

Elsewhere in the valley, we recommend Hochfügen, only a short distance from the autobahn exit. Drive to the town from Fügen along an eight-mile mountain highway. From there, lifts ascend to 2200 meters (7226 feet).

Take the Spieljoch cable car directly to the 2000-meter level above Fügen. From the top, at the Onkeljoch, there is a four-mile run back into the valley, the Zillertal's longest downhill run.

Zell am Ziller is a beautiful town, the most important in the lower part of the valley, but the skiing was too far from town to suit us. You can drive the 2.5-mile steep road up to the Gerlosstein lifts but if you are not accustomed to driving with chains, take the bus or try another resort.

Hintertux and the Tuxertal

The glacier opens at the end of the valley and from the ground station you can see most of the nearly 50 miles of trails above. The best run is the trail from the Grosse Kaserer (3268 m/ 10700 ft) down over a great steep field of bumps to the gondola. A nice intermediate run leads from the top of the Gefrorene Wand to the Spannagel house, a cozy alpine hut serving excellent food.

Opposite the glacier is the Sommerbergalm with skiing from the 2300 m/7544ft. level.

Mountain rating

Overall, Mayrhofen is known as an excellent area for beginners. The ski school especially for children is world-famous. The professionalism of the novices' ski instruction organization is even more important since the nursery slopes are not particularly convenient to hotel accommodation.

Attaching a rating to more than a dozen resorts in the valley is difficult. The majority of slopes are intermediate and lower-intermediate with very few exceptions where experts are challenged. In the Tuxertal it is more of the same but with a few more thrills for an advanced skier.

Ski school

Mayrhofen has a large ski school (tel. 2795) numbering 130 instructors, many of them English-speaking. Lessons here are comparable in price to schools in other parts of the valley.

The Hintertux ski school (tel. 363) has 20 instructors.

Individual lessons

for one hour	Sch. 320
for each additional person	Sch. 110

Group lessons

for one day (four hours)	Sch. 300
for three days	Sch. 580
for five days	Sch. 730
for six days	Sch. 790

Lessons are also available for cross-country. Contact the ski school for registration.

Lift tickets

Tickets for the individual resorts are available, as well as the regional Zillertaler-Superpass. We recommend buying the superpass.

	middle season	high season
for a half day	Sch. 155	Sch. 155
for one day	Sch. 230	Sch. 230

for two days	Sch. 440	Sch. 440
for three days	Sch. 650	Sch. 650
Zillertaler-Superpass		
for four days	Sch. 700	Sch. 840
for five days	Sch. 830	Sch. 1010
for six days	Sch. 950	Sch. 1160
for seven days	Sch. 1070	Sch. 1310

Accommodation

Finding rooms along the length of the Ziller Valley has been made easy with the help of the local tourist offices, which supply the usual brochures listing available housing and act as intermediaries in case you do not want to book your own reservation for an all-in plan or lodging.

In Mayrhofen, the tourist office (tel. 05285-2305) also provides a listing of local hotels that are particularly good for families with small children. These hotels, marked by the sign of the Zillertal mountain fairy, provide discounts for children, children's games, coloring books, special menus for children, etc.

Elizabeth Hotel (tel. 2929) The most luxurious hotel in the region, with excellent food.

Hotel Neue Post (tel. 2131) On the market square near the train station.

Hotel Neuhaus (tel. 2203) Also centrally located, closer to railway station than the Neue Post. One of the recommended hotels for families with children.

Sporthotel Strass (tel. 2205) Provides good lodging close to the Penken cable car. Excellent location for those who rate skiing as top priority.

Hotel Alpenhof Kristal (tel. 2428) medium price hotel on the main square. Popular with many English tour groups.

Hotel Kramerwirt (tel. 2216) Inquire at the nearby Hotel Bergland for more details on the Kramerwirt's half- and full-pension plans. Central location, short driving distance from the cable car.

Hintertux has several hotels right at the base of the glacier. If you're intent on skiing and little else they make a good choice.

Hotel Rindererhof (tel. 05287-501; telex: 053990) Excellent location right at the gondola going up to the glacier. Superb for the enthusiastic skier.

Hotel Neu Hintertux (tel. 05287-318; telex: 054643) almost as close to the lifts as the Rindererhof.

Badhotel Kirchler (tel. 05287-312; telex: 053990) Large hotel, located in the small town. It's a beautiful, expensive and comfortable place to stay.

Hotel Kirchlerhof (tel. 05287-431) A comfortable medium-priced hotel in Lanersbach catering to families. Excellent breakfast buffet.

Apartments

The tourist office booklet, "Hotels-Pensions-Apartments," has a complete section on apartment and chalet rentals in and around town. To find the place that suits your needs, write first for the booklet, choose a place and the tourist office will assist with reservations.

Child care

Mayrhofen's tourist association provides a baby-sitting referral service (evenings only). Call the tourist office at 2635.

The ski school provides day care and ski instruction for children. It was Austria's first children's ski school, its organizers told us, and its program provides instruction, meals and entertainment for the children during non-skiing time.

for three days	Sch. 965
for six days	Sch. 1400

Dining

At Mayrhofen, the 400-year-old farmhouse restaurant, Wirtshaus zum Griena (tel. 2778) caught our fancy and was kind to our wallet. The food was excellent, the atmosphere marvelous. Duck your head to avoid the old and low ceiling beams. On the Penkenjoch, the Vronis restaurant served excellent lunchtime meals and the service from the owner Martin Huber and his family was friendly.

In Lanersbach try the restaurant in the Kirchlerhof and in Hintertux test slightly-fancier offerings at the Badhotel Kirchler.

Nightlife

The evenings after skiing are cozy in the town's many hotel bars, but Mayrhofen will never be mistaken for St. Anton after dark.

There is life, however, in the Schlussel disco in the Brucke hotel. The group was mostly 18-25, while a slightly older crowd enjoyed the Andreas Keller in the Neue Post. Check the Tiroler Stuben of the Neuhaus, one of our recommended hotels. We enjoyed "five o'clock tea" with a visiting English friend in the hotel. He stayed on for drinks and dancing at the après-ski bar and recommended it highly.

This town does get rocking immediately after the slopes close with serious drinking and dancing. In general, make for the area around the marketplace and choose your own spot for the evening.

In Hintertux try the Batzenkeller disco and the Almbar.

Getting there

Travelers visiting the Zillertal fly into Munich. The valley lies along an autobahn exit (Achensee) between Munich and Innsbruck. The drive up the entire valley is easy and fairly short, only about 20 miles. There is both train and bus service in the valley.

Other activities

One reason we based our visit to the Zillertal in Mayrhofen was the enthusiasm of its tourist office, which promotes a regular series of events to entertain guests. These include tea dances, chess competitions, color-slide lectures and other entertainment.

Each week a puppet show is staged for children and on another evening games are scheduled for the kids.

An outing to Innsbruck for a museum and sightseeing visit is a must.

For the outdoor-minded who want to do more than ski, we recommend the Alpineschule Zillertal (tel. 2829), run by Peter Habeler, for mountain training and excursions into the region's rugged Alps.

Tourist information

Fremdenverkehrsverband A-6290 Mayrhofen; tel. 05285-2305; telex: 53850.

Fremdenverkehrsverband A-6280 Zell am Ziller; tel. 05282-2281.

Switzerland

For many, Switzerland *is* the Alps; *ergo*, Switzerland *is* skiing in Europe. Of course, Switzerland contains only a portion of the Alps and there are other places to ski in Europe. Still, as the heart of the Alps and the home of alpine skiing, Switzerland deserves the superlatives bestowed upon it: its skiing is excellent; its resorts are efficient, its tourist offices more than competent, its lift systems well-run and its hotels exceptional. Its skiing seems to go on forever.

A Note on prices

The prices listed in this section are valid for the 1987/1988 winter season in almost all cases. The 1988/1989 prices should be less than three percent higher this season. While prices were carefully researched, they always seem to change. Use them as a guide only; none of the prices in this book are guaranteed nor should they be construed as official. Ask for the latest prices before buying anything or staying anywhere. It will avoid most likely problems.

All prices are given in Swiss francs (SFR). As the book was being researched, the Swiss franc was at an exchange rate of SFR 1.4 to $1. Any subsequent change in the exchange rate will be the biggest factor affecting the prices.

When is high season?

In Switzerland the 1988/1989 ski season will be broken out as follows (based on the Flims/Laax region):

High Season: 24 December 88 to 6 January 89 and 29 January through February 26.

Low Season: January 7-29 and February 27 to April 2

Pre-season: December 10-24

Switzerland's Romantic Mountain Railways

The skier in Switzerland whose timetable is not completely filled with skiing adventures can take a scenic ride on one of the world's most advanced mountain railway systems in the world. The regional Swiss railroad lines and the Postbus system have organized three spectacular transalpine routes: the Glacier Express runs from St. Moritz to Zermatt; the Bernina Express traverses the Alps from Chur to St. Moritz to Tirano and on to Milan; the Engadin Express connects St. Moritz with Austria's Landeck and Innsbruck.

The Glacier Express

Perhaps the most famous of the Swiss rail trips, the Glacier Express is advertised as the world's slowest train. Indeed, the trip lasts seven and a half hours—spanning more than 291 bridges as well as burrowing through 91 tunnels—on its way from St. Moritz in Switzerland's southeast corner to Zermatt. Passengers are awarded a special "Glacier Express" certificate upon the completion of the journey.

Trains run from Zermatt to St. Moritz and vice versa. Both leave in the early morning and arrive in the late afternoon. In their elegant dining cars a complete three-course lunch is served during the Chur-to-Andermat leg. The meal costs approximately $20, excluding beverages. Reservations are required for the meals on the trains. Wine glasses on the Glacier Express are tilted to prevent one's wine from spilling due to the route's many steep turns and gradients. The tilted glass does mean that you have to regularly turn it to keep it tilted in the right direction.

Bernina Express

The Bernina Express, which crosses into Italy over the Alps in Switzerland's southeast corner, is Europe's highest transalpine railway. While the train trip follows the same route as the Glacier Express from Chur to St. Moritz, it then strikes off for the Bernina Pass, Poschiavo and on to Tirano in Italy.

Along one short, eight-mile stretch, the track runs through five looping, or corkscrew, tunnels, passes through two straight tunnels and crosses eight viaducts. The train crosses the Bernina Pass at 7405 feet and, in doing so, climbs the steepest gradient of any non-cogwheel train in the world.

The Engadin Express

This train and postbus route connects St. Moritz with Innsbruck, Salzburg and Vienna. The trip from St. Moritz to Landeck done mostly by postbus, lasts almost three hours and is considered by many to be one of Europe's most romantic trips.

After leaving St. Moritz, the train chuffs alongside a beautiful Swiss National Park, through the village of Scuol, then the post bus past the famous castle of Tarasp and on to Vulpera. This is the home of the fourth language of Switzerland, Ladin. The mountain folk here preserve the ancient language, but most still speak English as well as German or Italian. The express then ends in Landeck, Austria, in the Tyrol district.

Making reservations

These train trips can be booked in the USA through the Swiss National Tourist Office (tel. 1-800-223-0048; in NYC 1-212-757-5944); in Britain through the Swiss National Tourist Office (tel. 01-734-1921); in St. Moritz at the Rhaetic Railway station (telex: 693518); in Chur at the main train station (telex: 693158); and in Zermatt at Zermatt-Tours (telex: 472104).

Arosa

One of the longest-established ski resorts in Switzerland, Arosa was part of the development of skiing as a popular winter sport. Today, Arosa is known for relatively-easy, wide-open skiing and good off-slope activities. The town is tucked within a circle of mountains above Chur at the end of the Schanfigger valley.

Everything in Arosa is within easy walking distance. If you bring a car to the resort, leave it in the public parking area and forget about it, unless you decide to escape to some other area later in the week.

Where to ski

Situated at an altitude of 1800 meters, or 5900 feet, Arosa's lifts fan out to reach the two major peaks in the area, the 2512-meter Hörnli and the Weisshorn at 2653 meters. While there are only 16 lifts, their capacity exceeds 17,000 skiers an hour. Some 45 miles of runs are long and spread out, adding up to plenty of skiing. The entire resort is above the trees for wide-open skiing and perfect cruising. There are also nearly 20 miles of groomed cross-country trails.

Mountain rating

Arosa is Eden for beginners and intermediate skiers because of its wide and long runs. After several days without a snowfall, when skiers have broken new trails between the normally prepared runs, you can virtually ski across the entire mountain.

There is one run which requires an expert, and that is the descent from the top of the Weisshorn to the Carmennahütte. This very steep run is wide enough to allow a gutsy intermediate to traverse widely and make his way down the slope, but it also offers expert-level practice on the steeps with plenty of room for error.

Ski school

The Swiss Ski School in Arosa (tel. 311996) has more than a hundred qualified instructors, most of whom speak English. Special courses for children, deep-snow, cross-country and other events are organized by the ski school, including torchlight descents accompanied by fireworks, descents by full moon and ski races. The tuition for the ski school is as follows:

Individual lessons

for a half day (two hours)	SFR 80
for one day (four hours)	SFR 160

Group lessons

for a half day (two hours)	SFR 21
for three half days	SFR 59
for six half days	SFR 105
for six full days (M-Sat)	SFR 145

Note: Reductions for children are available.

If you are ready for a ski touring experience there is a group which has organized the Radiant Orbit Program which is a six day program of skiing with a mountain guide. The skiing is hard but the area covered is fantastic and the experience excellent. The programs normally run from January through April. Cost for half pension and six days mountain guide are SFR 1300 for a room with bath. For more information contact Erwin Lamm at the Hotel Haus Lamm, Arosa (tel. 311366).

Cross-country courses are also available for SFR 21 per half-day, SFR 40 for two half-days, up to SFR 89 for five half-days. A half-day is two hours. Private instruction is SFR 40 per hour for one to two persons.

Lift Tickets

All lift tickets issued for more than two days require a photograph.

	adults	children (to age 16)
for one day	SFR 37	SFR 26
for two days	SFR 70	SFR 49
for three days	SFR 98	SFR 69
for six days	SFR 145	SFR101
for seven days	SFR 156	SFR 109

The first three weeks of December, lift tickets are reduced an additional 15%. Senior citizens and one adult member of a family also will be given 15% reductions on lift passes.

Accommodation

Arosa has a hotel for everyone—from the most luxurious to the bargain one-star. Their all-in program, with prices ranging from SFR 600 to SFR 900, includes a special seven-day, half-pension, private bath or shower and toilet. In addition, special lift-ticket prices are offered to skiers taking advantage of these week packages. The low-season daily-prices for half pension with private bath are noted for the hotels listed below. Add 15 to 25 percent during high season.

Our recommended five-star hotels are:
    Kulm Hotel, tel. 310131. SFR 180.
    Savoy Hotel, tel.310211. SFR145.
    Tschuggen Grand Hotel, tel. 310221. SFR 180.

Our recommended four-star hotels are:
    Hohenfels, tel. 311651; telex: 74538. SFR 101.
    Posthotel, tel. 310121. Right in the center of the town near the train station. SFR 125.
    Sporthotel Valsana, tel.310275; telex: 74232. Modern by the lake with good restaurant and child care facilities. SFR 117
    Waldhotel National, tel 312665. This hotel is a bit back in the woods but considered to be excellent. SFR115

The three-star hotels most convenient to the lifts are:
    Anita, tel. 311109. SFR 90.
    Astoria, tel. 311313. SFR 89.
    Belvedere-Tanneck, tel. 311335. SFR 95.

Hohe Promenade, tel. 312651. SFR 95.
Obersee, tel. 311216. SFR 95.

Our recommended two-star hotels are:
Alpina, tel. 311658. Most of the hotel has just been restored and is beautiful. SFR 75.
Erzhorn, tel. 311526. SFR 85.

Apartments

Arosa is well organized to handle tourists who want to rent apartments during the ski season normally for a minimum of one week, Saturday to Saturday; during the Christmas and Easter seasons, a minimum two-week rental is required.

The tourist office keeps track of which apartments are available. When writing, include the number of beds required, the preferred number of rooms and your planned vacation dates. You will receive a quick response that lists a selection of apartments and prices. Select the apartment you want and return the information. You'll receive confirmation in writing and be directed to contact the owner upon arrival.

Several hotels in Arosa also provide apartments which are allowed to share the hotel facilities such as pool, steam room, tennis courts and TV room. Perhaps the best of these aparthotels is the Savoy followed by the Park Hotel, both with five-star hotel facilities. Hotel Savoy medium priced apartments, for four people, cost SFR 1200 in January; SFR 1500 in February. There is a charge for final cleaning of SFR 90. Guests can also sign-up for half-pension with the hotel for an additional SFR 48. Similar apartments in the Park Hotel cost SFR 950 during January, and SFR 1540 during February. The Hotel Alpina (a two-star) also rents out apartments for families.

Normally, linen and kitchen utensils are provided. Other communal or private amenities, such as swimming pool, sauna, TV or room phone all add to the costs. Standard apartments rent for between $12 and $20 per person a night. Prices vary significantly from low to high season.

Dining

The following restaurants come recommended by Arosa natives as being very reasonable and having excellent food:

Stuva, Hotel Alexandra Modern Art, Hotel Hof Maran Im Stubli, Hotel Central Arven-Restaurant Chez Andrè, and Gspan. For something different take the sleigh ride up to the Hotel Alpenblick above Arosa and enjoy a special meat platter which you grill at the table.

Nightlife

Arosa is not the "nightlife capital" of Switzerland. The fun is where you make it, usually with groups that seem to form on their own during any ski trip. Arosa's après-ski activities center around the hotels in the evening. Here you'll find smaller bars with hands or piano players. In addition to the more than 20 such bars,. Nuts is probably the hottest disco in town.

Other, more organized, after-ski activities include indoor tennis, squash, chess evenings, bridge and so on.

Child care

There are two public kindergartens for children from three to six years at the Park (tel. 310165) and Savoy (tel. 310211) hotels. The Park Hotel kindergarten is open Monday through Friday from 9 a.m. until 5 p.m. The rates are SFR 7 for a half day and SFR 20 for a full day with lunch.

The Savoy Hotel kindergarten opens at 9:30 a.m., closes at noon and reopens from 2 until 4 p.m. Prices are similar to the Park Hotle. There are reductions for child care on a weekly basis.

Another kindergarten is run by the Swiss Ski School in the Skihalle Kulm, Inner-Arosa. It is open daily, except Sunday, from 9:30 a.m. until noon and again from 2 until 4:30 p.m. Arrangements for lunch can be made at the school. This kindergarten does not include a ski school. The ski school (tel. 311996) can provide additional information on the children's ski course. Prices are approximately the same as for the kindergartens listed above.

Getting there

The closest airport is Zurich, nearly a three-hour train ride from Chur. There, catch a special train for Arosa just outside the main train station entrance. The train ride from Chur to Arosa takes about one hour.

Driving from Zurich to Arosa will take about two and a half hours in good weather. Follow the signs to Chur and after entering the city, follow the signs to Arosa. The road is steep and narrow and requires chains during most of the winter. Arosa has a car park for 460 cars.

Other activities

Arosa is known for its off-slope activities. There are indoor swimming pools; ice skating on three open-air rinks and one covered rink; more than 18 miles of walkways, which are maintained all winter; squash and tennis courts at the Park and Savoy hotels; and horse-drawn sleigh rides. The town is also active in arts and entertainment, scheduling concerts, lectures and exhibitions throughout the winter.

For horseback riding, contact E. Ritsch in Weierhof. Eight horses are available for hire, and the cost is SFR 17 an hour.

Want to learn about the strange game of curling? Arosa offers organized curling lessons every Tuesday starting in January for SFR 4 a lesson.

Ski racing fans can see the women's World-Cup slalom races in January and February.

Make sure to ask about the special "sunrise brunch" served at the top of the Weisshorn several times during each month.

Don't miss late January's horse races held on ice.

If you want to get away from Arosa, you must make an effort and it does take time. The train ride down the mountain to Chur lasts about an hour. However, in good weather Arosa is only about an hour and a quarter away from Klosters or Davos by car and within easy reach of other resorts, such as Laax, Flims or Lenzerheide.

Chur is worth a visit. So is the deepest gorge in Switzerland, the Via Mala, which leads to the St. Bernard Pass and is about another half-hour's drive from Chur. Tiny Liechtenstein, one of the world's smallest countries, can be reached from Arosa in just over an hour. Visiting provides a chance to send postcards to everyone back home.

Tourist information

Contact Tourist Office Arosa, CH-7050 Arosa; tel. (081) 311621; telex: 74271. Office hours are Monday through Saturday, from 8 a.m. until noon and from 2 until 6 p.m. (until 5 p.m. on Saturday).

Crans-Montana

These twin villages perched high on a plateau above the town of Sierre were the site of the 1987 Alpine Skiing World Championships. The new racing runs created, and the improved ski lifts erected in preparation for the World Championships resulted in one of the most accessible skiing areas in the world. Indeed, for the intermediate skier, Crans-Montana may be heaven on the slopes. Long challenging pistes coupled with virtually no waiting at lifts are is a combination most skiers will find hard to beat.

The history of skiing in this area was already inscribed in skiing lore long before the 1987 Swiss medal sweep. In 1950 the first Swiss ski championships were held here. And even earlier, in January 1911 the founder of modern downhill racing, Sir Arnold Lunn, had the idea to organize a race from the highest point on the Plaine Morte glacier down to Montana. Unlike today's closely-timed individual runs, in that race all racers started together and the first one reaching the town was declared the winner. The race eventually developed into today's famous "Kandahar" held in St. Anton, Mürren, Chamonix, Sestriere and Garmisch.

Crans-Montana has been recently connected with a budding purpose-built resort, Aminona. This Crans-Montana-Aminona area is served by 40 interconnected lifts with almost one mile vertical drop and 100 miles of prepared pistes.

Crans and Montana do have some distinctions, though both names are most often said in the same breath. Neither is a paragon of alpine architecture. It appears rather that an architects' convention was given free hand to erect as many different buildings as possible. Unappealing, square, concrete boxes stand beside massive triangular "Toblerone" shaped hotels with a smattering of traditional chalets seeming out of place amidst the concrete and glass.

Crans has a more concentrated city atmosphere while Montana's inner city dissipates quickly. The shop signs in Montana read simply—Cheese, Fondue, Real Estate or Restaurant. In Crans the signs read Gucci, Louis Vuitton, Piaget, Cartier. Crans is chic—Montana more for the family. Crans can be crowded with furs, while in Montana one is more at home in a ski outfit.

Be prepared to hike up and down hills since both towns are built on the side of the mountain. But this slope, though many curse it by day, provides many hotels with spectacular views to the Alps in the south.

Where to ski

The Plaine Morte trail starts atop the 3000-meter (9843-foot) Plaine Morte glacier, which also serves as a summer ski area. Sometime during your stay, take the gondola and then cable car up from Violettes and measure your time against the Kandahar ski pioneers, whose best time was just over one hour for the run. The run is a long nine miles of intermediate terrain with expert tendancies due to the chance for frequent off-piste shortcuts. The trail down from Plaine Morte is closely controlled for avalanche danger. After even a relatively light snowfall the run from the glacier back to Violettes is often closed, but opens as soon as precautions are taken.

The area of Crans-Montana-Aminona is reached from four major lifts. From Crans a gondola lift brings skiers to Chetzeron (2100m/6825ft) which was the starting point of the men's Super G. A gondola lift takes skiers to Cry d'Err (2206m/7173 ft) which is the hub of the entire area. From Montana a new 6-passenger gondola lift whisks skiers to Cry d'Err. Barzettes, a five minute bus ride from Crans or Montana, another new and fast gondola brings you to Violettes (2208m/7176 ft). Five minutes on the bus will bring you to Aminona where a gondola takes skiers to Pt. Mont Bonvin (2411m/7836 ft) where a wide-open above-treeline area provides fantastic uncrowded conditions.

The most crowded lifts in the morning are from Crans and especially the lift from Montana. But a short, free bus ride to

Barzettes and the Violettes or Aminona lifts will get you up the mountain faster.

The Cry d'Err sector of the mountain is the most crowded. Ten lifts bring skiers to Cry d'Err. After a long flat traverse a skier arrives in the Crans section of the mountain. From here the best bet is to take the Super G/Slalom run back into Crans then catch the gondola back to Cry d'Err. The runs below Cry d'Err heading to Montana are intermediate playgrounds but suffer from a serious bottleneck near Pas du Loop as the four trails merge and slip through a narrow gap before widening on the way to town. At the end of the day, realize that this bottleneck will be crowded—ski slowly and in control.

From Cry d'Err another trail traverses to the right bringing you into the Violettes section. This area is separated from the Montana section by a sheer cliff whose edge is marked generally by the National run on the ski map. The Violettes area is the favorite of many intermediates featuring twisting runs down through the trees to the gondola midstation plus four other lifts opening more great intermediate skiing.

Across the valley from Vilettes is the Aminona area and the La Toula lifts. This is my favorite section of the resort. La Toula offers challenging expert runs and Aminona boasts wide-open uncrowded cruising. Take advantage of the great skiing before the area gets "discovered."

Mountain rating

Intermediates will rate Crans-Montana one of the greatest places they've ever skied. The variety is outstanding.

Beginners are extremely limited on this mountain. In Crans, absolute beginners start on the golf course which is perfect, but the second step, directly to the mountain, is a big one. Montana's beginners start above the Signal restaurant. Instructors admit that the area is limited and after a few days it is up to Cry d'Err where the blue runs are really very wide lower intermediate slopes. Beginners manage through wide traverses and learn fast or crash. In Violettes there are no beginner slopes and the beginner sections of Aminona are for those who have been on skis at least three or four days—even then the gentle slopes are isolated in a sea of red pistes.

Only experts need worry at all about whether there are enough challenges to keep things interesting. Experts will find no real steep sections but there is plenty of off-piste and tree skiing. The championship runs are also a good test.

Ski school

The Crans-Montana area has more ski instructors (about 200) than some Swiss ski villages have permanent residents. There's a lesson being given somewhere on the slopes from Crans to Aminona nearly every hour of the day. For information on lessons, call 027-411320.

The Montana ski school is by far the most international. It boasts qualified Swiss Ski Instructors from the U.S.A., Australia and Britain. The Crans ski school is a relatively closed Swiss shop.

For private ski instruction, the cost is SFR 40 an hour for one or two students, and SFR 50 per hour for three to four persons.

Group lessons (three hours a day):

one half-day	SFR 19
seven half-days	SFR 90

Children pay SFR 18 for one day and SFR 75 for one week.

Cross-country lessons are offered and four different trails with a total length of 25 miles are prepared during the season.

Lessons are offered for two one-week periods each December before Christmas by the Swiss Ski School Association as part of its certification of teachers. The one-week package includes lessons, hotel with half-pension, plus bus and lift tickets. Prices start from SFR 725 weekly in a three-star hotel.

Lift tickets

The 88/89 Crans-Montana area pass is available at the following rates (Children between six and 15 enjoy a significant discount of approximately 40 percent):

half day	SFR 22
one day	SFR 36
two days	SFR 70

four days	SFR 123
five days	SFR 146
seven days	SFR 181
fourteen days	SFR 278

Accommodation

Crans-Montana can be very upscale. It doesn't claim many movie stars or much of the old rich. Crans-Montana is an oasis for the "corporate rich." The town boasts more five-star hotels than any other Swiss resort except St. Moritz and a dazzling selection of prize-winning, expensive restaurants. Finding the ritziest isn't difficult—digging for the good solid values for the middle-of-the-road crowd takes a bit more time.

Crans-Montana is an excellent resort to rent an apartment or chalet. Of the 30,000 people who may be staying during peak season, 25,000 of them can stay in vacation apartments or chalets. We'll list the traditional hotels first. The first price given is for the special ski week which Crans-Montana organizes during January, late March and early April. It includes seven days at half pension, seven days of ski passes and seven half-days of ski instruction. The last price noted is the normal high season price for half pension. Expect to pay approximately 20 percent less during low season.

Grand-Hotel Rhodania (tel. 411025; telex: 413754) SFR 1015—This is a Best Western Hotel call 1-800-528-1234 for reservations in USA. This is considered to be the most elegant hotel in the Crans side of town. It has almost everything a hotel guest could look for except a pool. Normal daily rate: SFR 185-200.

Crans Ambassador (tel. 415222; telex: 473176) SFR 1015—The best hotel on the Montana side of the town. It is next to the cable cars, has good nightlife and has an indoor pool. Normal daily rate: SFR 176-219.

Le Quatre Canetons (tel. 411698; telex: 473425) SFR 780—From the outside this looks like a converted box-shaped hospital, but once inside the doors you enter a world of cozy, quiet elegance. The large rooms look out to one of the most spectacular mountain range views in the world. The food is gourmet quality. The lounge has a crackling fire after dinner and the service is excellent. There is nothing fancy like saunas or pools—just top quality hospitality. Excellent English is spoken. Normal daily rate: SFR 82-97.

Etoile (tel. 411671; telex: 473195) SFR 780—This hotel is directly at the bottom of the Crans/Cry d'Err lift. The two ladies who run the place are a big help and will make your stay memorable. Normal daily rate: SFR 82-97.

De la Foret (tel. 413608) SFR 780—A bit of a walk to the downtown area but close to the Violettes lift. Has a covered swimming pool. Normal daily rate: SFR 82-97.

National (tel. 412681) SFR 780—This lower-priced hotel is near the Crans lifts. It is used by British tour groups but the owner can be cantankerous. Normal daily rates: SFR 82-97.

Cisalpin (tel. 412425) SFR 595—Right next to the lifts. Normal daily rate: SFR 53-60.

Pension Central (tel. 413767) SFR 595—Everything the name implies. Smack in the center of Crans. A family run pension. Normal daily rate: SFR 56-63.

Teleferique (tel. 413367) SFR 595—At the departure of the Cry d'Err lifts. If you want to take two steps and be on the lift, this is the place. Normal daily rate: SFR 56-63.

Vieux-Valais (tel. 412031) SFR 495—Small family-run hotel with only 15 beds. Normal daily rate: SFR 44 (B&B).

Olympic (tel. 412985) New hotel in the center of town. Normal daily rate: SFR 50.

Dining

This town, as noted has plenty of great eateries. These are some of our favorites from expensive to moderate to inexpensive.

For top gourmet cuisine head to "Le Chamois d'Or" (tel. 415553) where the chef works at Maxim's in Paris between seasons. The "Rostisserie de la Reina" (tel. 411885) is renowned for its fresh fish and shellfish and "Le Sporting" (tel. 411177) has top French and Italian food.

For the moderate meals try "Le Trappe" in the Hotel Cisalpine (tel. 412425). Try their *Fondue la Trappe*. The Hotel Aida (tel. 412781) has a beautiful rustic dining room.

The budget crowd should indulge at "Le Bistro" and "Mamma Mia" in Montana, and at the Ambassy Restaurant at the Montana edge of Crans.

On the mountain we liked the lunch menu at Des Violettes and Bella-Lui. Or if everything on the slopes is crowded try the restaurant at the lower station of the Montana/Cry d'Err gondola. The scenery from De la Plaine Morte restaurant (tel. 413626) on the glacier is the stuff memories are made of.

Apartments

Rental apartment and chalet listings in Crans-Montana are overwhelming. Twelve major rental agencies in Crans and 17 in Montana maintain listings.

Expect to pay SFR 720 for a two-bed studio during high season (February and Easter time); SFR 960 for a four-bed two-room apartment; SFR 1800 for a four-room six- to eight-bed apartment.

If you want to book, write to the tourist office in either town with details of what you want and the price range, and you'll get a prompt reply.

Nightlife

By American and British standards there isn't much. Immediately after skiing the only bar with a crowd is in Montana— Le Grange. It's small and very smokey. The Pub in Crans has been reported as an après ski spot but I can't confirm it.

Discos really don't get going until between midnight and one a.m. If you're determined and well-heeled head for "Le Sporting and "Pacha" in Crans but expect a SFR 20 cover charge which includes a drink. In Montana the place to be seen is the "Number One." There is no cover, but a beer is SFR 15.

If you have the urge to go out between 9 p.m. and midnight, try some of the piano bars which are normally quiet. Memphis Bar in Crans sometimes has jazz.

Child care

The ski school for children (six to 12) runs only half days. The cost for a half day is SFR 18; and seven days, SFR 75; all day nursery with lunch included is SFR 40. Telephone in Crans 411320, in Montana 411480. A new kindergarten has opened for children from three to seven years. It is located near the station for the Grand-Signal lift. The kindergarten is open from 8:30 a.m. to 5 p.m. Telephone is 412022. Rates are SFR 32 for full day with lunch, SFR 17 for half day and SFR 6 an hour.

Getting there

You'll most likely arrive at Geneva airport. From here, it's an uncomplicated car or train ride around the lake and into the mountains. From Sierre take the cable car around the corner from the railway station, or the bus from directly in front of the railway station.

Other activities

Crans-Montana is a center for hot-air ballooning and hang-gliding, with instruction in hang-gliding available. Call 413041 for information about both. A winter meeting of hot-air balloon enthusiasts is held annually, usually in February. A balloon ride for two costs SFR 600 and three SFR 750.

Sled-dog races are run several times during the season at courses in the area.

Tourist information

Check with the tourist office, Crans, CH-3963, Switzerland; telephone: (027)412132; telex: 473173 TURCH CH; tel. 412132. In Montana, the address is CH-3962, Switzerland; telephone: (027)413041; telex: 473203 TURM CH.

The tourist offices have automatic information service via phone at 41335. This automatic service provides snow condition reports during the season.

Davos

Davos is a queen among winter resorts, one of the first to be developed and still considered to be one of the best in the world. Located in Switzerland's Grisons region, in the southeast corner of the country, the town is dwarfed by mountains rising on both sides of the valley. The mountains have been developed into five separate ski areas.

The town is not quaint by any stretch of the imagination. Where a dreamer might expect to find wooden chalets, reality will produce square concrete hotels. But Davos maintains a sense of being comfortable. Traffic moves easily along the upper and lower main arteries without buildup. The hotels have a long distinguished tradition for excellence and practically every type of recreational possibility is available. If you want to buy a Rolex, pick up the latest in Gucci accessories or the finest Atomic racing ski, you'll find everything without the least problem. Residents are politely correct in dealing with visitors, perhaps not as warm as in small Austrian towns totally dependent on the influx of tourists, but friendly nevertheless.

At night the mix of people has unusual variety, from teen agers in town for the good skiing to elderly couples enjoying the crisp, clear mountain air and the restorative powers of an Alpine vacation. Nightlife is adequate, perhaps restrained. Everything seems done in moderation.

Davos will remind you of the best of Switzerland: beautiful, organized, tourist oriented, enjoyable to visit at any time.

Where to ski

Best known is the Parsenn area, one of the major reasons why Davos has become a premier European resort. It is reached by the Parsennbahn, a cable railway that leaves every 15 to 20 minutes during the ski season. It peaks at the Weissfluhgipfel, at 2844 meters, where it drops with two expert runs to the Parsenn. Here, runs are wide open and offer intermediate and beginning skiers a paradise for cruising. The Parsenn has 40 seemingly endless runs, including what was once Europe's longest—from Weissfluhjoch to Kublis.

The Jakobshorn area is the second major area in Davos, on the opposite side of the valley from the Parsenn. A cable car rises from the town to the lower station of the Jakobshornbahn, which peaks at 2590 meters. Here, 14 marked trails will keep a skier busy for at least a day. The area is more challenging than the Parsenn and often less crowded, but the runs are shorter and more limited. The other three areas are the Rinerhorn area at Glaris just up the valley from the main town, with thirteen runs and several good advanced-intermediate descents; the Pischa area, reached by a short bus ride from Davos and offering limited but uncrowded runs; and the Schatzalp/Strela area, which joins the Parsenn by way of a cable car that runs from the Strelapass to the Weissfluhjoch. This last area has significantly more difficult runs and offers a change of pace for several afternoons after one has warmed up on the Parsenn.

All of the runs end in the valley and most are within walking distance of the hotels. Where runs end in Kublis, Saas, Klosters, Wolfgang or, in Glaris, at the opposite end of the valley, frequent trains bring skiers back to the center of Davos. The train connection is included in the lift-pass price.

Mountain rating

Davos earns an A-plus when it comes to beginning and intermediate skiers. This is perhaps the ideal terrain for learning to ski and perfecting techniques. For experts, the Parsenn terrain can become somewhat boring and they should ask the instructors where the most challenging skiing—normally off the Parsenn—can be found.

The best expert runs on the Parsenn are from the top of the Weissfluhgipfel. Otherwise, stick to the trails that drop into town alongside the Parsennbahn, or take the Drostobel-to-Klosters run, which is narrow and sometimes steep. The Strela area, Rinerhorn and Jakobshorn all have some good expert runs but expect easy cruising for the most part. On days with good fresh powder, it pays to hire an instructor who will take you to the special spots for some thrills in the powder for the morning.

Ski school

The Davos ski school has more than 150 instructors. Almost every one of them speaks some English. There are some reductions for groups of senior citizens and for children. Inquire at the ski school to see whether such a group has been organized. Lesson rates are:

Individual lessons

one day (five hours)	SFR 190
five consecutive days	SFR 170 a day
half day	SFR 105
one hour (for one or two persons)	SFR 40

Group lessons

Note: one lesson equals two hours of instruction

one lesson	SFR 20
three lessons	SFR 55
six lessons	SFR 90
twelve lessons	SFR 160

A discount is offered for lessons given during the first three weeks of December. Children from four to 12 years get a 25 percent discount, depending on the length of the course. Ask when signing up.

Lift tickets

Separate passes are sold for each of the five areas outlined above, although there is a combination pass for Strela and the Parsenn area.

The most convenient pass, especially if you plan to ski for a week or more, is the all-inclusive regional pass. This pass gives you use of all lifts, as well as the train through the valley from Glaris to Kublis. The only restriction is that it's sold only for more than two days.

three days	SFR 120
six days	SFR 200
seven days	SFR 224
14 days	SFR 360

Note: A single-day ticket for the Parsenn area costs SFR 36. Children get a 25 percent discount.

Accommodation

Davos' hotels range from posh and plush to plain and priceworthy. The following hotels are our top recommendations in each category. They are listed with January "white-week" prices from the 88/89 ski season. Included is half pension, beginning Sunday evening and ending with breakfast the following Sunday. The special package six-day lift tickets price is SFR 200, and the special ski school price is SFR 138. Prices during the first three weeks of December are ten to 20 percent lower. All prices are with bath. The high season 87/88 normal daily rate is the last price quoted for each hotel.

Steigenberger Belvedere***   (tel. 21281; telex: 853110) No white week—Many consider this the best hotel in town. Normal daily rate: SFR 200.

Morosani Post Hotel**   (tel. 21161; telex; 853150) White week: SFR 890. A Best Western Hotel. Normal daily rate: SFR 178.

Sunstar Park Hotel**   (tel. 21241; telex: 853192) No white week special. Normal daily rate: SFR 165.

Sporthotel Central**   (tel. 21181; telex: 853188) No white week special. Normal daily rate: SFR 165.

Derby Hotel**   (tel. 61166; telex: 853236) White week: SFR 890. Normal daily rate: SFR 170.

Meierhof**   (tel. 61285; telex: 853263) White week: SFR 890. Normal daily rate: SFR 175.

Hotel Cristiana*   (tel. 51444) White week: SFR 560 Normal daily rate: SFR 105.

Hotel Des Alpes*** (tel. 61261; telex: 853241) No white week program. Daily room rate: SFR 118.

Edelweiss* (tel. 51033) White week: SFR 280 (Bed and breakfast). Normal daily rate: SFR 52.

Apartments

As at most Swiss resorts, the rental apartment business is well organized and bookings can be arranged through the tourist information office. Write to the office, and provide details about when you plan to arrive, how many people will be sharing the apartment and what facilities you desire. It will respond quickly with several apartment choices.

Keep in mind that you want to stay in Davos-Platz or Davos-Dorf. If you end up in Davos-Laret or Davos-Wolfgang, you will face a good walk to the lifts every day and may have to catch a shuttle bus. Make your selection and notify the tourist office or the individual owner, depending on the instructions you get from the tourist office.

Normally, linen and kitchen utensils are included in every apartment. Heat, taxes, electricity and cleaning services may be extra. Expect to pay between SFR 25 and SFR 42 per person a night, depending on how many are sharing the apartment, where it's located and its relative position on the luxury scale.

Dining

Davos has scores of restaurants. Try Ammann's Steakhouse, and the Rössli. Bündnerstübli at Dischmastrasse in Dorf is very local and very reasonable. Palüda-Grill is very rustic and located in the Derby Hotel in Dorf. In the Hotel Davoserhof, the Bündnerstübli is elegant with upper-level prices and high-class cuisine.

Just outside of the town try Hubli's Landhaus in Laret (tel. 52121), or the Hotel Post in Frauenkirch (tel. 36104); both are excellent and reservations are strongly recommended.

The best pizza in town is found at El Padrino in Platz. The best Italian restaurant is Trattoria Toscana in Hotel des Alpes in Dorf.

Nightlife

For nightlife, head to the "Postli Club," open every evening from 8:30 p.m. on; the "Cabanna Club," which gets started at 9 p.m.; or the "Central," which also opens its doors at 9 p.m. Don't expect many exciting things to happen before 11 p.m., though. Most discos stay open until 2 a.m.

Child care

Two organized kindergartens in Davos offer supervision for children between the ages of three and ten years.

The Bolgen Kindergarten (Tel: 34048) is in Davos-Platz, next to the Jakobshornbahn's lower station. It is open every day except Sunday from 9 a.m. until 4:30 p.m. The costs are:

for one hour	SFR 10
for one day	SFR 25
for six consecutive days	SFR 90

Lunch is served from 11:30 a.m. until 2 p.m. and costs an additional SFR 12. Advanced booking is required. Contact Davos-Jakobshorn Cable Airways (tel. 37001) for more information.

The Pinocchio Kindergarten in Bünda, Davos-Dorf, is open every day except Sunday from 9 a.m. until 5 p.m.. Its prices are:

for one hour	SFR 10
for one day	SFR 25
for six consecutive days	SFR 90

Lunch is served from 11:30 a.m. until 2 p.m. and costs SFR 12. If the school feeds the child, the charge for lunch is SFR 6. Reservations are required. Contact the Swiss Ski School of Davos, Promenade 83, 7270 Davos-Platz; tel. 37171.

Getting there

The closest airport is Zurich, nearly three hours away by train. You must change in Landquart if you decide to take the train to the resort.

If you opt for a rental car, follow the signs to Chur on an excellent superhighway until you get to the Landquart/Davos exit. The drive from Landquart to Davos is through the narrow valley and passes through Kublis and Klosters before arriving at Davos-Platz. The total distance from Zurich to Davos is about 150 kilometers, or just under 100 miles.

Other activities

Davos is a well-developed resort with a swimming pool, saunas and a solarium. The cost for the public pool and sauna is SFR 11 a visit; alternatively buy a ten-visit book of coupons for SFR 90. If you just want to swim, pay only SFR 4.50 a session, or SFR 35 for ten visits.

There is a new tennis and squash center in Davos-Platz with four indoor tennis courts and two squash courts, tel. 083-33131.

Europe's largest natural ice skating rink is open and skate rentals are available.

Horseback riding can be arranged by calling Hans Lenz at (083) 53888 or 52368.

Hang-gliding courses are taught by Werner Sieber in Davos-Dorf; tel. 52278.

Horse-drawn "sleigh rides to anywhere" can be arranged by calling 35135.

Both Zurich and Lucerne are only about a two-hour drive from Davos.

South, towards the San Bernadino pass, drive through the Via Mala, the deepest gorge in Switzerland, presided over by the recently restored castle of Hohen Rathien in Thusis. If the pass from Sils to Davos is open and you have tire chains, the drive that completes the loop around the mountains is beautiful.

Tourist information

The tourist information office is open daily from 8 a.m. until noon and from 1:45 to 6 p.m. On Saturday, it closes at 5 p.m. It is closed on Sunday. Write: Davos Tourist Office, 7270 Davos-Platz; tel. (083) 35135; telex: 853130.

Engelberg

When you ski at Engelberg, in central Switzerland, just remember that the Gerschnialp is for beginners and the Titlis is
for the advanced. It will save you a few difficult moments if
you're wary of the ski school of hard knocks.

Skiing in Engelberg is done in two major areas. The brunni
is on one side of the valley with slopes all the way up to the
Schonegg at 2040 meters (6691 feet). From Schonegg it's an
intermediate cruise down to the village.

The finest beginner and lower intermediate skiing is on the
opposite mountain below the Titlis glacier on Gerschnialp. Ski
out the doorway of the six-person gondola station and down
the mountain to the Gerschnialp lifts.

Because it is central Switzerland's major resort, Engelberg
is crowded on weekends. During the week, things are far less
hectic. Everyone but the rank beginner eventually makes it up
to the 3239 meter (10,624 feet) summit of Titlis. This is where
the best skiers sharpen their skills. To join them, take the gondola from the valley floor to Truebsee and then the two-section
cable car the rest of the way up to Klein-Titlis at 3020 meters.
You've spent over 90 minutes geting to this point, so enjoy the
view all the way to the Gotthard Pass in one direction and past
Lucerne to the Bernese Oberland and Interlaken in the other.

From Titlis there is a memorable run all the way to Truebsee
from what seems (on clear days) like the roof of the Europe.
The run crosses the summer ski area and becomes a black trail
as you begin the biggest part of the nearly 800-meter drop from
Station Titlis to Stand. Take it easy the first time down. The
glacial ice, sharp turns and the steepness of the slope can be
treacherous. Follow the trail markers and don't let the nets, set
out at the worst places, break your concentration.

After one run, some intermediates choose to stay on the

wider red run from Stand down to Truebsee. If you make this decision, take the horizontal T-bar across the frozen lake to Alpstuebli where you can go up to the 2583-meter Jochstock. The red run down to Jochpass and Alpstuebli is good before cruising down to the Kanonenrohr entrance.

The Kanonenrohr (cannon barrel) section is only a few hundred meters, but you'll turn enough to keep your thighs burning for a while. Lower intermediates should opt for the blue trail to the left of the toughest section. To repeat the best part of the run stop at the Untertruebsee cable car station and go back up. Jochstock down to the ground station is about six miles while from the Titlis peak to the ground station is eight miles.

The best off-piste skiing is on the Laub above the Ritz restaurant and below Titlis. The 1000 foot vertical drop is a challenge for even experienced skiers and a guide (cost: about SFR 120) is recommended.

Mountain rating

For beginners, the slopes of the Gerschnialp and Untertruebsee are best.

Intermediates will be challenged on both sides of the valley, particularly up top on Titlis.

Experts will discover whether they really merit that classification after several runs from the glacier summit. In short, Engelberg is an excellent ski destination for the broadest range of skiers.

Ski school

Two ski schools (for information, call 941161) with a total of 65 instructions offer both group and private lessons.

Individual lessons

one hour	SFR 36
half day (3 hrs.)	SFR 110
all day (5 hrs.)	SFR 170

Group lessons

Group lessons are offered in five full-day blocks. The Schweizer school offers four and a half hours of instruction for five days for SFR 108. The Neue school which guarantees small classes of no more than six, offers four hours of instruction daily for five days for SFR 120.

Cross-country lessons are offered by fifteen instructors (tel. 942255).

Lift tickets

The Engelberg ticket is good for all 24 lifts in the area, opening a total of about 32 miles of trails. There are discounts for children, senior citizens and families (ask about shoulder season rates). In addition, for day tickets the price drops three francs per hour after 10 a.m.

for one day	SFR 45
for two days	SFR 70
for three days	SFR 93
for six days	SFR 162
for seven days	SFR 170

Accommodation

Engleberg is a relatively small town (pop. 3100) with a major tourist capacity. Overall, there are nearly 10,000 beds available in hotels, guesthouses and pensions, plus another 6500 in private homes and apartments.

The all-in plan should be your first choice. The plan offera a week's accommodation and half pension, six-day ski pass, bus transfers and other extras beginning SFR 550 per week. Our choices:

Engelberg (tel. 941168, telex 866183) a pleasant Hotel in the car-free city center.

Hotel Central (tel. 941239; telex: 866269) Ideally located for all activities in town. Hotel has its own swimming pool and sauna.

Hotel Europaischer Hof (tel. 941263) Offers special ski package which includes seven days half board, five days general ski pass, five days ski school, courtesy bus to all lifts, reductions at sport center and swimming pool. Cost is about SFR 600 for the package. This is a Best Western Hotel (in USA, call 1-800-528-1234 for reservations).

The Dorint Hotel (tel. 942828) One of our favorite hotels in town. Special weekly all-in package available for SFR 590 or for SFR 480 without half pension.

Hotel Hess (tel. 941366, telex 866270) Here you get friendly staff, traditional, nice rooms and above all else, excellent food.

Sporthotel Trübsee(tel.941371) Hotel has a great location halfway up the Titlis bahn. Weekly plan is approximately SFR 600 without half pension.

If the hotels in Engelberg are fully booked, as they aften are in peak season, the lakeside city of Lucerne is a good alternative. It is only 30 minutes from the slopes by car. An excellent waterside hotel is **Bellevue et Balances**, a Best Western Hotel.

Dining

The Tudorstubli restaurant at Hotel Hess (tel. 941366) is the best restaurant in town and offers excellent lamb specialties.

Apartments

Engelberg has much to offer the person seeking apartment accommodation. Prices start at SFR 520 a week for one-bedroom apartment.

The tourist office has a computer list of available apartments and an inquiry will generate an answer mailed to you the same day.

Several agencies offer apartments in the city. Their names, total number of apartments offered by each and telephone numbers are listed below.

Interhome; 100 apartments, chalets; tel. 942340
Neuschwaendi organzation; 30; tel. 942516
Sunnmatt; 100; tel. 941461
Uto-ring; 35; tel. 01-2024310
Würsch; 40; tel. 943165

Nightlife

A pleasant place to meet is at the bar of the Bellevue Terminus Hotel opposite the railway station and ski school. Later in the

evening you can drop into the Spindle in the cellar of the Al-
penclub Hotel. It's crowded with the 18-25 set as is the nearby
Carmena club. Our favorites were Dream Life, an English pub
at the Central Hotel and Peter's Pub, just up the street.

The Casino, close to the ski school office, has a slightly older
crowd and a new nightclub.

Child care

The local ski school operates a ski kindergarten program for
children from three to six. The program runs in three-day blocks
and the price, SFR 111, includes a ski pass.

A second program, for children from seven to 14 is given in
three-day blocks and costs SFR 117. This includes instruction,
ski pass and lunch.

Getting there

The main international airport is Zurich, transfers by train or
automobile. Driving time from Zurich is about one-and-a-half
hours. If possible, make a sightseeing stop in Lucerne along
the way. Rental cars are available in Zurich, Lucerne and Engelberg.

Other activities

Engelberg is sunny most of the year. The biggest non-skiing
pursuits are hiking and sightseeing.

Engleberg has a sports center with indoor and outdoor ice
skating plus indoor tennis courts, a fitness center and a curling
competition area.

Horse-drawn sleigh rides are available throughout the winter, and on Friday from January through March nighttime sleigh
rides are a tradition.

Visit the beautiful 12th-century Benedictine abbey at the edge
of town. For more extensive touring, take the train for a tour
of Lucerne and the four lakes area.

On Friday during ski season there is a visitors' ski race. In
addition, there is a major ski jumping competition from the
Titlis 90-meter tower each February.

For the advanced skier, courses in trick skiing are offered
(tel. 941074).

The most scenic local excursion, other than the ride up the

Titlis bahn, is the trip to Schwand, about five miles away, where from the vantage point above the church you get the best view of the ring of mountains in the Engelberg area.

Tourist information

Check with the Kur-und-Verkehrsverein, CH-6390 Engelberg, Switzerland; tel. 041-941161; telex: 866246.

Flims/Laax

Flims/Laax is one of the truly undiscovered ski areas in Switzerland, at least as far as American and British skiers are concerned. Unlike the "best-known" Swiss ski resorts, which were patronized by English visitors during the early years of skiing's rise to popularity, Laax and Flims were discovered by the Swiss and the Germans, who know a good area when they find it.

Flims is a town in the traditional sense. The ski lifts start from the town center and the major hotels are spread throughout the town. Laax as far as skiers are concerned is limited to the new hotels and apartments which have been purpose-built at the base of the Crap Sogn Gion cable car. Not only the major hotels are centered here but also the major nightlife. Flims is perhaps a more Swiss experience. Laax is perhaps a purer ski vacation experience.

It is hard to describe the incredible expanse of skiing that surrounds a skier as he gazes from the top of the Crap Sogn Gion cable car station which rises from Laax. One thing is certain, that skier won't be able to stop grinning ear to ear. This is one wide-open area that cries out for all-day skiing.

Where to ski

Laax and Flims are at an altitude of about 1100 meters. One major lift from each resort town carries skiers to the snowfields, which are in turn linked by a far-flung, thirty-two lift system. These lifts are not tightly packed but efficiently service the trails belonging to four major sections: Cassons Grat, La Siala, Crap Sogn Gion and Vorab.

After the lifts split above Flims, one continues to Cassons Grat, a spectacular snowfield set on the Flimserstein. Here, powder and off-piste skiers can have a field day. The other fork of the lift takes skiers to Grauberg, which is linked with other lifts under the La Siala peak.

Above Laax, the cable car reaches the Crap Sogn Gion at 2220 meters and a second continues to Crap Masegn, 200 meters higher. From here, skiers can shoot back into the valley towards Falera, or to the lower cable car station. Other runs drop into the opposite valley, where more lifts bring skiers up to the La Siala area above Flims. High-altitude buffs head to the Vorab area, which, at over 3000 meters, presents a great panorama and beautiful skiing.

Mountain rating

The beginner will find the best areas under La Siala and on the Vorab and Flims-Foppa.

Intermediates will be overjoyed with the Crap Sogn Gion section and can find more than enough challenging runs anywhere in the resort area.

The expert skiers can stay busy when the mood strikes them, especially beneath the Crap Sogn Gion cable car, the back side of the Vorab, and through Cassons Grat's powder and trails.

Ski school

Ski school is available in both Flims and Laax. The prices are almost identical. Private instruction costs: SFR 100 for a morning lesson; SFR 90 for afternoon sessions; and SFR 160 for a full day

Group lessons for adults are: SFR 20 for a half day; SFR 38 for a full day; SFR 89 for five half-days; SFR 135 for five full-days.

Group lessons for children are: SFR 20 for a half-day; SFR 38 for a full day; SFR 43 for three half-days; SFR 64 for six half-days; SFR 95 for six full days.

A private instructor for powder work can be hired for SFR 115 for a half-day.

Lift tickets

The lifts are run by separate companies, one from each resort. The Flims lifts operate in the Cassons Grat and La Siala areas. The Laax lifts cover the Vorab and Crap Sogn Gion areas. 1988/

89 prices for a combination ticket that allows unlimited skiing in both areas are as follows:

	adults	children (6-16)
for one day	SFR 41	SFR 21
for two days	SFR 75	SFR 38
for six days	SFR 198	SFR 99
for eight days	SFR 248	SFR 124
for twelve days	SFR 324	SFR 200

Note: A photo is required for lift passes of four days or more, but the photo will be taken free of charge at the lift station.

Accommodation

These are our recommended hotels. We have visited each of the hotels. The price noted is the normal high season price with half pension based on double occupancy. Expect prices to be around 20 percent less during low season.

Note: the local phone prefix is (081).

Park Hotel Waldhaus (tel. 390181; telex: 851925) The best hotel in Flims/Laax. A beautiful hotel which is almost its own small village. The buildings are interconnected by covered paths and underground walkways. You can be elegant and formal or as casual as you please in this sprawling complex in the woods above Flims. Normal daily rate: SFR 175-215.

Adula (tel. 390161; telex: 851960) In Flims, this runs a close second to the Park Hotel. In fact, many people prefer it since it is much cozier and smaller. The Barga restaurant is considered to be one of the best in the entire region. It has an indoor pool, sauna and fitness room. The hotel is associated with Best Western. Normal daily rate: SFR 130-170.

Comfort Inn-Hotel National (tel. 391224, telex 851977) In Flims, this hotel is fun. The owner is a great cook and enjoys having a weekly ski barbecue in his mountain hut. The atmosphere is laid back and the hotel is just across the street from the main lifts in Flims. The hotel is part of the Comfort Inn group. Normal daily rate: SFR 85-95.

Arvenhotel Waldeck (tel. 391228) In Flims-Waldhaus, this hotel is known for a good restaurant. Rooms have been redone in knotty pine and the ambience is casual. Normal daily rate: SFR 76-102

Hotel Meiler-Prau da Monis (tel. 390171, telex 851901) In the center of Flims and close to everything. Normal daily rate: SFR 86-110.

Hotel Crap Ner (tel. 392626, telex 851908) This means Black Rock in the local dialect. It is a sport hotel five minutes from the lift station in Flims-Dorf. Excellent menu in the Stiva Crap Ner restaurant and cozy atmosphere in the cellar Tschuetta Bar. Normal daily rate: SFR 94-122.

Happy Rancho Complex (tel. 086-30131)

This is a group of three hotels: Happy Rancho (four-star), Little Rancho and Old Rancho (both three star). The Happy Rancho consists of similar-sized apartments, studios and hotel rooms. Ski Week here (with lifts and instruction) costs SFR 950. The Old Rancho and the Little Rancho are interconnected by underground passages and therefore share swimming pool and other facilities, all of which are first class. To tell the truth I think I would rather stay in one of the smaller Ranchos, Old or Little. The normal room rates are: Happy, Old and Little Rancho—SFR 114-137. This hotel complex is associated with Best Western.

Apartments

Flims and Laax are well organized to handle tourists who want to rent apartments during the ski season. Apartments are normally rented out for a minimum stay of one week, Saturday to Saturday; during the Christmas and Easter seasons, a minimum two-week rental is often required.

The tourist office keeps track, electronically, of which apartments are available. When writing, include the number of beds required, the preferred number of rooms and your planned vacation dates. You will receive a quick response that lists a selection of apartments and prices. Select the apartment you want and return the information.

Normally, linen and kitchen utensils are provided. Other communal or private amenities, such as swimming pool, sauna, TV or room phone all add to the costs. Standard apartments rent for between SFR 15 and SFR 20 per person a night. Prices vary significantly from low to high season.

Dining

Area restaurants are reasonably priced and most feature a good selection of international and regional specialties. The best in the region is the Restarant Barga (tel. 390161) in the Hotel Adula. In fact, Gault/Millau considers it one of the best in Switzerland. The other top restaurant is the Segnes und Post (tel. 391281). For good basic value and Swiss tradition in Flims, try the Waldeck (tel. 391228); the National is noted for its fish dishes. The Cabana is run by the family Hotz which also operates the Barga. In Laax, both the Capricorno (tel. (086) 35454) and Posta Veglia (tel. (086) 34466) are highly recommended for traditional Swiss cooking.

Nightlife

The best discos in the area are the Sardona in Flims which caters to a younger crowd earlier in the evening and then attracts an older clientel with special shows which start around midnight. In Laax, the Camona offers year-round disco action which will remind you of major big city discoteque. A live band starts at about 11:30 p.m. The Casa Veglia, in Laax, has a somewhat older crowd and is appropriately more sedate. Cover charges for all discos are around SFR 10 and expect to pay about SFR 10 for a beer, and SFR 15 for a mixed drink.

Child care

There are Swiss Ski School associated kindergartens in the area. In Flims and Laax, the children's ski school and kindergarten is open from 9 a.m. until 5 p.m. and normally includes skiing lessons for children old enough to learn. Rates are SFR 16 for a half-day; SFR 30 for one full day; SFR 43 for three half-days; SFR 74 for five half-days and SFR 100 for five full days including lunch. Lunch with any program will cost an additional SFR 7 unless specifically included.

Ski nursery prices are the same and children who do not wish to learn skiing can spend the day doing handicrafts, tobogganing and playing.

The Hotel Happy Rancho has an in-house kindergarten for families staying in the Happy Rancho complex. Non-guests may leave their children on a space available basis.

Getting there

The closest airport is Zurich. From there you can take a train to Chur, where you must change for a post bus to Flims and Laax. The entire trip will take about three hours.

If driving, take the main road to Chur and continue until you see signs for Flims to the right. Driving time is about two hours. Do not make the mistake of trying to approach Laax and Flims from the west—the pass is closed during the winter.

Other activities

Consider a trip to Chur, only a half-hour drive down the mountain. The Via Mala, Switzerland's deepest gorge, is just 45 minutes from Flims and Liechtenstein can be easily reached by car in about an hour.

There are horse-drawn sleighrides for SFR 80 for one to three persons, SFR 100 for four to five; or SFR 120 for six to seven. Riding stables are open with horse rentals for SFR 50 for 50 minutes or SFR 180 for a ten-hour ticket. Call 392435 or 392593.

Ice skating is available for SFR 3.50 per day; and SFR 25 for a ticket good for ten admissions to the rink. Skates are also available for hire for SFR 5 per day.

There are covered tennis courts for SFR 30 per hour in the Park Hotel in Flims and in the Hotel Signina in Laax.

A public swimming pool is open in Laax every afternoon from 1:30 p.m. to 9 p.m. except Saturday and Sunday when it closes at 6 p.m.; it opens from 10 a.m. to noon except Monday and Sunday. Entrance is SFR 5 for adults and SFR 2.50 for children.

Tourist information

Flims

Tourist Office, CH-7018 Flims-Waldhaus, Switzerland; tel. (081) 391022; telex: 851919.

Laax

Tourist Office, CH-7031 Laax, Switzerland; tel. (086) 34343; telex: 856111

Gstaad and the White Highlands Region

Gstaad is linked with the jet-set more often than with good skiing and that's a mistake because it has outstanding slopes for beginners and intermediates. This Alpine village tucked into a scenic valley, two hours from Geneva and 90 minutes from Interlaken, is part of a thriving ski circuit called *"Das Weisse Hochland,"* the White Highland. When you buy a lift ticket in Gstaad, or at one of the ten smaller resorts in the area, you can use any of 69 lifts opening up about 150 miles of prepared trails. The other villages lay stretched along the railway line (from east to west): St. Stephan, Zweisimmen, Saanenmöser, Schönried, Gstaad, Saanen, Rougemont, Chateau d'Oex, Les Moulins—with Launen, Gsteig and Reusch accessible by bus up the valleys fanning from Gstaad.

Where to ski

The skiing in the immediate area of Gstaad is fragmented. The relatively low Eggli (1672m/5494 ft) is the largest area and interconnected with the peak of Videmanette and the towns of Saanen and Rougemont.

The Wasserngrat (1940m) and the Wisple (1950m) are the two other totally separated areas. The Wasserngrat is the most challenging of the three areas, but is limited to two lifts. However, the skiing is superb and there is hardly ever a line. If the Eggli is crowded, this area offers skiing with no waiting. Beginners and lower intermediates may be out of their league here.

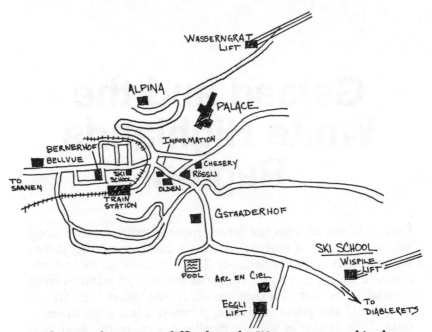

The Wisple is not as difficult as the Wasserngrat and is closer to town as well. This is a good intermediate area with limited lifts but long, enjoyable runs. Wide stretches of the slopes are left unprepared for powder hounds. It also has short lines and is within walking distance of the Eggli lifts. The Swiss Ski School is located at its base and the two drag lifts are used mainly by the ski school.

The Eggli shows two black runs—however, an intermediate skier should seldom feel anxiety here. The run through the trees from the chairlift at Eggli Stand to the ground T-bar station in neighboring Saanen has enough moguls and turns to hold your interest.

There is some genuine skiing adventure above Gstaad. The finest is La Videmanette. Ski over the Eggli and down to the Pra Cluen chairlift to reach the area above neighboring Rougemont, or drive there. From Rougemont, four-passenger gondolas ascend past rocky pinnacles to the La Videmanette summit at (2156 m/7071 ft). The run down through the rocks off the backside is strictly for experts.

On the Videmanette frontside, the first 300 meters straight over the edge (skittish types can take the traverse around the rim of the bowl) is also an eye-opener. There's a difficult mogul field to negotiate before beginning the remainder of the 3.5-mile intermediate run to Rougemont. Alternatively, ski around the corner to the top of the Pra Cluen chairlift and take the 3.5-mile *schuss* to the valley floor.

There is summer glacier skiing at Les Diablerets (3243 m/ 10,637 feet), which is reached via a three-stage cablecar from Reusch at the end of the valley.

The Hornberg section is the largest interconnected grouping of lifts in the "White Highlands." It is not directly connected with Gstaad but is easily reached by bus or train (both included with your ski pass). Take either the Horneggli lift from Schön-ried or the Saanerslochgrat gondola from Sannenmöser. Both lifts are opposite the respective railway stations, making getting lost impossible. This area, a lower intermediates' paradise, is served by 14 lifts which keep waiting time to less than five minutes.

For more challenging runs head for the St. Stephan lifts connected with Hornberg. Take the Saanerslochgrat gondola, and ski down to Chaltebrunne. Then take the chairlift up to the Gandlouenegrat which sits at the top of the St. Stephan section. The face of the mountain from Gandlouenegrat down to Chaltebrunne is one of the best slopes I've skied. There is something for everyone from expert to advanced beginner. Playing here can take up half the day. If you time it right for lunch make sure to eat at the Chemi Hütte at Lengebrand on the slopes above St. Stephan at the end of the chairlift from town.

Opposite the Hornberg section is the Rellerligrat (1934m/ 6285 ft) with what many claim is the most beautiful view of Gstaad. The slopes face the sun, meaning that they are the first to lose snow. Mornings can be icy and afternoons slushy, but skiing here on sunny days is a joy. The restaurant at the top is one of the best in the area. The runs back into the valley are long cruising trails with a long black run under the gondola for experts and advanced intermediates.

Zweisimmen offers an unfortunately isolated ski area flanked on the left by St. Stephan and on the right by the Hornberg lifts. There is no lift connection with either. The gondola from town to the Rinderberg opens up seven prepared runs served by five lifts. It is pleasant for a day's skiing. Most of the people who stay in Zweisimmen take the train to ski the Hornberg section.

Chateau d'Oex is another small area included in the regional ski pass. Here the La Braye gondola lifts skiers over a ridge behind the town to a mellow intermediate area of about a dozen runs.

The last area on the lift pass is reached from Les Moulins and is served by two long lifts. This area offers two very long beginner runs and one good intermediate trail back to the town from the top of Monts Chevreuils.

Despite the relatively low-lying intermediate slopes, Gstaad enjoys good snow most years from mid-December until mid-April.

Mountain rating.

If you are a beginner, Gstaad is an excellent destination. There are plenty of gentle inclines to practice snowplows and stem christies. The finest beginner run is the 1253-meter-long Skilift Schopfen slope from the gondola station on the Eggli.

Intermediate skiers will be overjoyed at the variety. Just when you think you've mastered everything, you can cut through the woods or go over the edge of a mogul field you've been by-passing and suddenly realise you haven't learned quite everything.

The expert can enjoy Gstaad if more emphasis is placed on technique than thrills. Plus, there are many opportunities to break through trees and ski through powder.

Ski school

Gstaad, with more than 100 ski teachers, has an outstanding reputation for English-speaking ski instructors and for private lessons. It is open from 8:30 am to noon and from 2:30 pm to 6 pm.

Indiviudal lesson rates: one hour (1-4 persons)—SFR 40; half day—SFR 100; all day—SFR 190.

Group lesson rates: half-day—SFR 21; full-day—SFR 36; six consecutive days—SFR 137; six non-consecutive days—SFR 163.

Many ski classes meet directly on the Eggli slope or at the entrance to the Eggli gondola station. Call 41865 for information and bookings. Lessons are available for cross-country.

In Chateau d'Oex the ski school (029-46848) offers half-day group lessons from only SFR 15 per day; SFR 40 for three days; SFR 72 for six days. Private lessons are only about 10% less expensive than in Gstaad.

Lift tickets

These tickets are good for the entire "White Highlands" area covering 69 lifts and 250 kilometers of runs. They are good on the railroad, on buses and for entrance to the covered pool in Gstaad.

for a half day (from 1:30 p.m.)	SFR 25
for one day	SFR 35
for two days	SFR 68
for three days	SFR 99
for six days	SFR 180
for seven days	SFR 203
for 13 days	SFR 299

Children from ages six through 16 get approximately a 40 percent discount if accompanied by an adult paying the full price.

A Chateau d'Oex limited area lift ticket for Chateau d'Oex/Mt. Chevreuils can be purchased for approximately 33% less than the "White Highlands" pass.

Accommodation

These hotels offer a special one week ski program which includes seven nights half pension and six days' lift passes plus entrance to the indoor swimming pool and use of the public transport. Add another SFR 48 for six days ski lessons. These weeks are available during from January 8 to February 5, and from March 5 to April 9. The package for cross country skiers without ski pass but with six days instruction is the price indicated, reduced by SFR 70. The final price is for the normal high-season (February) per person with half pension based on double occupancy.

Gstaad Palace (tel. 83131; telex; 922222) SFR 1790—The best in town. A chance to rub shoulders with the best of the movie, fashion and jet-set world if you can afford the entrance. Normal daily rate: SFR 285-400.

Grand Hotel Alpina (tel. 45725; telex: 922270) SFR 1050—Second best in luxury with excellent food, but no pool. Up the hill from town next to the Palace. Normal daily rate: SFR 140-190.

Hotel Bellevue (tel. 83171) SFR 980—Part of Best Western. One of the best hotels in town just below the luxury level. Normal daily rate: SFR 135-175.

Bernerhof (tel. 83366; telex: 922262) SFR 980—Centrally located, with swimming pool. Noted for spacious rooms, good service, with excellent kindergarten and many consider the hotel one of the best in town. Normal daily rate: SFR 129-141.

Hotel Arc-en-Ciel (tel. 83191; telex: 922286) SFR 980—Best location for skiing the Eggli. Opposite the gondola station and near a ski rental shop. Quiet, with a good restaurant. Normal daily rate: SFR 110-165.

Hotel Gstaaderhof (tel. 83344; telex: 922242) SFR 980—Good location relatively near lifts, station and downtown. Normal daily rate: SFR 95-120.

Hotel Alphorn (tel. 44545) SFR 980—Good location for skiers; near the lift for the Wispile. Across the highway from the Eggli gondola. Normal daily rate: SFR 95-120.

Posthotel Rössli (tel. 43412; telex: 922299) SFR 875. This is one of the hotel prizes in Gstaad, but is small and booked very early. The restaurant is one of the best in town. Normal daily rate: SFR 90-130.

Sporthotel Victoria (tel. 41431; telex: 922221) SFR 875—Excellent food; has two restaurants and a pizzeria. The most reasonable hotel in town. Normal daily rate: SFR 90-100.

Saanen

Hotel Steigenberger, in Gstaad-Saanen, (tel. 83388; telex; 922252) This is, after the Palace, the most luxurious accommodation in the Gstaad/Saanen area. It has everything—pool, sauna, good disco, and two restaurants. Normal daily rate: SFR 195-270.

Hotel Residence Cabana, in Gstaad-Saanen, (tel. 44855; telex: 922255) A Best Western Hotel. SFR 735—includes seven days half board, six days ski pass, six days ski school, free entrance to fitness center. Normal daily rate: SFR 143-180.

Landhaus (tel. 44858) A good middle-priced hotel in the center of town. Normal daily rate: SFR 70-80.

Krone, (tel. 41449) A low-priced bed and breakfast alternative in Saanen. Normal daily rate: SFR 50.

Saanenmöser

Hotel Hornberg (tel. 44440) SFR 830—includes ski school. Everything a good ski hotel should be: Near the lifts, with pool and sauna and an owner who helps his clients. Normal daily rate: SFR 85-150.

Schönried

Hotel Alpenrose (tel. 41238) SFR 800—includes ski school. You don't stay here for the luxurious rooms—this small hotel's only a three-star with 12 beds—you come for the great food, believed by many to be the best in the area. Normal daily rate: SFR 130-145.

Hotel Bahnhof (tel. 44242) SFR 700—includes ski school. This is the lowest priced major hotel in town. Nice rooms and close to the railway station. Normal daily rate: SFR 65-85.

Chateau d'Oex

This town down the tracks toward Montreux from Gstaad, is significantly less expensive than the Saanenmöser-Gstaad-Saanen area. The town is in the French part of Switzerland. It is not as charming nor as "alpine" as Gstaad. But, for overall savings of about 25% this might be the place to stay if you don't mind the half-hour train ride to the major slopes above Gstaad and Schönried.

These hotels have been doing good English-language business. The January week-long package is indicated first and includes half-board, lift tickets for all area lifts, train and bus transportation and entrance into Gstaad's indoor pool. The last price is the normal high season, half-board based on double occupancy.

Hotel Beau-Sejour (tel. 029-47423) SFR 552 This hotel is very convenient, across from the railway station and the cable car to the Chateau d'Oex area. Normal daily rate: SFR 72-93.

Hotel Ours (tel. 029-46337) SFR 552 Located in the center of town about three minutes from the lift and railway station. Normal daily rate: SFR 72-93.

Hotel Roc et Neige (tel. 029-45525; telex: 940097) SFR 472 This brand-new, sparsely furnished giant hotel does brisk group business and is located just downhill from the main town. It is a short five minute uphill walk to the lift and the train station. The restaurant is self-service which keeps prices down. Normal daily rate: SFR 47-57.

Dining

Even with Gstaad's jet-set reputation the best restaurants are just outside town. Naturally, the Palace has several world-class restaurants but then again most of us are not up to Palace prices. The "Cave" in the Olden Hotel in the center of town provides excellent dining by anyone's standards. Expect to be paying top price and you'll never know with whom you can expect to rub shoulders. Still in town, and considerably more reasonable, is the "Rossli" across the main street from the Olden—this is typical Swiss cooking at its best. Behind the Rossli try the "Chesery" which is good but not as exceptional as the Rossli. The "Arc-en-Ciel" opposite the Eggli gondola station has no atmosphere but serves excellent Italian food at low prices.

Out-of-Gstaad Places Schönried has the Alpenrose (tel. 41238) with a Relais et Chateau gourmet restaurant. This small nouvelle cuisine restaurant is one of the tops in Switzerland. An exceptional traditional Swiss restaurant is the "Bären" (tel. 51033) in the town of Gsteig on the road from Gstaad to Les Diablerets. Down the road from Gsteig try the "Rossli" in Feutersoey (tel. 51012 and 51180). Tucked into another valley in the tiny town of Lauenen enjoy a meal at the "Wildhorn" (tel. 53012). Finally, don't miss the 17th-century Restaurant Chlösterli (tel. 51045) just outside town on the road to Les Diablerets.

On the slopes

The best mountain restaurants above Gstaad are at the Eggli and Kalberhöni. Above Schönried try the Hornberg restaurants—one is slightly more upscale, the other has wonderful Rösti and plenty of pasta . . . both have great terraces to enjoy the sun. The Rellerli Mountain Restaurant on the opposite side of the valley from Hornberg enjoys a storybook view of Gstaad. The other mountain eatery worth heading for is the Chemi Hütte at Lengebrand above St. Stephan.

Apartments

Vacation apartment rentals are available in Gstaad and Saanen. Information on rentals is provided by the tourist offices. In middle season an apartment with one bedroom, living room and furnished kitchen costs approximately SFR 500-700 a week. Ample room for four people is typical.

Saanen and the other surrounding towns have apartments for about SFR 100 less.

Nightlife

The place for après ski just off the slopes is the Olden Bar. It's normally packed. Otherwise, even on Friday night, this town snoozes until midnight. The Chesery Bar and the Stockli Bar in the Bernerhof were recommended as the best places to have a beer or drink, but both are very quiet. The Taburi in Hotel Victoria offers a live Swiss folk group, but the crowd when we visited was deadly. If you come with your own group, though, you're sure to have fun.

The well-heeled enjoy an après-ski drink the Palace Hotel lounge above the city. Take along some money if you want to join them. For starters, the Palace disco cover is SFR 30.

After dark there's a lively crowd and live music at the Chlös-terli disco outside town. Also try the "Greengo" at the Palace Hotel and the Steigenberger Hotel disco in Saanen for dancing.

Child care

The ski school (tel. 41865) has all-day kindergarten. The cost for one day is SFR 20; for six consecutive days, SFR 90.

Hotel Gstaaderhof (tel. 83344 or 41055) has a child care center for children from two to six years of age. It is open from 9:30 a.m. to 5 p.m. Expect to pay SFR 5.50 per hour or SFR 30 plus meal-costs per day. Mornings from 9:30 to noon cost SFR 13, and afternoons from noon to 5 pm are SFR 17. Weekly rate for six days is SFR 150.

In Chateau d'Oex contact Mme. Blati at Les Clematites (tel. 029-473551). She takes children from two months old. The ski school also has children's lessons (tel. 029-46848).

Getting there

The most popular international airport is Geneva. From there, it is about two hours by train to Gstaad. Rental cars are avail-able in Geneva.

Other activities

Gstaad has an excellent covered swimming pool.

Gstaad is in a good location for train or auto excursions to Montreux, Geneva, Lausanne, Interlaken and Bern, all within approximately two hours by train.

A local air service provides sightseeing flights in the area (tel. 44025).

Ballooning over the Alps provides a once-in-a-lifetime thrill. Balloon rides can be arranged through Hans Büker, tel. 43250 or through the reception of the Palace Hotel or the Steigen-berger Hotel in Saanen. The average price is between SFR 350-400 per person for about two hours. This is based on SFR 1,400 per total trip with a minimum of four persons.

Ice skating and curling, with instruction for both, are avail-able (tel. 44368).

Tourist information

Information on the White Highland region is available through the tourist office in the center of Gstaad. Write CH-3780 Gstaad, Switzerland; tel. (030) 41055; telex: 922211.

Information on other towns in the area may also be obtained from the tourist office in Saanen, CH-3792 Saanen; tel. (030) 42597.

Tourist Office Chateau d'Oex: tel. (029) 47788; telex: 940022.

Jungfrau Region–
Grindelwald, Wengen, Lauterbrunnen, Mürren

The Jungfrau region is near Interlaken and at the end of the Alpine rainbow for intermediate skiers. A network of 185 miles of trails is spread over a vast expanse of slopes, all set in two majestic valleys about an hour's drive from Bern, the Swiss capital.

The backdrop created by the Jungfrau, Mönch and Eiger mountains is one you'll see on travel posters the world over.

The Jungfrau region has three major ski areas accessible from its twin-valley towns. The best-known resort is Grindelwald, a picture-postcard settlement nestled at the foot of nearly 10,000-ft. peaks about 30 minutes by train or car from Interlaken. There is skiing at Grindelwald First, reached by chairlift (to your left as you enter town), and on the slopes beneath Kleine Scheidegg (on your right), reached by cog train or gondola.

The second area is just beneath the Eiger. Here Wengen and Kleine Scheidegg offer car-free villages on the mountain and Lauterbrunnen is in the valley on the opposite side of the Lauberhorn. It is also a second starting point for the cog train up the mountain. The auto-free resort, Wengen, is halfway up the mountain along the train route overlooking the Lauterbach valley. Up on the ridge plateau is Kleine Scheidegg at the base of the Eiger, a settlement with railway station and hotels.

The third ski area, Mürren/Schilthorn, is across the Lauterbach Valley and is also reached by cog train or cable car.

Where to ski

Mürren—For ski challenges in this region, savvy downhillers head for the Schilthorn. Take the cog train from Lauterbrunnen to Mürren and then go by cable car the rest of the way; or take a direct cable car from Stechelberg, outside Lauterbrunnen.

There is less good skiing but more challenges on the Schilthorn than at any of the other locations. Overall, there are eighteen slopes with about thirty miles of runs. The eye-opener is the black run from the 2971-meter (9744-foot) Schilthorn. Start by quaffing an extra-strong cup of *espresso* in the Piz Gloria revolving restaurant atop the Schilthorn, then tackle the famed "Inferno," also called the "007 Run" in honor of the stunning ski scenes from the Bond movie. The lower section, called the "Kanonenrohr," or cannon barrel, sends you hurtling down a narrow, steep, rutted and often icy chute.

If you visit in late January, watch at least a part of the "Inferno-Renne," the traditional (since 1928) Schilthorn race that pits nearly 1500 (as many as 4000 apply) would-be champion skiers against the clock and the 12-kilometer course. It takes a world-class skier almost 15 minutes to come down.

Adventurous skiers also tackle the black runs from the 2145-meter (7035-foot) Schiltgrat. Connecting lifts take you to the Winteregg and Almendhübel, the mountain's other two ski areas, where intermediate skiing—with an occasional black run—is the rule.

Grindelwald First—The 2928-meter (9609-foot) Schwarzhorn on your left as you enter town is the backdrop for the Grindelwald First slopes. Intermediates, this is your territory with a few challenges and lots of cruising. The upper runs descend over an open, treeless slope from the Oberjoch T-bar at 2468 meters (8095 feet). The Schilt T-bar, in the shadow of the Schwarzhorn at 2250 meters (7381 feet), offers more of the same. Trails continue all the way into town.

The First is a place to work out those kinks before moving on to tackle the runs over on the Kleine Scheidegg side of the valley.

Grindelwald/Kleine Scheidegg/Wengen The cog train, which takes about a half hour to reach Kleine Scheidegg. Across the

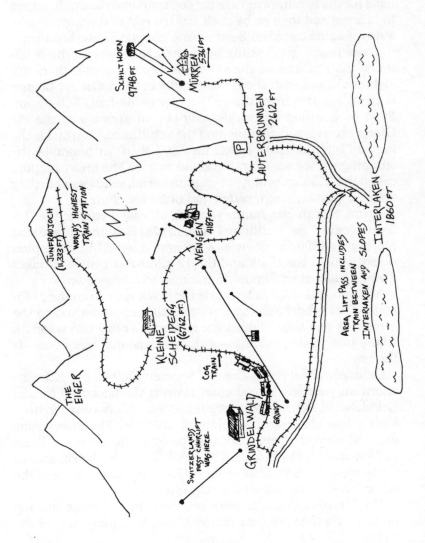

SCHILTHORN 9748 FT.

MÜRREN 5361 FT.

LAUTERBRUNNEN 2612 FT.

JUNGFRAUJOCH (11,333 FT)

WORLD'S HIGHEST TRAIN STATION

WENGEN 4187 FT.

THE EIGER

KLEINE SCHEIDEGG (6762 FT.)

COG TRAIN

GRUND

GRINDELWALD

SWITZERLAND'S FAST CHAIRLIFT WAS HERE

INTERLAKEN 1860 FT.

AREA LIFT PASS INCLUDES TRAIN BETWEEN INTERLAKEN AND SLOPES

parking lot from the Grindelwald Grund station is the Männlichenbahn, a gondola lift. In 25 minutes the gondola deposits you near the summit of the Männlichen at 2235 meters (7333 feet). Before you is a marvelous 15-minute run to Grindelwald or a series of trails and interconnecting lifts that take you around to Kleine Scheidegg. The Männlichen T-bar run to the left of the top gondola station takes you down a challenging mogul field. And the wide runs off the Gummi chairlift between Männlichen and Kleine Scheidegg are challenging for most intermediates.

The finest intermediate run is reached by the Lauberhorn lift from the Kleine Scheidegg train station stop in the Eiger's shadow. The cog train continues through the Eiger north face to the highest slopes of the Jungfrau (a supplementary ticket is necessary for the final section).

Ski both outstanding runs from the 2472-meter Lauberhorn above Kleine Scheidegg. One leads to Wengen along parts of the famed World-Cup Lauberhorn run. It's a delightful ski experience with a seemingly endless variety of dips, turns, mogul fields and occasional ice patches, perfect territory for the advanced intermediate. Try the run from the Lauberhorn to the Wixi chairlift, picking your way through the mogul fields. When the snow is good, this run is exceptional.

The run down the opposite face of the Lauberhorn brings you down into Grindelwald passing Arvengarten before a network of intermediate trails which offer a touch of adventure—there is always an easier way around the tough places for the less advanced. This 30-minute run to the car park of the Männlichen gondola or to the cogwheel train station, may be the highlight of your stay in the Jungfrau region, unless you're counting the chills of Mürren's "007 Run" as a fun experience.

For variety, take the cog train to the Eiger glacier stop and ski from near the glacier's base at 2320 meters (7621 feet) all the way down into Grindelwald.

Mountain rating

Mürren—Don't plan to ski the Mürren area extensively if you're a beginner. There are some intermediate slopes that the beginner may be able to handle after a few days, but just barely.

Grindelwald—First should present no difficulties for the lower intermediate. Beginners use the short Bodmi lifts above town with ease while everyone from advanced beginner and above goes right to the top.

Kleine Scheidegg/Wengen—The Männlichen side offers no surprises and intermediates will handle everything but the toughest mogul fields with ease. Working one's way around the mountain toward Kleine Scheidegg from the Männlichen requires more skills but can be handled by most intermediates. The Wengen side with the Lauberhorn run is perhaps the most challenging. But Wengen, with its position on the slopes and good nursery slopes, may also be the best spot other than Grindelwald First for beginners.

Experts will find challenging runs in all three areas.

From May until September a 300-meter (984-foot) lift operates on a slope of the Jungfrau above Kleine Scheidegg. Expect "more sunshine than real skiing on this run."

Ski school

More than 70 ski instructors are assigned daily to individuals and groups seeking lessons on the Wengen and Grindelwald slopes.

The Mürren ski school has 25 instructors giving group and private lessons.

Prices are uniform in all three ski areas, with Mürren having the highest rates by a few francs a week. These prices are for the Wengen Ski School.

Individual lessons
half-day (2.5 hrs)   SFR 95
all day   SFR 190

Group lessons normally two hours of instruction each day.
for one day   SFR 17
for a full-day   SFR 34
for six full-days   SFR 140
for 12 half-days   SFR 156

Cross-country instruction is available. The best circuit is the seven-mile loop around the outskirts of Lauterbrunnen. Wengen does not have a cross-country run and Mürren has a simple half-mile circuit.

Check with the ski school for information on Alpine ski touring and powder skiing:

Grindelwald ski school, tel. 036-53202;
Wengen ski school, tel. 026-552022;
Mürren ski school, tel. 036-551247

Lift tickets

A special Jungfrau region ticket for a minimum of three days includes Mürren, Kleine Scheidegg and Grindelwald First. Individual tickets good only for one of the areas are also available.

Jungfrau region

for three days	SFR 114
for six days	SFR 198
for seven days	SFR 202

Grindelwald First

for one day	SFR 36
for three days	SFR 82
for six days	SFR 136
for seven days	SFR 142

Kleine Scheidegg/Männlichen

for one day	SFR 38
for three days	SFR 98
for six days	SFR 168
for seven days	SFR 172

Mürren

for one day	SFR 36
for three days	SFR 86
for six days	SFR 148
for seven days	SFR 152

Accommodation

These hotels and pensions are recommended for accommodation. Prices, unless otherwise noted, are for seven days at half pension (breakfast and one meal, normally dinner) during January.

Grindelwald

Hotel Spinne, (tel. 532341; telex: 923297) Best Western Hotel. SFR 860—Includes seven days half pension, six-day ski pass, and entrance to the sport center and swimming pool. Ski School is an additional SFR 135.

Derby Bahnhof Hotel (tel. 545461; telex: 923277) SFR 741— Excellent location adjacent to the Jungfrau cog railway station. Daily rooms cost SFR 60.

Scheidegg Hotels (tel. 551212; telex: 923235) No Ski Week— the finest lodging in the area for the skier; overlooks Kleine Scheidegg station in the shadow of the Eiger. 30 minutes by train into the mountains from Grindelwald. Reserve well ahead.

Sport-Hotel Jungfrau (tel. 531341; telex: 923297) SFR 629.

Wengen

Hotel am Waldrand (tel. 552855; telex: 32340) SFR 700— Popular with ski racers, particularly during Lauberhorn race week.

Hotel Eiger (tel. 551131; telex: 923296) A Best Western Hotel. SFR 655—Includes seven days half board, seven-day ski pass, six days of ski school.

Alpenrose (tel. 553216; telex: 923293) SFR 630—A lift is directly outside this hotel. Noted for its quiet setting and traditional meals.

Mürren

Hotel Alpina (tel. 551361) SFR 717—Good hotel with reductions offered for families. Excellent view of the valley and a quiet setting.

Hotel Alpenblick (tel. 551327) SFR 617—Small hotel two minutes from the cog-train station.

Jungfrau (tel. 552824) SFR 733—Excellent location near both the slopes and the sports center and indoor pool.

Lauterbrunnen

Hotel Silberhorn (tel. 551471) SFR 587 (includes ski pass and ski school)—Ten minutes' walk from the cog trains to Kleine Scheidegg and Mürren.

Hotel Staubbach (tel. 551381; telex: 923255) SFR 677 (includes ski pass and ski school)—Comfortable; eight minutes' walk from the cog-train station.

Hotel Alpenrose SFR 450—In Wilderswil at entrance to Lauterbach valley, 15 minutes by car from Lauterbrunnen. Family-run hotel three minutes from ski train to Lauterbrunnen or Grindelwald and two miles from Interlaken.

Ask your travel agent to check the Switzerland all-in package plan for the Jungfrau area. The Wengen all-in plan, for example, includes seven nights half pension, plus a week's ticket for the Kleine Scheidegg-Männlichen runs (Mürren not included) beginning as low as SFR 400. However, most visitors choose all-in packages ranging between SFR 500 and SFR 700.

Staying in Interlaken

Interlaken has begun to emerge as a hotel center for skiers planning to ski the Jungfrau area. It is only a 30 minute bus ride from the lower lift stations and as a relatively large city it has nightlife and good dining. The reasons for staying in Interlaken fall into two categories. First reason—Interlaken hotels and ski packages are much less expensive than those to Wengen, Mürren and Grindelwald. Second reason—if you are traveling with a non-skier, Interlaken has more to offer than the liveliest Jungfrau resort, Grindelwald, and it is in a perfect position for day trips to many Swiss cities such as Bern, Lucerne, Zurich and even Zermatt. If one of these two reasons don't suit you then head into the mountains.

Dining

Hotel restaurants offer typical dishes with emphasis on meat, potatoes and cheese specialties. In Grindelwald you can choose from more than 30 restaurants.

For a special (and expensive meal), try the dining room in

the Grand Hotel Regina (tel. 545455). The restaurant at the Hotel Spinne has good Swiss and international specialties, complemented by a full wine celler.

Near the slopes in Wengen we like the restaurant in the Hotel Victoria-Lauberhorn (tel. 565151).

In Mürren, enjoy at least one midday meal inside the Piz Gloria, a revolving restaurant (tel. 552141) on the Schilthorn.

Apartments

There are many apartments, chalets and chalet apartments for rent in the Jungfrau region. The local tourist office has price and location info and will assist in a booking.

A typical rental apartment in Grindelwald with one-bedroom, living room (with sleeping space for two more people), kitchen and all utensils, costs about SFR 825 a week during high season; SFR 550 in midseason. Expect to spend another SFR 50 for electricity, cleaning service and linen fees.

Nightlife

Take a walk along Grindelwald's main street and choose the atmosphere you want to enjoy, from quiet pubs to raucous discos. The disco in the celler of the Hotel Spinne is probably the hottest spot for nightlife and dancing, but very crowded. Another lively meeting place is often Le Farme club in the Hotel Regina.

In Wengen, check out the Eiger Hotel's Eiger Bar. Nightlife is more limited here since after dark only the group staying on the mountain will usually be around, although trains run until late evening.

At Lauterbrunnen, the Tiffany Disco in the scenic Hotel Silberhorn is lively, while on the mountain, in Mürren, the Inferno bar-disco in the Palace Sporthotel is a good choice. If you want to meet new people each night, choose Grindelwald. Wengen and particularly Mürren tend to cater to sedate habitués.

Child care

Grindelwald and Wengen offer ski kindergarten for children from ages three to seven. The school begins at 9:30 a.m. and lasts until 4:30 p.m. Hourly rates are SFR 3. The cost for one day is SFR 22. The price for lunch is SFR 10.

Wengen with its no-traffic situation is one of the premier resorts for families with children. It also has good nursery slopes and plenty of easy tracks back to the town from all over the mountain.

Other activities

Interlaken is an international tourist center and starting point for excursions in the Bernese Oberland, one of Switzerland's most beautiful regions.

The smart shops in Bern and the rustic center of the old capital city merit a side trip.

Scenic Lucerne, at the foot of Mount Pilatus, is a little over an hour's train ride through the Alps.

The Jungfraubahn cog railway, which takes skiers up the mountain, is also a delightful outing for the non-skier. The train goes up through the Eiger's north face to the Jungfrau slopes. The stop inside the north face gives passengers a chance to look through protective glass windows at the treacherous mountain face. Special reductions are offered for non-skiers who use the train.

Grindelwald offers the widest range of non-skiing sports activities, including horseback riding, ice skating, curling, hang-gliding and hiking.

One of the most exciting excursions is a sightseeing tour of the area via plane or helicopter from the Männlichen summit. For more information, check at the Grindelwald tourist office.

Getting there

The most frequently used international airports are Geneva and Zurich. Rail connections are excellent to Interlaken and then on to Grindelwald, Lauterbrunnen, Wengen or Mürren.

Tourist information

Interlaken Tourist Office, 3800 Interlaken, Switzerland; tel. (036) 222121; telex: 923111.

Verkehrsbüro Wengen, CH-3823 Wengen, Switzerland; tel. (036) 551414; telex: 923271.

Verkehrsbüro Grindelwald, CH-3818, Switzerland; tel. (036) 531212; telex: 923217.

Verkehrsbüro Mürren, CH-3825 Mürren, Switzerland; tel. (036) 551616; telex: 923212.

Klosters

The English royal family, most notably Prince Charles, has chosen Klosters as its winter ski center for several years. they come for the excellent skiing and also for Klosters' relaxed, elegant atmosphere. those are the same reasons you will probably choose the resort. the houses surrounding the town proper are a bit more elaborate than most other places you'll visit, giving an immediate tip-off that Klosters is a cut above. the small central town area is quaint but packed with specialty stores.

Think of Klosters as Davos' little sister resort. Smaller, quainter and not as modern (it could be called a small, chic resort that has been kept a secret), Klosters is little more than a suburb of Davos. Both resorts share the Manhattan-sized, wide-open snowfields of the Parsenn, but Klosters has more challenging runs into town than Davos. Klosters also has its own ski runs and lift system in the Madrisa area, which is on the opposite side of the valley from the Parsenn. The entire Klosters/Davos ski area offers 200 miles (320 kilometers) of ski runs served by more than 50 lifts.

Where to ski

From the 1200-meter-high village the lift system takes you to 2844 meters on the Parsenn side at the Weissfluhgipfel, and up to about 2400 meters on the upper lift of the Madrisa area.

The Parsenn is the best-known area and is reached by the Gotschna cable car, which leaves every 15 to 20 minutes during the ski season. The cable car lets you off at the Gotschnagrat, where skiers can either traverse over to the Parsenn or ski beneath the cable car to a T-bar and chairlift. The Parsenn peaks at the Weissfluhgipfel (2844 meters) where it drops with two expert runs. Here it is wide open, offering both intermediate and beginning skiers a paradise for cruising. The Parsenn has 40 seemingly endless runs, including what was once Europe's longest—from Wcissfluhjoch to Kublis. If you like carefree cruising, you will love skiing the Parsenn above Klosters and Davos.

The Madrisa area is much smaller: approximately 30 miles (50 kilometers) of runs served by six ski lifts. The area is reached by cable car from Klosters-Dorf, which is a hike from the center of town. The area's runs are mostly of the intermediate and beginner level. When there is sun the Madrisa slopes are bathed with warming rays the entire day, something to remember when it's quite cold, but sunny. The longest and most scenic Madrisa run is from St. Jaggem at (2542 m/8340 ft) down to the Schlappin overlook and down to the Madrisa cable car.

For the jaded, Madrisa is a springboard for an exciting ski mountaineering trek to Austria, which combines both skiing and climbing. The Swiss Ski School can line you up with a guide for this adventure if the snow quality is good.

Mountain rating

Klosters earns an A-plus from beginning and intermediate skiers. The Parsenn is perhaps the ideal terrain for learning to ski and perfecting technique.

Experts may find the Parsenn terrain somewhat boring and should ask instructors where the most challenging skiing can be found. The best expert runs on the Parsenn are from the top of the Weissfluhgipfel. Otherwise, stick to the trails that drop into town alongside the Parsennbahn, or take the Drostobel-to-Klosters run, which is narrow and sometimes steep. The Wang trail, which runs directly under the Gotschna cable car, is one of the toughest expert runs in Europe. Unfortunately, it seems it is closed more than it is open. If the trail is open and there is no avalanche danger, you're in for an experience. On a day after a good, fresh snowfall it pays to hire an instructor for the morning to find those special spots for some thrills in the powder.

The Madrisa area is strictly for intermediates, beginners and sunworshipers.

Ski school

The Klosters ski school is divided into six levels and in addition offers special children's courses and cross-country instruction. Depending the skiers' level, classes are held either on the Madrisa or on the Gotschna side of the valley. Check with the ski school (tel. 083-41380) in order to arrive at the proper area for your level.

Individual lessons (one to four people)

one day (4½ hrs)	SFR 180
half day (2¼ hrs)	SFR 105
one hour	SFR 40

For each additional person there is a fee of SFR 10.

Group lessons

half day	SFR 22
three half days	SFR 54
six half days	SFR 90
six full days	SFR 138

Lift tickets

The most convenient lift pass to purchase is the Kloster/Davos all-inclusive pass. This pass includes the Madrisa side of the valley, plus use of the train that runs between Davos and Klosters and as far down the valley as Kublis. The tickets are only available for periods of three days or more.

three days	SFR 120
six days	SFR 200
seven days	SFR 224
14 days	SFR 360

There are discounts of about 20 percent for children and for lift passes purchased for the pre-season—before December 22, 1988.

Daily lift passes for the Gotschna are SFR 38; for the Parsenn, SFR 38; and for the Madrisa, SFR 32.

Accommodation

The best time to ski Klosters is during one of its special organized "ski weeks." These take place during the low seasons.

Quality Royale-Aaba Health Hotel (tel. 48111; telex: 74801) is a five-star hotel and is considered by many to be the best in town. A double room with half-pension is SFR 240-460 during low season and SFR 440-560 during high season. This is part of the Quality Royale group.

For my money the Hotel Alpina (tel. 44121; telex: 74547), a Best Western Hotel, is the finest place to stay in Klosters. It has a great location, classy indoor pool, the people are nice and it is easy to make reservations. Double room costs with half pension are SFR 250-330 low season and SFR 360-400 during high season.

Perhaps the most traditional hotel is the Chesa Grischuna (tel. 42222; telex: 74248). It is a Romantic Hotel, but though it has ambiance and is cozy, the rooms are small and there is no pool. Expect to pay SFR 310-360 during low season and during high season for a double with half-board.

Also available at the upper end of the scale is the Hotel Pardenn, (tel. 083-41141; telex: 853364). A five-minute hike from the ski shuttlebus and 10 minutes from the center of town, but with plenty of 5-star comfort including pool, sauna, and fitness room. Rates: Low season—SFR 280-360; high season —SFR 320-420.

The less expensive hotels are located in Klosters-Dorf which is near the lifts for the Madrisa area but a long hike from the Parsenn lifts.

Apartments

Klosters has plenty of apartments for rent. In fact, apartments outnumber hotels by more than three to one. The apartments are normally rented out for a minimum of one week, Saturday to Saturday; during the Christmas and Easter seasons a two-week minimum rental is required.

The tourist office keeps track of available apartments. If you write and supply all the information, including the number of beds required, the preferred number of rooms and the period for which you are planning your vacation, you'll get an immediate response with a choice of apartments and prices. Select the apartment you want and return the information.

Normally, linen and kitchen utensils are provided, while extras, such as swimming pool, sauna, TV or room phone all add to the cost. Standard units rent for between $16 and $28 per person a night. Prices vary significantly from low to high season.

When making reservations, make sure that your apartment is in Klosters or Klosters-Platz, *not* Klosters-Dorf. They are a good distance apart. Not only is Klosters-Dorf dead, it also requires a good hike to reach the Gotschna cable car, which serves the major skiing areas.

Dining

For restaurants featuring good local specialties, try "Hotel Alpina," "Hotel Rufinis" and "Restaurant Steinbock." Other restaurants recommended by Klosters natives are "Alte Post Aeuja" (for lamb specialites), "Casanna," "Madrisa" and "Porta." For pizza and a great lunch buffet head to the cellar Pizza in the Vereina Hotel. We recommend the Chicago-style thick crust deluxe. It's a meal in itself.

Nightlife

Klosters' nightlife centers around its major hotels. For discos, there are "Funny Place" and "Casa Antica." The Funny Place is a great place to meet people, but it charges a hefty SFR 10 cover charge, has overpriced drinks, even by Swiss standards, and the staff is not particularly pleasant, even with a guide from the tourist office there.

The bar in the Pardenn for a late evening visit is intimate and relaxing, but a bit stuffy. Save it for impressing a stuffy friend. Better still is the bar of the Chesa Grischuna where there is quiet piano entertainment.

Child care

A kindergarten associated with the ski school operates inside the Hotel Vereina from 9:15 a.m. until 4:30 p.m. Call 41380 for further information.

Getting there

The closest airport is Zurich. Klosters is two-and-a-half-hours by train ride and you must change in Landquart.

If you decide to rent a car, follow the signs towards Chur until you get to the Landquart/Davos exit. The drive from Landquart to Klosters is through the narrow valley and passes through Kublis before arriving at Klosters-Dorf and then Klosters. The total distance from Zurich to Klosters is about 140 kilometers, just under 90 miles.

Other activities

Klosters is rather quiet. Visitors who are looking for other activities should take the train to Davos, which is only fifteen minutes away. Davos has a public heated outdoor swimming pool and an open-air skating rink. In addition, there are seven covered hotel pools in town and two heated outdoor pools; you will have to check with the hotel to get the rates for using their facilities. The hotels also have several squash and tennis courts, as well as saunas and solariums. Again, check with the concierge for the charges.

If you want to leave town, both Zurich and Lucerne are only about a two-hour drive away. Or drive to Landquart, then south towards the St. Bernard Pass, where you can drive through the Via Mala, Switzerland's deepest gorge, and see the recently restored castle of Hohen Rathien in Thusis. If the pass from Tiefencastle to Davos is open and you have chains, the drive that makes a loop around the mountains is beautiful.

Tourist information

Tourist Office, CH-7250 Klosters; tel. (083) 41877; telex: 74372. Normal hours are Monday through Saturday, from 9 a.m. until noon and from 2 until 6 p.m. (until 5 p.m. on Saturday).

Portes du Soleil
Champéry
Les Crosets
Champoussin

The Portes du Soleil ski area nestled just south of Lake Geneva and straddling Switzerland and France claims to be Europe's biggest ski area. Though the Trois Vallées region makes a similar claim the skiing in Portes du Soleil is seemingly endless. Where a skier in the Trois Vallées may be able to easily transfer from valley to valley, transfers in the Portes du Soleil area take time and effort. Where the lift system in the Trois Vallées forms a tight web linking miles of prepared slopes, the lifts through the Portes du Soleil are more of a gossamer strand linking far-flung pistes. I remember, after a long morning of continuous skiing from Champéry in Switzerland to Chatel in France, having my guide point out a peak which seemed somewhere on the other side of Mont Blanc. When he announced to me that was where we started, I was incredulous and forgot any notions about a relaxed afternoon cruising home.

The Portes du Soleil area is made up of more than a dozen different resorts. Four to six lie on the Swiss side of the border and the remaining eight or ten, depending on how one counts resorts, are in France. The key resorts are Champéry in Switzerland and Avoriaz in France. Les Crosets and Champoussin tucked high on the mountain between Champéry and Avoriaz also offer an excellent central location for exploring the Portes du Soleil.

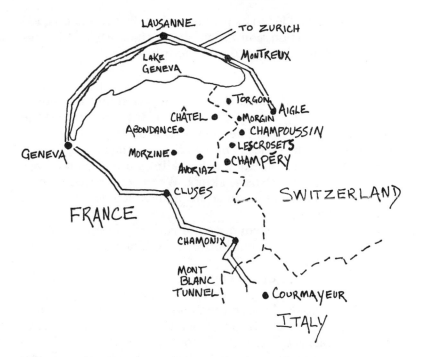

Champéry is a mountain town which has not realized it is an international ski resort. The old chalets look lived-in, the odor of cow manure wafts across the main street, a plucky kid goat prances in the back of a station wagon, the discos look like a throwback to the 50's and no tour buses are packing the center of town. Unfortunately, Champéry will probably be nudged into the mainstream of tourism in the next five years, but until then it is an unpretentious change of pace.

Les Crosets set in the midst of the ski area is a cluster of apartments which provide easy access to the slopes and little else. But, this enclave is also earmarked for growth. With plans for underground garages, new apartments and new lifts, it is the major topic of discussion among the local families which own the land and are planning the developments.

Champoussin has already started in the direction of a purpose-built resort but stopped recently due to a shortfall of capital. Champoussin, unlike Les Crosets, was developed by outsiders which added to its problems, but the town has a good ski-in/ski-out location, controlled alpine chalet-style buildings with restaurants, discos and an indoor pool.

Where to ski

This is a real skier's area. But not only is skiing the slopes challenging, finding your way from resort to resort can test the skills of an Eagle Scout. The area does provide good lift maps with suggested itineraries to make crisscrossing the region less difficult. With such an expanse of skiing no one map allows sufficient detail for extensive skiing. When you arrive in a new section stop and pick up a local lift map which details runs in the immediate area.

Note that the lift system does not perfectly interconnect. In Chatel there is a shuttle bus between the Linga and the Super-Chatel cable car.

Experts can strike out in any direction but will find the biggest challanges dropping down runs in the World Cup section of Avoriaz, yoyoing through the Plaine Dranse and Linga, and daring the "wall of death" or Chavanette. No expert will leave feeling complacent after any of those experiences.

Intermediates should be ready for an endurance challange of the first order. Forget any attempts to ski every run during a week-long vacation. It is just not possible. There are plenty of intermediate circuits which will provide a very full day of skiing. Try from Champéry to Avoriaz and back, or vice versa. On another day, take intermediate runs from Avoriaz to Chatel and return.

Beginners will not have a chance to really enjoy the expansive skiing Portes du Soleil. The best bets for beginners are Le Crosets, Champoussin, Avoriaz and Chatel.

Mountain rating

Score this one as a test of any expert, extensive enough for every intermediate on your list and more than any beginner can handle. Chavanette, known as the "wall of death" and the "Swiss wall," between Avoriaz and Les Crosets has lured experts for decades. As you stand at the lip of the drop, due to the steepness, you cannot see the slope which falls under the tips of your skis. Once you gather the courage to drop off the rim, it's a wide open expèrt steep. As I stood above Chavanette I recalled reading that snow would not stay on a slope so steep. Those snow scientists obviously didn't study in the class I was about to attend. Don't be ashamed to take the path around the "wall" at this point—more skiers choose this option here than at any other place I've skied in Europe. If you are in shape you can get the most from this far-flung area. If you're not, get ready to suffer or limit your skiing.

Ski school

The Swiss Ski School in Champéry offers both downhill and cross-country lessons.

Downhill group courses cost: half-day—SFR 17 (SFR 15 for children under 12); one week—SFR 80 (SFR 68 for children). Private one-hour lessons: SFR 35—for one person; SFR 40—for two persons; SFR 50—for three or four. Half-day private lessons for groups of one to four persons cost SFR 120. Full-day lessons for groups of 1-4 cost SFR 230.

Cross-country lessons are a bit less expensive. Group lessons are given in one-and-a-half hour segments. One lesson—SFR 14; two lessons—SFR 30; six lessons—SFR 65. Private cross-country lessons per hour are: one person—SFR 30; two persons—SFR 36; three to four persons—SFR 42. Half-day private lesson—SFR 90. Full-day private cross-country lesson—SFR 190.

A good way to get to know the area is through organized "Discover the Portes du Soleil" groups of five skiers on Saturdays and Sundays for SFR 40. The groups, organized by the Swiss Ski School in Champéry, normally make a loop through Les Crosets, Champoussin, Morgins, Avoriaz and return to Champéry.

A ski-safari across the Portes du Soleil is normally organized in late January and again in late March and April. These ski safaris are either seven-day or 14-day. The seven-day price—SFR940— includes four nights in Switzerland, three nights in France, six-day lift ticket, hotel with half-board, a guide, luggage transfers between hotels and swimming pool passes. The 14-day program—SFR 1850—is similar with seven nights in

Switzerland and seven nights in France. The ski-safari groups are of 8-10 skiers and are open to good skiers only.

Lift tickets

The Portes du Soleil ski pass (for adults 12 years and older) will cost: one day—SFR33; three days—SFR88; six days—SFR165; 13 days—SFR274.

A pass for only the Champéry, Les Crosets, and Champoussin lifts costs: half-day—SFR 16; one day—SFR27; two days—SFR49.

Both passes are discounted for children under 12 years of age.

Accommodation

Champéry, Les Crosets, and Champoussin have only a handful of hotels but plenty of apartments. There is also an excellent weekly program which includes seven days half-board, six-day lift tickets for the entire Portes du Soleil area, free entry to the covered pool, ice rink and the thermal baths in Val-d'Illiez. The 1987-88 special weekly price is noted and the normal high season half-board rate is also noted for each hotel.

Champéry

Hotel Suisse tel. (025) 791881, telex: 456412. My choice as the best place in town. The Hotel Suisse was completely redone between the 85/86 winter and the 86/87 winter. Special week: SFR780. Normal rate: SFR 84-174.

Hotel de Champéry tel. (025) 791071, telex:456285. Special week: SFR 820. Normal rates: SFR 93-172.

Beau-Séjour tel. (025) 791701, telex: 456284. A nice hotel with good restaurant and reasonable prices. The change in the location of the lifts will have an impact on this hotel. Last year is was the closest place to the main lifts up to Planachaux, but with the new cable car being located next to the sports center the Beau-Séjour will lose this advantage. Special week: SFR 695-750. Normal rates: SFR 81-101.

Hotel de la Paix tel. (025) 791551. An almost legendary hotel for young people. It's friendly, helpful and has great food and lots of it. The crowd is usually young and very international.

It also used to be very close to the main lift, but will be about a five minute walk away when the new cable car is in place further down in the valley. Special week: SFR 595-650. Normal daily rates: SFR 56-72.

Hotel des Alpes tel. (025) 791222. More upscale than the Paix with a fancy and expensive a la carte restaurant. This hotel has the possibilities to creep in the next higher category with some planned renovations. Special week: SFR 595-650. Normal daily rates: SFR 75-85.

Les Crosets/Champoussin

Télécabine tel. (025) 791421. There aren't many other choices in Les Crosets but this fills the bill. There is an Anglo/Swiss staff who are very helpful and who speak excellent English. Special week: SFR 685. Normal daily rates: SFR 70-85.

Alpage tel. (025) 772711, telex: 456254. This is the center of Champuossin and a great ski-in/ski-out location. If you are traveling by yourself I'd suggest somewhere in Champéry rather than up here but with a group it can be a great time. Special week: SFR 685. Normal daily rate: SFR 79-112.

Apartments

Champéry has a special weekly rate including apartment, six-day lift ticket, free entrance to the pool, skating rink and termal baths in Val-d'Illiez as well as cleaning fees. This special offer is effective from 10-23 January and from 13 March to the end of the season.

Studio apartment will cost SFR 430 per person for two persons and SFR 390 per person for four persons sharing.

Two-room apartment (means one bedroom and 2 beds in the living room) will cost for three persons sharing—SFR 410 per person; and for four persons sharing—SFR 370 per person

Three-room apartment (means two bedrooms and two additional beds in the living room) costs for four persons—SFR 410 per person; five persons—SFR 370 per person; Six persons—SFR 320 per person.

The normal January weekly rates for apartments: Studio— SFR 500; two-room—SFR 650; three-room—SFR 750; four-room (often an entire chalet)—SFR 900. In February prices jump: Studio—SFR 600; two-room—SFR 850; three-room—SFR 1050; four-room—SFR 1330. These prices are from one agency only. Other rental agencies may be more or less expensive depending on location and luxury.

In order to reserve apartments you may write to the tourist office, however they will only send you a listing of the agencies in town. Try these:

In Champéry: Agence Immobilière de Champéry—tel. (025) 791444; or Agence Mendes de Leon—tel. (025) 791777. I found the people in Mendes de Leon much more helpful than in the other.

In Les Crosets: Try Bureau Dents-du-Midi, V. Rey-Bellet—tel. (025) 791893; or Les Cimes—tel. (025) 791867.

In Champoussin: Location Services—tel. (025) 772681.

Child care

The ski school (tel. 791615) has a special "Mini-Club" for children from four to seven years of age. It is open from 9 am to 5 pm daily. It includes ski lessons, games and lunch. Half-day cost—SFR 22; Full-day with lunch—SFR 43.

For younger children from three months to four years a nursery has been organized. It is open from 8:30 am to 5:30 pm. One day with lunch costs SFR 28. A half day with lunch from either 8:30 to noon or from 11 am to 5:30 pm costs SFR 24. A full day without lunch is SFR 22. A half-day without lunch is SFR 18. the nursery school telephone is 791969, or contact the tourist office at 791141.

Dining

Champéry's cooking benefits from its proximity to France. For the best meals in town try the Restaurant le Mazot in the Hotel de Chapéry, the Restaurant Victor Hugo in the Hotel Suisse or the Restaurant des Alps. Slightly more reasonable, the Vieux Chalet was repeatedly recommended by locals and the La Paix which also garnered many local recommendations. For Italian food and pizzas head to Cime de l'Est or, if desperate, try the pasta in the Pub. For traditional food try Restaurant le Centre or the Restaurant Grand-Paradis. Chez Gabi, on the slopes above Champoussin, also had excellent food and makes a great mid-day stop or a good evening meal after a ride up the mountain on a snow cat.

Nightlife

Champéry, Les Crosets and Champoussin are not known for their nightlife or aprés ski. After skiing the meeting place of choice seems to be Le Pub in the middle of Champéry. To me it is dingy and depressing but the place to be if you hope to score any action. Later, after ten p.m., the disco opens and begins to fill up near midnight. The crowd is normally very British. The locals seem to congregate in Dancing le Levant after having the compulsory beer in "le Pub."

In Champoussin try the disco in the basement of the hotel or head for Le Nid for a quiet place to drink and meet other lost tourists. Expect to pay SFR 7 for a mixed drink and between SFR 3 and 6 for bottled beer.

Other activities

Champéry is a bit out of the way to allow easy access to major cities but if one doesn't mind the half-hour winding drive down the mountain Montreux and Lausanne are within an hour's drive. Monthey in the valley has a covered bridge and open-air market.

A visit to the thermal baths of Val-d'Illiez is a relaxing must, especially with free entrance included in most of the special packages which bring tourists to this area. Normal entrance is SFR 7. Buses run from Champéry to Val-d'Illiez twice a day—check with the tourist office for exact times.

For those interested in para-gliding contact Catherine Crevoisier at (025) 772083 or the tourist office in Champoussin (025) 772727.

Tourist information

Champéry: Office du Tourisme, telephone: (025) 791141, telex: 456263.

Champoussin/Les Crosets/Val-d'Illiez: Sociætåae de Dévelopment, telephone: (025) 772077; Val-d'Illiez/Champoussin, telephone: (025) 772727; Les Crosets, telephone: (025) 791423.

Saas-Fee

Saas-Fee is a village of very narrow streets, chalets and small hotels, and year-round skiing. Saas-Fee is for serious skiers: those who place more importance on the number of black-rated runs on the mountain than on the number of discos in the village. Nestled in the neighboring valley to Zermatt, Saas-Fee allows no private cars in town. You park on the outskirts and take public transport.

Saas-Fee has its own snow-making equipment on the lower beginner slopes. Combined with the glacier runs above there's never a danger that poor snowfall will threaten your vacation. In fact, its tourist office guarantees snow for visitors.

The town occupies a magnificent site at 1800 meters (5904 feet), ringed by 18 separate peaks of 4000 meters (13,120 feet) or more. Snowcaps on these mountains are permanent, as is skiing on the 3000-meter (9840-foot) Felskinn.

Where To ski

Saas-Fee's nearly 50 miles of downhill trails are superbly divided among beginning, intermediate and expert levels. Absolute beginners will start on the Saas Fee town lifts where they will stay for about three days. The ski instructor then takes them up either the Plattjen lift or the Felskinn.

For all other levels of skiers, Saas Fee offers four distinct areas. The Hannig area gets the first sun in the morning and normally has the smallest crowds. The lifts are very limited but the gondola and the two drag lifts open long runs back into town.

The next section to get the morning sun is the Spielboden/Längfluh area. These runs are on good-intermediate to expert terrain. The first section of the mountain under Längfluh down

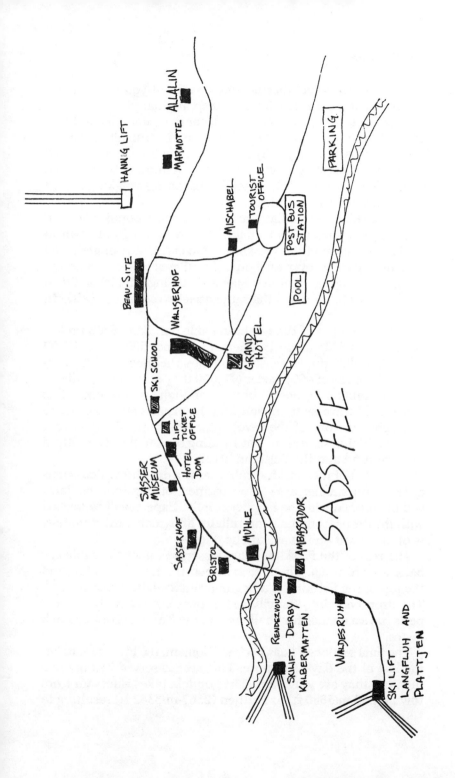

to the chairlift is the intermediate terrain. If you ski past this middle station get ready for the steep and narrow.

From the top of the Längfluh cablecar the unique "Fee-Chatz" connects this area with the Felskinn and Mittelallalin areas. The "Fee-Chatz" is basically a bus on runners which is towed behind a snow cat. This creative lift system must be used due to the 30 meter flow of the glacial ice each year making a fixed lift system an impossibility.

The Felskinn/Mittelallalin area is the most popular section of Saas Fee's pistes. Two small lifts tow skiers from town to the lower station of the Felskinn cable car. Unfortunately, the wait here can be over an hour. Creative skiers can take the quickly moving, less-crowded Speilboden/Längfluh lifts and then the "Fee-Chatz" to reach the same area served by the Felskinn lift.

Once at the top of the Felskinn cable car, Saas Fee's underground Metro Alpin whisks skiers up another 500 meters (1600 ft.) to Mittelallalin. Here, stop to enjoy the magnificent panorama of dozens of 4000 meter (13,000 ft.) peaks. Intermediates and beginners (those brave enough to come this far) should traverse to the left and the experts should cross to the right, in front of the revolving restaurant. Skiers have a choice of doing several runs or heading back to the Metro Alpin underground and the Felskinn area.

To the left of the Felskinn cable car is a drag lift which opens a delightful smaller area—the Egginer. Strong intermediates will be satisfied with the Egginerjoch lift. Experts will be thrilled with the drops from the Hinterallalin lift which, unfortunately, is often closed due to avalanche danger.

The rest of the Felskinn runs crisscross under the cable car back toward town. The area between the middle station and the top of the Felskinn is a beginner/intermediate playground. The drop back into the village steepens considerably and experts have a chance for challenge on the Kanonenrohr or Bach pistes.

The final section of Saas Fee's ski domain, the Plattjen, catches the last of the day's sunshine. This area is served by only two lifts, but they are long ones. The gondola takes skiers up from town (1800 m/5850 ft) to Plattjen (2567 m/8342 ft) resulting in a run of almost 2500 ft. vertical drop. There are trails for all abilities. This section not normally crowded.

Mountain rating

Experts will never complain about the runs at Saas-Fee. There's enough black to make things interesting.

Intermediates may think that the lift network and trails were laid out with them in mind. Most trails above Saas-Fee start with a red or blue leg, often with the option of taking a black-rated stretch.

Beginners can work toward becoming advanced beginners on the Saas Fe town slopes; then the slopes above the valley beckon.

Ski school

The Saas-Fee school (tel. 028-572348) has approximately 100 instructors. English is no problem in this resort.

Group lessons (three hours a day)

one half-day	SFR 20
six days (full days of instruction)	SFR 145
twelve half-days	SFR 175

Lessons for children are SFR 17 per half-day; SFR 133 for twelve half-days; and SFR 110 for the six-day ski course. Children can be fed looked after by the ski school during lunch for an additional SFR 16 per day.

Private lessons costs SFR 40 per hour for one or two persons; SFR 50 per hour for three to four people; SFR 185 for a full day.

Cross-country lessons are also offered, but only a five-mile loop around Saas-Fee is prepared. They cost SFR 70 for five half-days.

Special ski-mountaineering off-piste adventures were organized the past two winters for climbs to the top of the Alphubel and Allalin. These treks start with a two to four hour climb on skins. And end with long high-altitude powder cruises through virtually virgin snow. Tours are limited by both the weather and a shortage of qualified instructors. From mid February through the end of the season the treks depart approximately once a week.

"The Haute Route" is a classic ski adventure trek between Saas-Fee, Zermatt, Courmayeur and Chamonix. These treks are organized from mid-April until the end of May. This is a tough physical trek and participants should be in good shape for high altitude ski-climbing and must be able to ski in deep snow. The mountain climbing school conducts the Haute Route tour from early May to the first week in June. Contact: Bergsteigerschule Saastal, CH-3906 Saas Fee, tel. 028-572348 or the tourist office at 028-571457. The cost for the classic "Haute Route" tour is approximately SFR 750 which includes guides, accommodation in mountain huts, meals, hotel expenses during the tour, mountain railway and bus fares.

Lift tickets

Saas-Fee lifts (88/89 prices)

for one day	SFR 42
for two days	SFR 80
for three days	SFR 110
for six days	SFR 190
for seven days	SFR 215

Beginners need only purchase tickets for the Saas Fee town lifts for SFR 18 per day for adults and SFR 14 for children.

Children from six to 16 get approximately a 40 percent discount on the normal lift fees.

Note: The Fee-Chatz, which is a shuttle between the Längfluh and the Felskinn area is not included in the lift pass prices. If you decide to take the snowcats, which serve as the lift system shuttle, the price per ride is SFR 4 for adults and SFR 1 for children. This "lift"—really a snowcat-bus—is used since a permanent lift cannot be built acorss the glacier which mover approximately 30 meters each year. The "Fee-Chatz" is not included in the lift ticket since the snowcats may be needed on another section of the mountain during an emergency and their operation cannot be be guaranteed.

Accommodation

The first prices listed are special ski week rates normally available in January. They include hotel, half pension, ski pass, ski lessons, entrance to the pool. There is also an active entertainment program of ski racing, fashion shows, fondue and raclette parties, and tourchlight processions. The final price noted is the normal high season half pension price based on double occupancy.

The Best

Walliserhof (tel. 028-572021; telex: 472221) SFR 994—The best hotel in town. For a sensuous splurge try the suite with livingroom, round bed, white marble bath and private sauna. Daily normal rates: SFR 133-173.

Ambassador (tel. 028-571420) SFR 861—Renovated with new pine furniture. In town near the ski school assembly point. Has indoor swimming pool. Normal daily rate: SFR 107-139.

Allalin (tel. 028-571815; telex: 472208) SFR 791—This beautiful three-star hotel is really four-star quality. It is located at the far end of town from the ski lifts, but with ski storage facilities at the lifts there is no need to drag equipment back and forth. The food is some of the best in town. Normal daily rate: SFR 77-99.

Moderate

Mischabel (tel. 572118) SFR 791—A Best Western Hotel. Located as you enter the town about a seven minute walk to most lifts. Normal daily rate: SFR 77-99.

Hotel Marmotte (tel. 028-572852) SFR 791—The rooms could be bigger, the decor could be more traditional mountain Swiss and the location could be closer to the main lifts. This hotel shines because of its mad owner, Karl Dreier, who makes everyone feel at home. Karl is also the chef and he cooks some of the best hotel food I've eaten. There is a free ski storage arrangement with the Waldesruh Hotel opposite the Felskinn lift plus a free babysitting arrangement with Hotel Alphubel which is considered one of the best hotels for children in Switzerland. Normal daily rate: SFR 77-99.

Derby (tel. 572345; telex: 472207) SFR 765—Family hotel with excellent location on the road to Felskinn and Plattjen lifts. Normal daily rate: SFR 73-95.

Hotel Europa (tel. 572791; telex: 472229) SFR 728—A small hotel (fifty-five beds) with good location for those planning to do most of their skiing on the Hannig. Normal daily rate: SFR 65-84.

Hotel Waldesruh (tel. 572295; telex 472214) SFR 765—Good location on the way to the Plattjen and Längfluh gondola ground stations. Caters to families. Normal daily rate: SFR 73-95.

Budget
Mühle (tel. 572676) SFR 679—Very small hotel offering basic accommodations. Normal daily rate: SFR 59-77.

Feehof (tel.572308) SFR 546 (bed and breakfast only). A bargain basement garni. No telephone, no public restaurant, no credit cards. Normal daily rate: SFR 33-42.

The hotels in this town are all good. We've picked out some exceptional ones which we know. The best way to select a hotel if you're traveling with a group or tour package is to decide whether close to the main lifts of in the center of town (and the nightlife action) is more to your liking. Or perhaps you want to be near the Hannig lift and in the sunniest part of town.
   Near Felskinn, Plattjen and Spielboden lifts: Waldesruh, Derby, Burgener, Bristol, Ambassador, Fehof, Mistral, Muhle, Rendezvous, Saaserhof.
   Center of Town: Beau-Site, Britannia, Christiana, Dom, Gletschergarten, Grand, Mischabel, Park, Walser, Walliserhof, Zurbriggen.
   Near Hannig on the sunnyside: Allalin, Alphubel, Domino, La Collina, Marmotte, Sporthotel, Tenne.

Dining
The best restaurant in the area is the Fletschhorn (028-572131) about a 30 minute walk out of town or a ten minute taxi ride. This restaurant is considered to be one of the best in Switzerland and features nouvelle cuisine.

Perhaps the second best eatery is the Hohnegg (028-572268) just about a 10 minute walk above the town or call for their taxi service which will bring you up. Also nouvelle cuisine.

The Walliserhof "Le Gourmet" restaurant (028-572021) is also a top nouvelle cuisine restaurant.

For excellent traditional Walliser food try the Saaserhof Restaurant (028-571551) and the Schäferstube. For cheese specialties and Swiss specialties the top recommendations are the Vieux Chalet (572892) and the Arvu-Stuba.

For good less-expensive meals try the Hotel Allalin (028-571815)—a rebuilt 300-year old room with wooden beams and hand-carved chairs, make it magical by candlelight; Hotel Dom (591101) for great Röstle; La Gorge (572641); the Hotel du Glacier (571244) also has excellent fondue and raclette.

For pizza try the pizzeria/steakhouse under the Hotel Beau-Site, the Boccalino—in front of the Saaserhof—or the pizzeria in the Walliserhof. Pizza costs from SFR 8-12 and pasta about the same.

On the slopes make sure to have one lunch in the revolving restaurant at the top of the Metro Alpin lift. It is the highest revolving restaurant in the world and, amazingly, the prices are reasonable. The mountain restaurant Berghaus Plattjen a third of the way down the National run from the top of the Plattjen lift is great for a late lunch when it catches the sun. On the opposite side along the Längfluh run, where it meets the Gletschergrotte trail cutting off from the Kanonenrohr, is the Gletscher-Grotte which catches sun most of the day.

SFR 20 will cover a good lunch with beer and coffee.

Apartments

Apartments are the way to go if you really want to save money. Saas-Fee alone has about 1500 chalets and apartments for rent. Write to the tourist office and ask for a list of apartments that will be available during the time you will be in Saas Fee. Also, include your requirements, such as the number of people in your party. The office will send a list of available apartments in town, plus a map showing apartment locations. You then select the apartment you want and correspond either with the tourist board or directly with the apartment owner.

The apartments normally include linen and kitchen utensils.

You will be charged a visitor's tax and there may be an extra charge for the electricity and heat you use during your stay.

Expect to pay between SFR 25 and SFR 40 per person a night, depending on the number of people sharing the apartment and its location.

Nightlife

Saas-Fee is known as a town for young skiers and those who think young. You'll meet a lively crowd in the evening.The three main live-music places are within a stone's throw of each other. The Walliserhof "Le Club" has a good band and an older clientele—25-45 years old. The San Souci across the street also provides good music but with a younger crowd (18-25). During the low season when there is no school break neither disco is overrun with teen agers. For slightly more traditional dancing, and the place most locals go, try the Yetti in the basement of the Hotel Dom. At discos expect to pay about SFR 7 for a beer or glass of wine. As of press time no disco in Saas Fee had a cover charge.

There is also a good group of bars: Pic Pic is a Swiss locals' spot, the Fee Pub across from the Yetti normally has a good crowd, Walliser Stübli under the Hotel du Glacier and the Metro Bar near the Hotel Beau Site are lively.

Après ski as the slopes close is an early affair since the sun drops behind the mountains early. If you're off the mountain at around 3 p.m. the terrace bars at the Derby, Mühle, Rendezvous and Christiana do a great business. After four when the sun drops out of sight, the crowd evaporates. Most gather in bars such as Chemi Stube in the Christiana, the Saaserhof or inside the Rendezvous which have live music, but I didn't find anywhere with good dancing music and really wild après-ski merriment.

Child care

Saas-Fee's ski school (tel. 574348) is for children ages five to 12 with a half-day fee of SFR 16. The six-day course of all-day lessons is SFR105. Lunch costs an additional SFR 15 per day.

Children from three to six will be taken care of by a nurse in the town kindergarten. Enroll children at the tourist office.

Prices for guests with visitors card: full day with lunch—SFR 16, without lunch—SFR 12; half-day with lunch—SFR 11, without lunch—SFR 6; one week with lunch—SFR 80, without lunch—SFR 60; one week of half-days with lunch—SFR 55, without lunch SFR 30.

Getting there

By train: From Zurich airport via Bern, Spiez, through the Lötschberg tunnel to Brig. At Brig you change to the Post Bus which meets the train and leaves from the front of the railway station about 15 minutes later.

From Geneva, trains run directly to Brig.

By car: Travel via Montreux then up the Valais pass through Sion to Visp where you turn south and follow signs to Saas Fee.

If you are driving from Zurich or Basel you can choose to take the Löschberg tunnel from Kandersteg to Goppenstein, above Brig and Visp. This tunnel requires that you load your car onto the railway. Trains transit the tunnel every half-hour from 5:35 a.m. to 11:05 p.m. The trip takes only fifteen minutes. Cost per car (including 9-seat vans), is SFR 15. From Goppenstein continue your drive to Visp then on to Saas Fee.

Park in the car park at the entrance to the town. Either call your hotel from the phone on the wall of the tourist office or take a taxi to your hotel. Taxis from parking/bus station to town cost SFR 13 for two people, SFR 16 for three, and SFR 17 for four.

Other activities

Visit the Saaser Museum, open from 2 p.m. to 6 p.m. with entrance of SFR 3 for adults and SFR 1 for children. It is packed with photographs of the old Saas valley, plus old tools, kitchen utensils, and furniture of a mountain people.

For exercise the Bielen Sports and Leisure Center offers a 25-meter (80 ft.) heated indoor swimming pool, children's pool, 2 tennis courts, exercise room, whirlpools, steambath and mixed sauna. Entrance costs, with the visitors card, are SFR 9.50 (except sauna) or SFR 14 (with sauna). Discounts are available for repeat visits. Tennis courts are should be reserved in advance and cost, with the visitors card, SFR 22 per hour from 8 a.m. to 4 p.m. and SFR 28 per hour after 4 p.m. until 10 p.m.

Tourist information

Write Verkehrsbüro Saas-Fee, CH-3906 Saas-Fee, Switzerland; tel. 028-571457; telex 472230.

St. Moritz

When you have visited all the other great resorts, enjoyed the fine hotels elsewhere claiming to pamper guests to the ultimate, when you've seen all the mountains said to be grand and great, then and only then journey to St. Moritz. You'll find that although there is elegance and alpine beauty everywhere in Switzerland, nowhere is it concentrated in such huge amounts as it is on the rooftop of Europe in St. Moritz, the original Swiss winter resort.

In winter the great expanses of snow-covered lake provide a massive, scenic foreground for the celebrated town whose name has become a synonym for quality and luxury. The most elegant aspect of St. Moritz, the great hotels, are expensive, almost prohibitively so, but everything else, restaurants included, is there for nearly everyone.

The central area of St. Moritz Dorf is compact, really only a mesh of two main streets with a few sideroads and a single, small main square. Sports shops abound and prices are surprisingly low. There are actually true bargains in February and March when sales are offered. Movies are up-to-date, nightlife superb, moonlight strolls on the lake wonderful. The range of entertainment fits every pocketbook and taste.

Where to ski

Until you have experienced St. Moritz, your education on Alpine Switzerland is incomplete. Exclusive, expensive, exciting: That's the two-time Olympic site (1928 and '48) which is home to some of the finest intermediate skiing anywhere.

Altogether there are 150 miles of groomed trails. The setting is stunning, 6,000 feet high in the southwestern corner of Switzerland, near the Italian border in the twin shadows of the 3,057 meter (9,270 feet) Piz Nair and the 3,303 meter (10,833 feet) Piz Goravtsch.

The main runs are clustered around the summits of the two mountains. The Corviglia runs come downhill near St. Moritz Dorf and the Corvatsch into St. Moritz-Bad (the Hahnensee run only) on the valley floor.

The finest run is the Hahnensee, a black trail which is intermediate for most of the five-mile-length. The run boasts a vertical drop of over 1,500 meters.

It's a five-minute walk from the end of the Hahnensee run to the Signalbahn cable car which takes you up to Corviglia.

On the second time down the Hahnensee break off the run at the Mandras t-bar and go back up to the Murtel cable midstation. Here, the run down to Surlej is peppered with moguls and dips and all the while the panorama includes the frozen lakes of Champfer and Silvaplana. The adventurous work their way along the slopes via the t-bars at Alp Margun to the 2,800 meter Culoz de las Furtschellas. From here, there is an interesting run to Sils-Maria on the Silvaplana lakeshore. Be sure you have the regional lift ticket or there's a 5 franc surcharge for the Sils-Maria lifts.

The longest, and favorite run of many, is from Piz Nair, either down the front side to St. Moritz or over the ridge at the 2,486 meter (8,154 feet) level at the cable car station in Corviglia and down past Marguns to the Celerina gondola. The Celerina run is superb lower intermediate skiing along a stream, through woods and finally down a short but challenging mogul field 300 yards from the ground station. For greatest length along an intermediate trail, climb all the way to the top of the Fuorcia Glisha t-bar behind Piz Nair for the run to the valley floor.

The single most challenging run in the valley is "The Hang," a chilling drop from the top at Lagalb on the Bernina Pass. It's rated black-plus. On the other side of the pass approach is Diavolezza where the skiing is average but there's a stunning glacier ski trek after a 25-minute walk on skis to the mountain bar run by Otto Rohner and then onto the glacier. On full moon nights there is a unique Alpine experience, night glacier skiing at Diavolezza.

There is also summer skiing on the summits at Corvatsch and Diavolezza.

Mountain Rating

Eighty percent of the slopes in the St. Moritz area are for intermediates. Beginners will start to feel at home after several runs on one of the longer trails. When in doubt, follow the advanced beginners of a St. Moritz ski class for the best slope that day.

Experts will head for the toughest parts of the back side on Piz Nair, plus the summit of Corvatsch and the super challenge of the black run at Lagalb.

Ski Schools

St. Moritz area ski schools have 145 instructors (plus 30 additional temporaries). In 1927 the world's first ski school was established here. The main ski school (tel. 082-34980) is in the center of town with a booking station in the tourist office.

Individual lessons

one hour	SFR 50
half day	SFR 90
all day	SFR 180

Group lessons
(normally three hours of lessons daily)

one day	SFR 45
three days	SFR 110
six days	SFR 168

Lessons are available for cross country, which is extremely popular because of the nearly 75 miles of well-maintained trails in the valley. If you do cross country you probably want to ski the Engadine Marathon course, a 26-mile cross-country circuit. Come in mid-March and take part along with as many as 12,000 others in one of the world's great cross-country ski races.

Helicopter ski transport for off-piste skiing and powder skiing (plus deep snow skiing instruciton) are available.

Lift Tickets

Engadine regional pass (includes St. Moritz and Corviglia, Sils Maria, Silvaplana, Surlej, Champfer, Celerina, Samedan, Pontresina and Zuoz)

for three days	SFR 114
for six days	SFR 190
for seven days	SFR 211

Day tickets for the individual areas are priced

Corviglia	SFR 34
Diavolezza	SFR 33
Corvatsch	SFR 36

Accommodation

Over half of the hotels in St. Moritz are four and five star, the highest concentration of quality hotels in Switzerland. The best of the best is the **Suvretta** in neighboring Champfer. This wonderful monument to Swiss hotel expertise is overshadowed in reputation by the Palace in St. Moritz dorf. The **Suvretta** (tel. 21121, telex 74491) is a model of understatement, a great hotel on the mountainside with its own lift connection to Corviglia. Half pension daily rates are SFR 150 to SFR 315 with high season rates about 25 percent higher.

Second on our ranking list of the five, five-star hotels in St. Moritz is the **Kulm** (tel. 21151, telex 74472), on the road to the bob and Cresta runs. Rooms are SFR 150 to SFR 295 half pension.

Badrutt's Palace (tel. 21101, telex 74424) is still the place to stay if you want to be seen. It is one of the most famous and elegant hotels in the skiing world where if you have to ask the price you should be staying somewhere else. Prices range between SFR 210 and SFR 270 per night with half pension during low season. In addition, Badrutt's has a ski week package which includes breakfast, dinner at a different restaurant each night and a regional ski pass, with prices (per person, double occupancy) from SFR 1600 for a room facing the mountain to SFR 2300 for a large room facing the lake. Come prepared with a dark suit and tie or you will not be allowed to wander through the public areas after 7 p.m. For reservations call Leading Hotels of the world in the U. S. at (800) 223-6800 or (212) 838-3110; and in Britain at (800) 181-123.

Hotel Albana (tel. 33121, telex, 74465), Best Western Hotel, SFR 1070—Low season rate, including ski pass for one week. Excellent downtown location with superb staff and a very good kitchen.

Schweizerhof (tel. 22171, telex 74447) SFR 800 weekly. One of the most comfortable hotels in town.

Hotel Steinbock (te. 36035) SFR 525 weekly. Small hotel (26 beds) with good restaurant, reputation for making guests comfortable.

Hotel Nolda (tel. 082-35855) SFR 630 francs weekly. Does not include any meals, but this family hotel with 70 beds has good location at the end of the Corviglia run and adjacent to the Signal cable car lift. Has its own sauna, swimming pool, solarium and whirlpool.

Neues Posthotel (tel 22101, telex 74430) SFR 630 weekly. Within short walk of main tourist office.

Steffani (tel. 22101, telex 74466) SFR 770 weekly. Comfortable midtown hotel around the corner from the parking garage.

National Hotel (tel. 33274) SFR 400 weekly.

Waldhaus am See (telex 74759, tel. 37676) SFR 560 weekly. Quiet location directly on the shore of St. Moritz lake although only three minutes' walk from the train station.

Sporthotel Bellaval (tel. 33245) SFR 380 weekly. Near the lakeshore. Full pension, if desired, 105 francs additional.

The **Reine Victoria** and the **Roi Soleil**, both in St. Moritz Bad, are Club Med hotels.

The St. Moritz all-in plan is the Sunshine Ski Week. The 1988-89 plan, beginning Nov. 26 (arrival Saturday, start Sunday morning), ranges from SFR 1025 weekly for five star hotels down to SFR 640 for bed and breakfast places.

The week includes half pension (b&b at garni hotels), 6-day lift ticket, 4 hours ski instruction daily for 6 days plus a ski party and a race. There are also special plans for combination ski and tennis weeks. Price for January through the spring of 1989 are about 10 percent higher, ranging from SFR 685 to SFR 1280.

Chesa Guardelej (tel. 23121; telex 74781) SFR 175 high season price per person, double occupancy, including half pension)—One of the best hotels you'll find in the Alps. The hotel is made of a group of small building connected by underground passages. Rooms are excellent and there are several different dining areas and restaurants, plus the hotel is equipped with a full exercise room and swimming pool.

Albana in Silviplana (tel. 49292 or through Best Western). High season half board rate per person: SFR 100. The hotel has an award-winning restaurant.

Dining

One dining experience you should enjoy is the excursion to Muottas Maragl, a mountain hotel restaurant near Pontresina at Samedan on the way to the Bernina Pass. You take a funicular up to the hotel, which has a truly spectacular location overlooking the valley. Go up on the funicular (runs every half hour from 7 until 11 p.m.) just before sunset and watch the lights come on in the valley. Reserve in advance (tel. 082-33943) and ask for a window seat.

The great hotels of St. Moritz, which incidentally cost SFR 1,500 to SFR 2000-plus weekly for half pension, boast equally famous dining rooms, with the same high prices. Opt instead for something down to earth like the Italian specialties in the basement pizzeria at the Chesa Veglia. The Chesa Veglia restaurant is also superb although considerably more expensive.

For a wild game specialty like deer steak, try Talvo (Tel. 34455), a restaurant in nearby Champfer (take highway 27 out of town). The menu here ranges from 26 to 40 francs.

Try also the restaurant Steinbock in the hotel of the same name listed above for tasty, reasonably priced Swiss specialities.

To demolish your budget and add an unforgettable dining experience, have lunch (reservations required) at La Marmite, a gourmet restaurant atop Corviglia. It's in the funicular station near the self-service restaurant.

The Stuvetta, a cozy corner of the restaurant building at the Marguns lift station, is great for lunches, particularly pasta dishes. And the last stop of the day should be the Alpina Hutte, the St. Moritz ski club hut in the shadow of Piz Nair where you should order a Grischa, a traditional hot-wine filled pot with drinking spouts for up to four. One of the most reasonably priced restaurants in the area is Veltlinerkeller, down the hill from Dorf toward Bad.

Apartments

Vacation apartment rentals are popular but expensive here. Altogether there are about 6,500 apartment beds but only about 2,900 are available for rental. In some cases you'll pay 25 percent more than you would in other Swiss resorts. A typical two-room rental apartment within walking distance of the lifts rents for approximately 1,000 francs. The local tourist office will provide you with a list of apartments. In addition, Interhome operates an office in the town opposite the Kulm Hotel. You can arrange for an apartment there.

Nightlife

At 1 a.m. most evenings the streets are still full of visitors sampling St. Moritz's great nightlife. The most famous address is the King's Club disco at the Palace where 30 francs (men, bring a tie) gets you in plus a drink. The most fun we had, by far, was the Stubli, the typical Swiss wood-paneled bar in the lower level of the Schweizerhof. The ski instructors come early and stay late. There's usually so little room you are crowded, shoved, and shuffled from one spot to another. You'll like it.

The Cresta Bar in the Steffani is a good meeting place after the walk down the hill from the Corviglia funicular, but from there you might move on after 10 p.m. to the nearby Vivai, a disco with a young following. Nearby also is Cascade, a sort of combination bar/pub you'l like almost as much as the Stubli in the Schweizerhof. Another disco, the Spotlight, is near the tourist office. And there's not a cozier place than the bar/sitting room of the Albana after a day on Corviglia.

It's chic in late afternoon to order a hot chocolate and a whipped cream-covered slice of Black Forest cake at Hanselmann, the famed chocolate specialist adjacent to the Hotel Albana in the center of the town.

Child Care

The Ski School for children 6-12 runs half days and full. A half day is 14 francs. Six half-days are 98 francs. The full day price for three days is 60 francs and 100 for six days of instruction.

Getting There

You'll most likely come in via Zürich airport and then train to St. Moritz station. There is regular turboprop service from Zürich to St. Moritz and return for 370 SFR via Air Engiadina. Train costs: Zürich to St. Moritz—SFR 116 (first class), SFR 74 (second class). Rental cars are available in Zürich and St. Moritz.

If you are driving, the easiest route is Zürich-Chur-Thusis, then a 30-mile stretch over the Julierpass (chains needed only in the worst weather) or through the Thusis-Samedan car-train tunnel when the pass is closed.

Iff you stay in St. Moritz and not one of the outlying towns, you'll pay a stiff fee for parking, about 14 francs a day unless you are staying more than a week. In that case, there is a discount card available. The main garage is located centrally, however, two minutes down the hill from the Corviglia funicular. If you buy the regional ticket, the ride on the PTT Sports Bus to any of the slopes is free.

Other Activities

If possible, ride the Glacier Express, a 150-mile crossing of the ice-covered landscape between St. Moritz and Zermatt. The train leaves St. Moritz shortly before 9 a.m. and crosses 291 bridges and goes through 91 tunnels before arriving at Zermatt at approximately 4:45 p.m. Going the other way the train leaves Zermatt at 10:05 a.m. and reaches St. Moritz at 5:52 p.m.

It's possible to go down the famed Cresta Bob run without

risking your life. Sign on as a guest rider on non-racing days. The fee for five rides as a passenger on the one mile course is about 400 francs; one ride costs 100 SFR. The ice track closes in early March. Horse-drawn sleigh rides range from a run down the lake (about SFR 100) to a romantic trip into the Rosegg Valley (about SFR 250).

The first "Skijoring" races, with horses pulling skiers on the frozen lake race track, were run in 1901. The competition continues. Try to see one of the events during the first three weekends in February.

For information on hand gliding instruction telephone 34980. You can take a Delta hang glider taxi ride for SFR 180.

Excursions to Italy, over the Bernina Pass at one end of the valley and the Maloja at the other, are easy and bus tours are available if you are not driving.

St. Moritz has two museums, the Engadine, with an emphasis on local history and the Segantini, an art museum.

If you are looking for mountain hiking gear or climbing equipment Testa Sport (down the hill toward St. Moritz Bad) or Scheung Sport (just off the main square) are well-stocked.

The local movie, across from the Kulm Hotel, shows current films in the original language.

Tourist Information

Check with the Kur-und-Verkehrsverein, CH-7500 St. Moritz, Switzerland, Telex 74429 Tel. 082-33147.

In neighboring Pontresina the address is Verkehrsverein, CH 7505 Pontresina, Switzerland, tel. 082-66488

Verbier

This world-class resort is located in Switzerland's southwest corner, roughly between Zermatt to the east and Courmayeur and Chamonix to the west. Verbier itself is the major town in an area comprised of four valleys that have been interconnected by a spectacular lift system. The highest peak, Mont-Fort at 3328 meters, is the nexus for lift systems that rise from Verbier and Super-Nendaz. Some eighty lifts within the network service more than 180 miles of runs.

Verbier, the town, is upscale, chic and very well known, but reasonable accommodation can be found. Super-Nendaz is connected with Verbier and offers considerably less expensive accommodation. The lower lodging costs are offset by a slow and arduous lift system, which starts at Super-Nendaz and brings you to the top of the Tortin, where you can connect with the rest of the Verbier lift system.

Mountain rating

Verbier is considered tops by expert skiers. The expert runs are steep and hair-raising. We don't recommend runs such as the Tortin from Col des Gentianes for non-experts or for skiers who are not at least advanced-intermediates; if you fall, there is no stopping for at least a hundred meters. Other expert steep runs are not as long.

Intermediate skiers will find challenging terrain and technique perfecting runs.

Beginning skiers can glide down easy bunny slopes. However, they shouldn't expect the rest of the mountain to be conquered by week's end.

The lifts and the runs in the Nendaz area are shorter and easier than those in Verbier (except for the expert-level Tortin). This area will provide a nice break from Verbier's more crowded

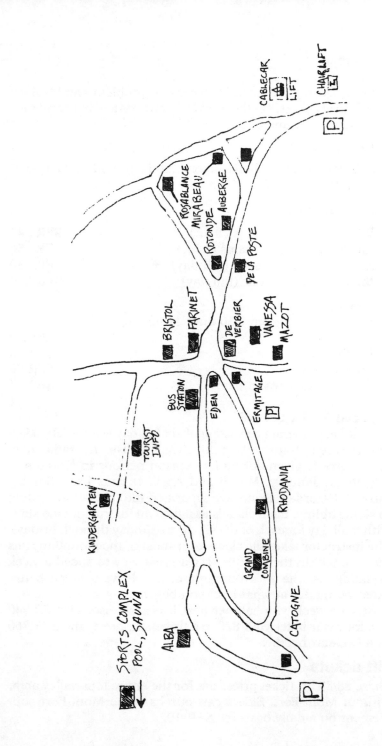

sections. During the week Verbier is no problem and lift lines are relatively short. On the weekends crowds arrive from Montreux, Lausanne and Geneva.

Ski school
The ski school has 170 instructors and is located in the Chalet Orny. Telephone: (026) 74825.

Individual lessons

for one or two persons (1 hr.)	SFR 42
for three or four persons (1 hr.)	SFR 56
for one or two persons (full day)	SFR 230
three or four persons (full day)	SFR 270

Group lessons
These are offered from 9:30 until 11:45 a.m.

for one day	SFR 19
for three days	SFR 50
for six days	SFR 90
for six days (consecutive)	SFR 82

"Special Wedel Course"
A week-long program consisting of six full-day lessons lets skiers tour the area's trails while honing their skills at the same time. The course is given during low-season periods in November, December, January, March and April. It runs from Sunday through Saturday. Skiers are separated into classes according to skiing ability. Each class is assigned an instructor who stays with it all day for each of the six days (Sunday through Friday). The instructor takes the skiers over most of the mountain runs that are within their ability. It's a great way to spend a week of skiing, ski the entire mountain, and leave a much better skier, no matter at what level you began.
Cost: One week with half pension, lifts and lessons is SFR 940 in a four-star hotel; SFR 820 in a three-star hotel; and SFR 760 in a two-star hotel.

Lift tickets
These 88/89 lift ticket prices are for the entire four-valley area, without Mont-Fort. Skiers can purchase the Mont-Fort supplement on a daily basis for SFR 10.

for one day	SFR 42
for two days	SFR 80
for three days	SFR 116
for six days	SFR 208
for seven days	SFR 236
for fourteen days	SFR 400

Half-price tickets are available for skiers over 60 years and for children younger than 16 years. The lifts are also discounted during certain low-season periods.

Family vacationers should be sure to ask about discounts, because a formula is used to calculate a healthy discount for families. For example: if two parents bring two children between the ages of six and 16, they must only purchase two full tickets and the children's tickets are free. Or, if two parents are traveling with two children between the ages of 16 and 25, they get all four tickets for the price of only two and a half tickets. Similar discounts apply to single parents.

Accommodations

The basic costs are (the normal high season rate with half pension based on double occupancy is noted after each hotel): Four-star hotels with package: SFR 990.

Four-star hotels:
Rosalp (tel. 76323; telex: 473322) SFR 180-200.
Vanessa (tel. 70141; telex: 473621) SFR 160-190.
Grand Combine (tel. 75515; telex: 473795) SFR 112-142.
   Three-star hotels:
Rhodania (tel. 70121; telex: 473392)—A Best Western hotel. Normal daily rate: SFR 145-153.
Chamois (tel. 76402; telex: 473247) SFR 93-110.
Mazot (tel. 76812; telex: 473812) SFR 110-140.
de la Poste (tel. 75681; telex: 473357) SFR 93-110.
Rotonde (tel. 76525; telex: 473247) SFR 88-205
de Verbier (tel. 75346; telex: 473846) SFR 93-110.
Vieux-Valaise (tel. 75955; telex: 473247) SFR 93-110

Two-star hotels:
Auberge (tel. 75272; telex: 473357) SFR 80-96.
Rosa Blanche (tel. 74472) SFR 67-78.

Crystal (tel. 75349) SFR 67-78.
Note: Rosa Blanche and Crystal can be reached by telex at 473247.

The following are bed-and-breakfasts.
Bristol (tel. 74022) SFR 60-75.
Ermitage (tel. 74977) SFR 62-80.
Farinet (tel. 76626) SFR 75-85.
Mirabeau (tel. 76335 SFR 65-84.

Apartments

Verbier is extremely well organized to handle apartment seekers during the ski season. Minimum stays are normally one week, Saturday to Saturday; during the Christmas and Easter seasons, a minimum two-week rental is required.

The tourist office's computer keeps track of which apartments are available. Write and give details on the number of beds required, the preferred number of rooms, and the dates you plan to be there. An immediate response with a selection of apartments and prices will follow. Select the apartment you want and return the information to the tourist office.

Bed linen and kitchen utensils are usually provided in each apartment. Other communal or private amenities, such as swimming pool, sauna, TV or room phone all add to the cost. Standard apartments rent for between $15 and $25 per person a night. Prices will also vary significantly from low to high season.

Dining

In Verbier's excellent restaurants prices vary depending on the establishment's relative position on the luxury scale and the quality of the food. But with their strong French influence, it is difficult to find a poorly prepared meal. The following restaurants come recommended by locals: Rosalp and Vanessa for a splurge; also, Au Vieux Valais and Le Mazot. Head to the Refuge under the Hotel Rhodania for good spaghetti and other Italian food. They serve "spaghetti by the meter" which guarantees a good time.

Nightlife

The most popular pubs are **The Pub** which is very English, **Nelsons, Fer a Cheval** with great hot wine, and **La Luge.**

The best discos in town are the **Tara Club** and the **Farm Club Disco**. The **Scotch Club** is not as popular. Expect to pay about SFR 20 for entrance charge including a drink.

Child care

A kindergarten, "Chez les Schtroumpfs" (the Smurfs' Place), is located in Chalet Lesberty, just a short distance from the tourist office. Its rates are SFR 32 a day, including lunch; SFR 26 for a half day with lunch; and SFR 16 for a half day without lunch. The kindergarten accepts infants as well. Call for details on the exact ages accepted (tel.77555). The kindergarten is open daily from 8:30 a.m. until 5:30 p.m.

The ski school also runs a ski nursery (tel. 74825 or 77469), which offers beginning ski lessons for children from three to ten years. Rates are SFR 32 for a half day, including lunch; SFR 43 for a full day with lunch; SFR 118 for three days; and SFR 215 for six days. Its hours are from 8:30 a.m. until 5 p.m.; closed Sunday.

Getting there

The closest airport is Geneva. Train service runs from Martigny on the Simplon line to Le Châble, where you can either take the cable car to Verbier or a direct bus from the station during the winter.

If your airline cannot arrange free or direct transfer from the airport to the resort, a rental car shared by several people makes the trip much easier; the car can also be used for side trips back to Montreux or Lausanne. The drive from Geneva should take about two hours. Follow the signs to the St. Bernard Pass (yes, home of the famous St. Bernard dogs) until you reach Sembrancher. There, turn left and drive up the hill to Verbier.

Other activities

Verbier has recently built an extensive sports center, which features an indoor swimming pool, ice rink, curling rinks, squash courts, whirlpools, saunas, solariums and two indoor tennis courts. The resort is approximately an hour's drive from Montreux and Lausanne, two of the most beautiful and interesting Swiss cities.

On lake Geneva, just before Montreux, visit the castle of Chillon. The town of Sion is very picturesque with a beautiful castle dominating the center of town. In the spring, a stop at the monastery at the St. Bernard Pass to visit the dogs makes for a pleasant tour.

For a change of pace, skiers may want to visit Villars, Leysin or Crans-Montana, all within an hour's drive from Verbier.

Tourist information

Tourist office, 1936 Verbier l; tel. (026) 76222 or 77181; telex: 473247 TURVE CH.

Villars

Villars is a gentle postcard town huddled on the side of the mountains overlooking the Rhone Valley with spectacular views of Mont Blanc. The spectacular views across the Rhone Valley from the winding approach to the town, either along the road or on the train from Aigle, are a beautiful introduction to the resort. The quiet village still retains its alpine character with only a handful of square concrete buildings marring the harmony of chalet-style architecture. Villars is a town which for years has successfully balanced different generations—the older, upscale vacationer and teen-age students at private schools and colleges. Except for those looking for extremes—steeps that leave you breathless by day and wild parties that leave you exhausted by night—Villars is a resort for everyone. It has one of the largest sports centers in Europe with plenty of activities for the non-skier as well as slopes for every level of skier.

Where to ski

The major ski area of Villars is reached by either the Roc d''Orsay gondola or by the cog train which leaves from the center of town and reaches the major mountain hub at Bretaye (1800 m). Either ascent will allow similar explorations of the ski area. For those starting at Roc D'Orsay (2000 m) the first run is a gentle warmup reaching Bretaye. From here three chairlifts and three drag lifts fan out to open the slopes surrounding Bretaye. Head up the Grand Chamossaire (2120 m) and the Petit Chamossaire (2034 m) for the morning hours. The runs down from the Grand Chamossaire are gentler and a bit longer than those from the Petit Chamossaire, but both can be handled by all but the absolute beginner. Petit Chamossaire offers significantly more challenging terrain, both on- and off-piste, for

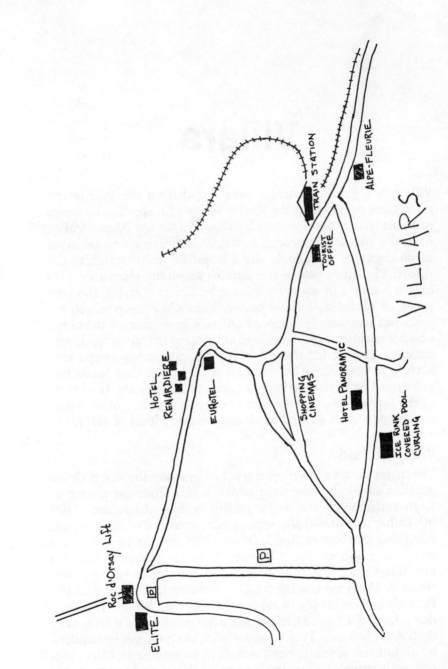

the expert. The opposite side of Bretaye topped by Chaux de Conches (2027 m) and Chaux Ronde is an intermediate joy with virtually unlimited off-piste possibilities for both intermediates and experts. Once again trails allow even beginners to enjoy the skiing. The piste map of the backside of Chaux Ronde and Chaux de Conches stretching down to La Rasse looks like a dozen blue threads streaming to one point, however the impression of only easy slopes is misleading. Here experts can find jumps and tree-skiing—especially directly beneath Chaux de Conches—and intermediates can push themselves off-piste virtually anywhere in this area.

Reaching the Gryon area is an easy two-step process. From La Rasse a short lift brings skiers to Sodoleuvroz where a long drag lift reaches Les Chaux (1750 m) and another stretches even higher to Croix des Chaux (2020 m). Here skiers of every level can enjoy the snow and the views including very long off-piste runs down to the Gryon gondola.

The other major area of Villars is the connection with Les Diablerets. Dropping behind Meillerets and Les Mazots is a web of between-the-tree runs which link up with a lift bringing skiers to Isenau and then another gondola reaching Pierres Pointes just beneath the glacier. Skiing under the Pierres Pointes gondola is some of the most challenging within miles. Two cable cars bring one to Scex Rouge (2970 m) where the actual glacier skiing opens up. The required adventure is the long run around the Oldenhorn and down to the cable car station at Oldenegg. Take the cable car up to Cabane then ski back down to Oldenegg beneath the lift. Note: This all-day adventure takes time—make sure to start early and head back by around two in the afternoon in order to make the series of lifts needed to reach Villars by late afternoon

Mountain Rating

Villars though predominately a fantastic place for beginners to learn and for intermediates of all levels to frolic is also a playful mountain for experts. There is adequate terrain to keep most adventurous skiers happy for an entire week. Some mountains play with expert skiers and in some resorts the experts play with the mountain—Villars is definitely in the latter category. Though I would not send the dedicated expert skier to Villars for a week, the resort would be wonderful for a mixed-level group of skiers and friends.

Ski school

Villars has two ski schools—the traditional Swiss Ski School and the more avant-garde "Ecole de ski moderne."

Swiss Ski School: For groups, a half-day—SFR 18 (SFR 17-children); three half-days—SFR 50 (SFR 45-children); six consecutive half-days—SFR 80 (SFR 70-children). Private lessons will cost SFR 40 per hour for one, SFR 45 per hour for two, and SFR 50 for three and four persons. A private instructor for a full day costs SFR 200. Cross-country lessons are the same prices as downhill.

"Ecole de ski moderne" This school is very English oriented. It used the GLM, (graduated length method) instruction. This has skiers starting on short skis and then using long skis within a week. There are also hot dog ski lessons, ski ballet, surf, telemark, and off-piste opportunities. Group lessons cost: SFR 15 for adults and SFR 12 for children. Private lessons: SFR 35 for one person; SFR 40 for two persons; SFR 45 for three persons; and SFR 50 for four persons. A private insturctor for a half-day is SFR 120; and for a full day SFR 220.

Lift Tickets

The lift tickets include Villars, Gryon, Meilleret and Isenau. Tickets for the Diablerets glacier cost extra.

88/89 prices: Half-day—SFR 25; Full day—SFR 32; Six days—SFR 155. Children get a 20% discount.

Accommodation

Villars does not have thousands of hotel rooms—that's part of its charm. The hotels in town are quality establishments. Correspond directly with the hotels or the tourist office will be happy to make reservations—tel. (025) 353232. The prices for hotels noted here are for half-board based on double occupancy.

There is also a special "White Week" program which links the lifts of the Lake Geneva region and includes seven days half-board, free entrance to the pool, skating rink and fitness center, plus unlimited skiing in Villars, Chateau-d'Oex, Les Diablerets, Leysin, Les Mosses and La Lécherette. The low season prices are noted for each hotel.

Grand Hotel du Parc tel. (025) 352121, telex: 456218. One of the leading hotels of the world. Very posh, very upscale, very formal—requiring a jacket at dinner and in the public areas of the hotel after seven p.m. Swimming suits acceptable in the covered pool. Rates: SFR 130-222. White week price: SFR 1175.

Panoramic tel. (025) 35211; telex: 456228. This is the newest hotel in town. Beds fold into the wall to allow more room during the day. Though the restaurants are considered some of the best in Villars the half-board menu quality varies greatly. Covered pool. A Best Western Hotel. Rates: SFR 78-165. Ski a GoGo price: SFR 860.

Elite tel. (025) 351341; telex: 456203. A modern but soulless hotel at the bottom of the Roc d'Orsay gondola. This is Villars' ski in—ski out hotel. No pool. Rates: SFR 72-141. White week price: SFR 770.

Eurotel tel. (025) 353131; telex: 456206. The bottom of the four-stars. This hotel seems to have been designed for groups. It has a pool but I would try the other four-stars before bedding down here. Rates: SFR 81-151. White week price: SFR 770.

Le Renardière tel. (025) 352592; telex: 456215. Considered by most as the best-kept secret in Villars. Well, not that well-kept, rooms are hard to come by. Make reservations early. Tucked between trees this hotel is a cluster of three chalet-style buildings. Rates: SFR 78-118. White week price: SFR 825.

Alpe Fleurie tel. (025) 352494. This hotel looks like one on the postcards you send home to friends and family. Very family oriented, the hotel is located directly across from the train station and close to everything in town. Rates: SFR 90-120. White week price: SFR 825.

Gold et Marie-Louise tel. (025) 352477; telex: 456212. Though there are plenty of rooms with private bath, this hotel also has less-expensive rooms with bath down the hall. Rates (with private bath): SFR 80-135. White week price: SFR 825.

Ecureuil tel. (025) 352795. This very traditional bed and breakfast has some rooms with kitchenettes, allowing preparation of meals in the room. A good budget choice. Rates (with bath): (B&B) SFR 37-65. White week program: SFR 670 (half-board).

Villars-Palace tel. 352241. One of the most prestigious Club Meds in Europe. French, as you might expect, is the language. Particulars from Club Med.

Apartments

Apartments are the best choice if you really want to save money. Apartment rentals are normally only available for stays of one week or longer. Villars alone has about 7000 chalet and apartment beds for rent. Write to the tourist office and ask for a list of apartments that will be available during the time you will be in Villars. Also, include your requirements, such as the number of people in your party. The office will send a list of available apartments in town, plus a map showing apartment locations. You then select the apartment you want and correspond either with the tourist board or directly with the apartment owner.

The apartments normally include bed linen and kitchen utensils. You will be charged a visitor's tax and there may be an extra charge for electricity and heat.

Expect to pay between SFR 25 and SFR 40 per person a night, depending on the number of people sharing the apartment and its location.

Apartments are also available through rental agencies such as **Interhome** with representatives in the United States and offices in Britain and Germany as well throughout most of Europe.

Child care

The Swiss Ski School has a special children's program for kids from 3 to 10 years of age. Open Monday through Saturday from 9 a.m. to 4:30 p.m. It is located behind the train station in Villars. Telephone: (025) 353907. Prices (inlcuding lessons, lifts and lunch): one day—SFR 45; three days—SFR 120; six days—SFR 230.

Club Pré Fleuri, tel. (025) 352348, takes care of skiers and non-skiing children from the ages of three to eleven. Prices (including lunch): half-day—SFR 28; full day—SFR 45; six days—SFR 240.

Le Nid, tel. (025) 351518, takes children from 2 and a half through 5 years. Open from Monday to Saturday from 8:30 a.m. to noon and from 2 to 5 p.m.

Nightlife

Villars is a town where most people bring their good time with them. But for those who insist on leading the disco frenzied nightlife, Villars boasts one of the glitziest and best discos in the Alps, the **New Sam**. New Sam is built on multi-levels and claims one of the best light shows in Europe. As all French-influenced discos in Europe, New Sam doesn't start to roll until very late—translated, this means after midnight.

A much smaller disco with prices not much smaller, but with a younger crowd is the **El Gringo**. It starts up late and claims the smallest light show in Villars.

Depending on whether the crowd is lively, the **Bridge Pub** can be a nice hang-out.

Other Activities

Villars has some of the best-developed non-ski activities in Switzerland. The Sports Center has six covered tennis courts, two squash courts, sauna, and Turkish bath open from 8:30 a.m. to 10 p.m.

There is a covered pool, a covered skating rink, a special fitness club, bowling and horseback riding.

Geneva, Montreux and Lausanne are only a short drive away.

For hang gliding or para-gliding lessons call Denis Giraud or Pascal Balet in Gryon (025) 682683.

Tourist information

Office du Tourisme Villars, CH-1884 Villars, Switzerland. Telephone (025)353232; telex: 456200.

Zermatt

Zermatt, Switzerland's best-known ski resort, was the base from which the famous assaults of the Matterhorn were launched. The killer mountain still casts its shadow over the storybook town, which has developed into one of Europe's premiere winter playgrounds.

Fortunately, Zermatt is a destination resort, that is, the village is difficult enough for weekend skiers to reach to keep most of them away. The town has a total of about 17,000 beds and a lift capacity on the slopes of almost 29,000 people an hour, with more than 93 miles of marked ski trails. Even during the busiest seasons lift lines are not impossibly long and uncrowded slopes can be found.

The town itself is everything a quaint Swiss village is imagined to be: Tiny chalets line the roads and the hotels in the center of town are picturesque. No cars are allowed; a train connection is the only way to arrive in Zermatt. All cars are parked in a large lot outside the village. Unfortunately, the horse-drawn sleighs which carry tourists and townsfolk alike through the town, along with bags of groceries or ski equipment, have been replaced for the most part with speeding electric trucks and carts. When you hear a ringing bell, get to the side of the street.

Where to ski

Zermatt sits at the end of a long valley and is bounded by three major skiing areas. Each area will keep skiers busy for at least two days' worth of thrills.

The Sunnegga area (2290 meters) is quickly reached by an underground cable railway and has ski lifts that reach the Unterrothhorn at 3103 meters (10,170 ft.). This area is the least

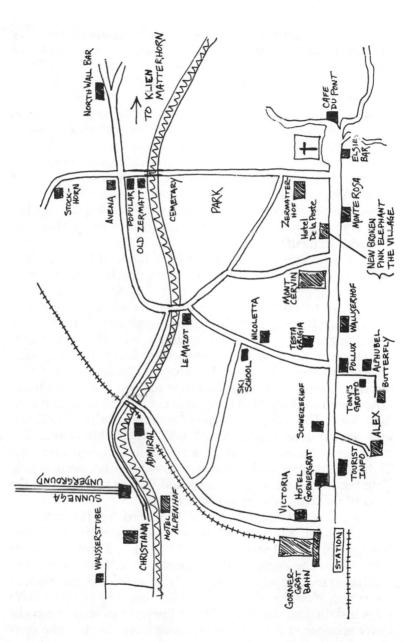

time-consuming to reach. It also gets the most sun in the valley and has recently been equipped with snow-making facilities which stretch from the top station down to Sunnegga. From the Unterrothorn avoid the run returning to Blauherd if you only plan to return back to Unterrothorn. The cable car is the slowest lift on the Sunnegga area and normally has a wait. A better area to explore for intermediate skiers is the Kumme side where a triple chair allows almost continuous skiing and long runs back down to Tuftern will keep experts and intermediates happy. The Fluhalp run down to the lower station of Gant offers good initial skiing but long runouts at the lower levels. For those planning to connect with Gornergrat—it's the only connection, but not recommended for other than advanced-intermediates.

The Gornergrat area is served by a cog railway, which is convenient to get to but the ride takes nearly 45 minutes to reach the upper station. The wait in line at the Gornergrat station can be up to an hour-and-half. However, I have normally found that when the line at Gornergrat is long walk over to Sunnegga and head up the mountain with almost no wait. The Gornergrat area features wide-open skiing at the top back toward Riffelberg and on to Landtunnel. Exciting expert-only terrain is found on the side dropping to Gant from Stockhorn, Rote Nase and Hohtälli. A new cable car links the Hohtälli with Rote Nase. This eliminates the 15 minute hike that until last year adventurous experts faced while their skis were being transported between peaks on a suspended trolley. This new lift is also important in that it now makes the connection possible between the Sunnegga area and Gornergrat without the need to make the above-mentioned hike.

The Klein Matterhorn (Little Matterhorn) area is reached by a series of cable cars. The last one, which reaches the Klein Matterhorn at 3820 meters, or 12,530 feet, is Europe's highest cable car. It can easily take 45 minutes to an hour in order to reach the area's upper stations, but here you can ski throughout the summer on the glacier. New snow-making facilities have been installed on the slopes above Furgg in order to keep the lower sections of the summer ski area open. My favorite runs on the Klein Matterhorn sector are to the far right side of the area, below Hörnli.

From the Klein Matterhorn, skiers shouldn't miss the opportunity for a special adventure involving skiing over to the Italian side of the mountain, visiting Cervinia and having a good Italian meal. Make sure to check weather conditions first, since excessive winds often close the cable cars. This can make the return trip impossible except by a four-hour bus ride. Change your money before you strike out for Italy—the rates are better on this side of the mountain if you plan on changing Swiss francs into Lira. Remember that your lift ticket is not good on the Cervinia lifts—a special lift pass must be purchased on the Zermatt side which will allow use of the Cervinia lifts.

Mountain rating

Every level of skier will find thrills in Zermatt. Each area has runs that make beginners feel like experts, as well as runs that make experts wonder just how expert they really are.

Experts will enjoy the Kumme-side of the Unterrothorn and some of the steep drops back into the village from the Sunnegga area. There are a half-dozen steep, bumpy and exciting runs in the Gornergrat section from Stockhorn, Rote Nase and Hohtälli down to Gant into the valley between Sunnegga and Gornergrat. And although the Klein Matterhorn area is wide open with gentle slopes, the runs from Schwarzsee back into town can be testing. Experts also have almost unlimited opportunities for off-piste skiing; for example, skiing over to Saas Fee is an option with proper equipment and the assistance of a guide or instructor.

Intermediate skiers can be happy in any area but should avoid many of the black runs, which are really for experts. If you take the cable car over to the Stockhorn, Rote Nase and Hohtälli be aware that there is no easy escape from the steep and bumpy.

Beginning skiers will find easy slopes on the Gornergrat and on the Klein Matterhorn glacier. Plus, the Sunnegga area has a good long beginner/lower intermediate trail network from Blauherd down into town.

Ski school

The Zermatt ski school has more than 175 qualified instructors and mountain guides who teach in the traditional Swiss ski-school system. These are 88/89 prices. Telephone: 028-672451.

Individual lessons

for one day	SFR 180
for each additional person	SFR 10
for half day	SFR 90
for each additional person	SFR 5

Group lessons (age 12 to adult)

for one day	SFR 40
for three days	SFR 100
for six days	SFR 210

Children from six-12 get an additional discount from 20-40%.

Zermatt also offers a special "Wedel-Ski Course" lasting a full week. The course includes a seven-day ski pass and an instructor for six full days (Sunday to Friday). The major difference between this program and standard group lessons is that the instructor stays with the group for the entire day, instead of only three or four hours in the morning, and accompanies the group down almost every run within the skiers' abilities. The courses are conducted during the last weeks in November, the first weeks in December, the last three weeks in January, and—a special spring skiing course—the last week in April. Cross-country classes are also available.

To enroll in one of the "Wedel Courses," write in advance to the tourist office and request enrollment forms. The price (including seven-day ski pass): SFR 300.

"The Haute Route" is a classic ski adventure trek between Saas-Fee, Zermatt, Courmayeur and Chamonix. These treks are organized from mid-April through the end of May. This is a tough physical trek and participants should be in good shape for high altitude ski-climbing and must be able to ski in deep snow. The Haute Route tour is normally conducted from early May to the first week in June. Contact: Franz Schwery, mountain guide, 3920 Zermatt, tel. 028-672880. The cost for the classic "Haute Route" tour is approximately SFR 750 which includes guides, acommodation in mountain huts, meals, hotel expenses during the tour, and mountain railway and bus fares.

Lift tickets

The Zermatt lift system has fairly complicated tariff formulas. You can buy ski passes for each of the areas separately or in any combination. You can also buy coupons, which may not be a good deal if you plan to do any serious skiing, since you have to purchase varying amounts of these depending on the area in which you'll be skiing. The coupons are designed for skiers who can spend only a limited time on the slopes. For those who will be skiing the entire day, the best deal is the full combination pass. The 88/89 prices for it are listed below:

for one day	SFR 40
for two days	SFR 86
for three days	SFR 122
for six days	SFR 212
for seven days	SFR 224
for 14 days	SFR 384

Note: If you are plan to ski to Cervinia, you must pay an additional surcharge in order to use Cervinia's uphill lift system. The surcharge for the combination ticket is SFR 46

Accommodation

Zermatt may not be the sort of European resort that offers inexpensive hotels, but compared to resorts in the United States even Zermatt's best hotels are a bargain. When you request rooms do yourself a favor and request a room not facing the main street. For some reason the disco denizens feel compelled to yell and sing at the top of their lungs as they stagger down Main Street after emerging from the music-filled cellars between one and three in the morning.

The prices noted are the middle season prices effective during 10-30 January 1988 and from 10 April to 1 May 1988. Prices for February to 9 April 1988 are approximately 30% higher. Prices are based on double occupancy with half-board.

If you want the best that Zermatt has to offer head for the Mont Cervin (tel. 661121, telex: 472129) or to the Zermatterhof (tel. 661101, telex: 472145). Both are SFR 178. The Hotel Alex (tel. 671726, telex 472112) and the Hotel Nicoletta (tel.661151, telex 472108) are considered the next best in town. The normal daily rate: SFR 162-210.

The hotels listed below feature lower rates and special packages, which are available during low season—early December, January after New Year's and the end of April.

Hotel Alpenhof (tel. 674333; telex: 472139)—By all reports, one of the best hotels in town. A chalet-style hotel located just across from the main Sunnegga lift and only minutes from the center of town. SFR 119

Hotel Admiral (tel. 671555; telex: 472155)—Shares the pool with the nearby Christiania. Friends who have stayed here have nothing but praise for the place. SFR 109-141.

Hotel Monte Rosa (tel. 661131; telex: 472128) Also a Best Western hotel—One of the grand hotels in the center of Zermatt with access to one of the best pools in town. SFR 137.

Hotel Walliserhof (tel. 671174; telex: 472123)—A Best Western hotel. First-class rustic lodgings with an excellent restaurant. SFR 119.

Hotel Butterfly (tel. 673721; telex 472121)—A Best Western hotel. Located in the center of Zermatt with whirlpool and fitness room. SFR 101-141.

Hotel Gornergrat (tel. 671027; telex: 472122)—A fairly modern hotel located in the heart of Zermatt across the street from the train station and adjacent to the Gornergrat station. SFR 101-141.

Alphubel (tel. 673030)—A relatively small two-star hotel located in the middle of Zermatt. SFR 74-96

Burgener Pensione (tel. 671020)—A small, traditionally rustic hotel. SFR 82.

Testa Grigia (tel. 672501; telex: 472108)—This is a bed-and-breakfast which is attached to the Hotel Nicoletta. Through a passageway guests have access to Hotel Nicoletta's swimming pool; a good way to get some of the goodies of a big hotel at bed-and-breakfast prices. SFR 85-110.

Dining

In a resort as highly developed as Zermatt, your biggest dining out decision will be which of the numerous excellent restaurants to visit.

For high-gourmet, high-priced meals try "Le Mazot" where even normally taciturn Germans go out of their way to compliment the owner on great food and service. "Zamoura" in the Hotel de la Post (tel. 671932) has excellent seafood. Then try "Belle Epoque" in the Hotel Nicoletta (tel.661151).

For the middle-of-the-budget crowd test the fare at Tony's Grotto (tel. 674454) tucked up a tiny street between Hotel Pallux and Hotel Derby. For steaks try Victoria (tel. 673871) opposite the railway station. Cafe du Pont has excellent fondue, raclette and wine. The Walliserstubli in the Wiesti section of town (tel.671151) is known for good steaks, filled porkchops and huge portions.

If you're trying to hold down the spending and still get a great meal head for Averna, the Walliserkanne or the Bahnhof Buffet in the railway station. Northwall Bar in the Steinmatte part of town under Hotel Rhodania makes the best pizza in town according to many locals.

One of the other joys of a vacation in Zermatt is stopping in at one of the excellent mountainside restaurants that offer lunch and snacks during the day. Our favorites are the mountain restaurants at Findeln (especially Enzo's), just below Sunegga, the new restaurant at the top of Unterrothorn, and the restaurant at Furri, on the way back from skiing the Klein Matterhorn area.

Nightlife

The fun starts as the lifts close. For après-ski action from 4 p.m. to 6 p.m. stop at the Olympia Stübli on the way back to town from the Sunnegga area. In town try the Popular Pub (younger crowd), Old Zermatt (slightly older and quieter), and Elsie's Bar (most pretentious crowd). Zum See is also a good after ski watering hole.

The night action revolves around the discos in town. For the 18-27 crowd head for The New Broken or the Village—both located in the Hotel de la Poste complex. The Pollux also has an excellent disco. The 27-40 group should go to the Alex which is a beautiful disco with relatively subdued music allowing conversation. The crowd here is a very sophisticated international set. Check into the Pink Elephant in the Hotel de la Poste which has a café atmosphere and often features great jazz.

Child care

The ski school (tel. 672451) offers a program that includes ski instruction for children who are old enough to ski. A one-week course costs about SFR 115.

There is also a kindergarten, which can be contacted through the tourist office or through the hotel where you are staying; It offers baby-sitting services for about SFR 25 a day, including lunch.

Apartments

Apartments are the best chioce if you really want to save money in Zermatt. A well-organized rental system offers apartments for more than 10,000 people a night in town. Write to the tourist office and ask for a list of apartments that will be available during the time you will be in Zermatt. Also, include your requirements, such as the number of people in your party. The office will send a listing of available apartments in town, plus a map showing apartment locations. You then select the apartment you want and correspond either with the tourist board or directly with the apartment owner.

If you are fortunate enough to find an apartment in the Obere-Steinmatte section of town, you'll literally be able to put on your skis at your door and ski to the Sunnegga lifts or the Gornergrat when the snow is still on the streets.

The apartments normally include bed linen and kitchen utensils. You will be charged a visitor's tax and there may be an extra charge for the electricity and heat you use during your stay.

Expect to pay between SFR 25 and SFR 40 per person a night, depending on the number of people sharing the apartment and its location.

Getting there

By train: From Zurich airport via Bern, Spiez, through the Lötschberg tunnel to Brig. At Brig you change to the speical Brig-Zermatt train which leaves from the front of the Brig station. Time: Zurich-Brig—about three-and-a-half hours, Brig-Zermatt—1hr. 20 mins.

From Geneva, trains run directly to Brig in two hours.

By car: Travel via Montreux then up the Valais pass through Sion to Visp where you turn south and follow signs to Zermatt.

If you are driving from Zurich or Basel you can choose to take the Löschberg tunnel from Kandersteg to Goppenstein, above Brig and Visp. This tunnel requires that you load your car onto a train. Trains transit the tunnel every half-hour from 5:35 a.m. to 11:05 p.m. The trip takes only 15 minutes. Cost per car including 9-seat vans, is SFR 15. From Goppenstein continue your drive to Visp then on to Tasch outside of Zermatt. The car park, just outside of the village of Tasch, is about three miles from Zermatt. Buses and trains connect Tasch with Zermatt approximately every 20 minutes; the ride takes eleven minutes.

From the railway station in Zermatt, take a horse-drawn taxi to your hotel or apartment. It's a great way to start a vacation.

Other activities

Zermatt is up to handling non-skiers on vacation, though activities are much more limited due to its distance from other tourist sights and its dedication to skiing. The town has 12 hotel indoor swimming pools; most can be used by non-guests with payment of a daily fee. Also available are 18 saunas, a salt-water swimming pool, two ice skating rinks, curling rinks, covered tennis and squash courts, miles of marked walking trails and cross-country ski circuits.

Tourist information

Tourist information, CH-3920 Zermatt, Switzerland; tel. (028) 661181; telex: 472130.

Italy

Italy has more of the Alps than any other country. Its high-altitude skiing means good snow. Mont Blanc, the highest mountain in Europe, straddles the France-Italy border and the Matterhorn is right on the Switzerland-Italy border.

Italy also has the entire Dolomite mountain range, which many consider to be among the world's most spectacular mountains. Many Italian ski areas here are world-class and the skiing is augmented by the Italian love of life and matchless cuisine and wines.

If the weather changes, there is always a beautiful city, such as Milan, Turin, Verona or Venice, just a few hours away from the slopes.

A note on prices

The prices in this section are from the 1986/1987 winter season. As we went to press, new lift prices arrived, which showed an increase of about five percent. Figure that they will increase approximately five to seven percent during the 1987/1988 winter season. Remember, since prices do change, these should be used as a guide only. Hotels are expected to increase by ten to thirteen percent.

All prices are given in Italian lire (L). The book was researched when the lira was at an exchange rate of L. 1300 to $1. Any subsequent change in the exchange rate will be the biggest factor affecting the prices.

When are the seasons?

Some Italian resorts have adopted a rather complicated series of mini-season. Basically the seasons have remained in tact with the introduction of some in-between seasons. If you follow these season breakouts for planning you will not go too far wrong:

High season: 21 December to 7 January and 5 February to 2 April.

Low season: 8 January to 4 February and 2-30 April.

Pre season: 6 December to 20 December.

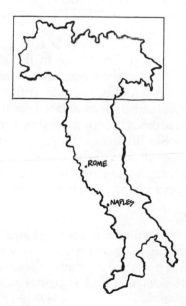

Cortina d'Ampezzo

Ever since hosting the 1956 Winter Olympic games, Cortina's wide, sunny valley in the eastern part of the Dolomites, has come to qualify as one of the world's top ritzy ski resorts.

The town's picturesque square is framed by two massive mountain ridges: To the east lies the connected area formed by Cristallo (2930 meters) and Faloria (2344 meters); to the west, Tofana (2840 meters) and Pocol (2282 meters) form another connected area that is accessible from the town. Further to the west, approaching the Falsarego Pass (2105 meters), the areas of Cinque Torri (2572 meters) and Langazuoi (2746 meters) beckon the adventurous skier.

These areas are loosely connected by a system of buses and taxis, none of which are very expensive.

Where to ski

One suggested approach to Cortina is to ski Faloria in the morning, then ski down to Tre Croce in the afternooon and take the lift up to Son Forca or Staunies in order to ski the rest of the day. Day two could be spent at Tofana or Pocol. Day three might be the Falzarego area and subsequent days could offer repeats of the areas. Or, since Cortina is connected into the Dolomiti Super Ski lift ticket, there is also the choice of skiing down the opposite side of the Lagazuoi, skiing the Corvara area and returning to Cortina by taxi or bus at an extra charge. Whatever your choice, there is plenty of skiing.

Mountain rating

This area is an advanced-intermediate skier's paradise. It is probably a bit too challenging, except for a few slopes, for most beginners and it will push most intermediate skiers.

The intermediate skier will find Tofana, Faloria and Cinque Torri an enjoyable area.

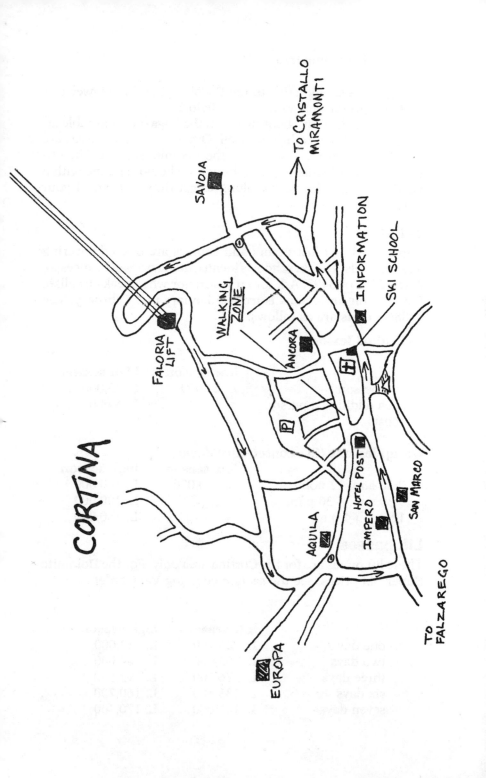

Beginners should stick to the Pocol area and the lower lifts on Cristallo, as well as several at Faloria.

Experts will enjoy shooting down the Lagazuoi; the cablecar ride to the peak is a thrill in itself. Other good expert areas are the Tofana and the last lifts of the Cristallo section. The off-piste skiing is exhilerating, although it should be done with a good guide and instructor along to get the most out of your day.

Ski school

Cortina has 140 instructors and courses are offered covering all skill levels. The ski school is located at Piazza San Francesco, 2; tel. 2911 or 3495. Ask for an instructor who speaks English. Low season for lessons is from 9 January to 4 February. The 1988/98 costs are as follows:

Individual lessons

	low season	high season
one person	L. 28,000	L. 35,000
each additional person costs		L. 5,000

Group lessons (Six consecutive days)

	low season	high season
9:30 a.m.-12 noon	L. 120,000	L. 140,000
9:30 a.m.-4:30 p.m.		L. 300,000
12 noon-4 p.m.		L. 180,000

Lift passes

These lift prices are for the Cortina area only. For the Dolomite Super Ski prices, see the section covering Val Gardena.

	low season	high season
one day	L. 25,100	L. 32,000
two days	L. 53,000	L. 64,000
three days	L. 76,100	L. 91,800
six days	L. 133,500	L. 160,700
seven days	L. 141,600	L. 170,400

Children born after January 1, 1975, get a 30-percent discount; seniors born before December 31, 1928, receive about a 20-percent discount. Bring proper IDs.

Accommodation

Cortina is a fairly mature resort so its hotels in some cases show their age. The quality is uneven in terms of room size and furnishings. If you plan to take a room, make sure that you see it before accepting it. If you have already made a reservation, ask if it is possible to see several rooms from which to make a decision.

The following hotels are centrally located, offer good value and have been visited by a Ski Europe representative. Prices are for "white-week" packages, which include seven days at half pension in a room with bath, per person, double occupancy. A seven-day ski pass costs L. 141.600 extra and ski school for six days is L. 120.000 additional. The low-season (7-21 Jan.) price is given first with high season (4 Feb. - 18 March) in parentheses.

Note: the telephone prefix for Cortina is (0436).

Hotel Miramonti (tel. 4201; telex: 440069) L. 1,120,000 (L. 1,470,000) This is the most luxurious and elegant hotel in town. A bit out of the center of the town.

Hotel Cristallo (tel. 4281; telex: 440090) L. 980,000 (L. 1.260,000) A close second in luxury to the Miramonti.

Hotel Ancora (tel. 3261/3254; telex: 440004) L. 700,000 (L. 1,176,000)—Our favorite hotel in Cortina is located directly on the famous central square. There are more luxurious hotels, but staying at the Ancora is an experience you will savor long after your vacation is over.

Make sure to meet the proprietress, Signora Flavia, who speaks good English and will make your stay memorable.

Europa (tel. 3221; telex: 440004) L. 630,000 (not available) Corso Italia

San Marco (tel. 66941) L. 490,000 (L. 756,000) An absolutely beautiful hotel which has recently been restored with fantastic woodwork. Don't let the price fool you.

Hotel Aquila (tel. 2618) L. 455,000 (L. 700,000)

Hotel Impero (tel. 4246) L. 224,000 (L. 350,000)—Bed-and-breakfast only; some rooms have kitchenettes.

Apartments

There are no rental apartments listed but some18,000 rooms in private houses are available to rent. Prices for these rooms range from L.15,000 to L.25,000 in low season and from L.20,000 to L.35,000 during high season. For more information, contact the local tourist office.

Dining

The following restaurants, recommended by several natives of Cortina, offer good food for a relatively low cost; each offers a meal that costs between L.25,000 and L. 40,000, including house wine.

Tivoli Lacedel, 34; tel. 866400—Overlooking Cortina, Tivoli is rated as one of the best in town. It offers prize-winning home-made pasta dishes. Call for reservations. Closed Mondays.

Baita Fraina Fraina; tel. 3634. Closed Mondays.

Da Beppe Sello Ronco, 68; tel. 3236. Closed Tuesday.

Lago Scin Lago Scin; tel. 2391. Closed Wednesday.

Bellavista Meloncino Gilardon; tel. 861043. Closed Tuesday.

Da Ferruccio Ronco, 115; tel. 866741. Closed Wednesday.

Nightlife

For all its glitzy reputation, Cortina is relatively quiet at night. There is an old wine bar, the Enoteca, which is packed with merrymakers.

The disco at the Europa hotel, The VIP Club, seems to be the main action place. Lub Club, Metro Club and the Bilbo Club are discos that mainly cater to a young crowd earlier in the evening and an older group later on.

Child care

Child care in Cortina is not a school affair. There are scores of private baby sitters and baby-sitting services available through the hotels or private homes where skiers may be staying. Baby-sitting services are relatively inexpensive and children seem to get more than their share of affection from the Italians who take care of them. The ski school also runs a children's ski course for those old enough to begin skiing.

Getting there

We suggest going by car. The closest airport is in Venice (about a two-hour drive). The closest train station is in Calalzo, which is connected to Cortina by a regular bus service. Trains from Innsbruck and Munich arrive at Dubbiaco, a 50-minute bus ride from Cortina. A daily bus service connects Cortina with Venice and with Innsbruck. Both trips take about four hours. Check with your travel agent, since there are some packages that arrange for a special bus to meet incoming skiers at the Milan airport and bus them directly to Cortina.

Other activities

Regular tours to Venice and Verona are scheduled most days. There is also excellent ice skating, bobsledding, horseback riding in the snow, curling championships, World Cup ski races, ice hockey, and more. The tourist office publishes a list of activities and the local paper, *Il Notiziario di Cortina*, provides daily activity summaries in Italian.

Tourist information

The main office is located on Piazzetta S. Francesco, 8. A second, smaller information office is located on Piazza Posta. Call (0436) 3231 or 2711; telex: 440004 AZIENT I.

Cervinia

Walt Disney's film, "Three Men on the Mountain," about the dangerous climb of the Matterhorn created an image of grandeur that characterizes the best of the Alps. That film added to the mystique of the Matterhorn and Zermatt, but there is an other side to the mountain—the Italian side. Cervinia is a forerunner purpose-built resort in Europe. Born through a decree by Mussolini that a ski resort should be developed where the town of Breuil stood, energetic Italians enthusiastically took up "Il Duce's" mandate. However, unlike other purpose-built resorts which have a semblance of central architectural control, Cervinia is the product of a score of fathers. The architecture is the worst of the southern-Italian-square-apartment technique combined haphazardly with neo-modern circular and triangular buildings. A friend, Suni Mallow creator of the Skiing in Europe Newsletter states, "Cervinia has all the charm of frozen pizza."

Despite being ravaged by architects and developers during its infancy, Cervinia manages to delight skiers year after year. The wide-open slopes, the certain snow, and the chance to ski Zermatt on the cheap bring groups of Germans, British, and Americans who zip across the slopes during the week until the weekend hoards from Milano and Torino arrive for their days in the snow.

One other point which is important to note at this juncture in Cervinia is the quantum improvement of the lifts from the village to Plan Maison. Once famous as one of the worst lifts in Europe, the parallel cable cars have been replaced by a sleek six-person gondola. The final stage of the present parallel cable cars should be opened this winter from Plan Maison to Plateau Rosa.

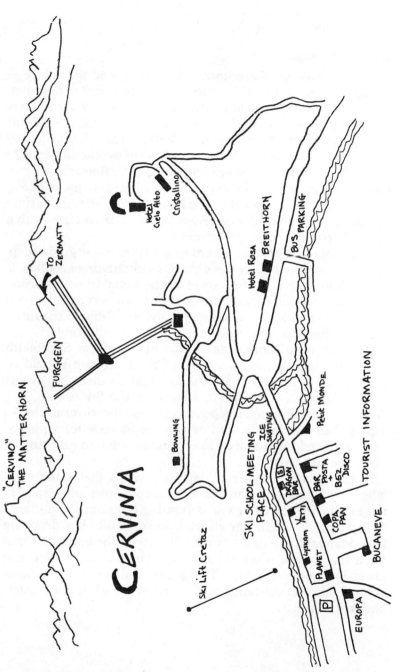

Where to ski

To the Italians the Matterhorn is *Il Cervino,* and the village at the base of the Italian side of the mountain is called Cervinia. Cervinia, without the old charm and beauty of Zermatt, has hotel and lift prices which are about 30 percent lower. Its lift system has been connected with Val Tournanche, a nearby village, so that, today, those who choose to ski the Italian side of the Matterhorn experience more than 100 kilometers of prepared ski runs, which are served by six cable cars, one gondola, five chairlifts and 23 ski lifts. The longest run covers more than 20 kilometers—from Plateau Rosa to Val Tournanche—with a vertical drop of about 1500 meters.

One problem affecting where to ski is the poor guide map. There are at least two or three versions circulating around the resort, but none is useful except in the broadest sense. Don't expect to find well-marked trails either, but fortunately, with relatively easy slopes and access to anything difficult requiring focused effort, anyone can eventually feel comfortable.

The descent to Zermatt starts from Plateau Rosa. Special lift tickets for use on the Swiss side of the mountain should be purchased before you go up the mountain; otherwise, expect to pay double to take the lifts back up the Swiss side. The Zermatt side has much steeper terrain and narrower trails. An expert skier can have a field day on the Swiss side, while the beginning and intermediate skier can find enough easy runs to make the trip enjoyable.

In the Cervinia area experts can perhaps find some challanges with good snow and an adventurous spirit off-piste. Try the Furggen if the cable car is running (you have less than a 50% chance based on my efforts), do some off-piste dropping from Plateau Rosa, or try out the lifts above the Cristallo Hotel for a few bumps. Cervinia is really paradise for novice and lower intermediate skiers. The gentle, wide-open snow fields above Plan Maison build confidence and with a good international image.

Mountain rating

The Cervinia/Val Tournanche slopes support beginner and intermediate skiing skills. Wide open and excellent for practicing, they offer an adequate number of challenging steeps.

Expert skiers may enjoy several great days of cruising the wide slopes but may also become bored. The Furggen (11,360 feet) offers excellent, albeit limited, expert-rated skiing. However, should a group of experts invest in the services of a ski instructor, they'll find the most challenging slopes. Experts will also have a great time on the Zermatt side, and this is the part of the allure of Cervinia as a resort: it lets you take advantage of the savings made possible by staying in Italy and skiing the wilder-and-woolier Swiss side.

Ski school

There is an excellent ski school at Via J. A. Carrel; tel. 949 034. Arrangements can be made at any hotel reception desk, or visit the school.

Ask for an English-speaking instructor.

Daily lessons are available at the approximate rates listed below:

Individual Lessons

one person	L. 24,000 per hour
two people	L. 28,000 per hour
three people	L. 32,000 per hour
four people	L. 34,000 per hour

Group Lessons (includes three hours per day of instruction with about 6-10 skiers per group).

one day:	L. 30,000
three days:	L. 68,000 (low)
six days:	L. 103,000 (low)

A ski instructor for an entire day costs approximately L. 180.000.

Lessons are also available for cross country, ski competition (six-day course), off-piste skiing and summer skiing.

Lift tickets

half day	L. 22,500
one day	L. 29,000
three days	L. 79,000
six days	L. 130,000
seven days	L. 146,000
14 days	L. 224,000

The supplement payable in addition to the Cervinia ski pass to ski in Zermatt costs Lire 20,000. If you do not have a Cervinia pass and want to ski to Zermatt you will have to pay Lire 40,000 for an international lift. If you want to try and ski all of Zermatt in a day, forget it. But realize that the supplementary ticket you purchase in Cervinia is only good for the Klein Matterhorn section of Zermatt. It is possible to strike out for Gornergrat or Sunnegga. In that case wait to get to Zermat to buy a day-pass.

Skiers with a weekly pass in Courmayeur can use it one day in Cervinia and vice versa, the Cervinia week pass is good for a day in Courmayeur.

Accommodation

These hotels and pensions have been visited by a *Ski Europe* representative and offer good value for the money. Prices are per person and include seven days at half pension in a double room with bath during low season (with the middle season—February/March—price following in parenthesis). Where no telex number is listed, reservations can be telexed (in English) through the Cervinia tourist office; telex: 211822 ASTCER I.

Hermitage (tel.948918 or 948998) L. 710,000 (L. 910,000)—A beautiful hotel which is the best choice in Cervinia. Everyone who stays here loves it. Make reservations early since it is very popular.

Cristallo (tel.948125; telex: 210626) L. 770,000 (L. 980,000)—Located up the hill from the main part of town. A hotel shuttle bus takes guests to the town and to the lifts in the morning. Ski directly back to the hotel in the evening. This is a modern luxury hotel which is comfortable but by no means cozy.

Europa (tel.948-660 or 948-661) L. 420,000 (L. 595,000)—Located in the center of town, just a few minutes' walk from the lifts; clean and modern with parking.

Breithorn (tel. 949-042) L. 374,000 (L. 455,000)— Recently renovated, furnished with knotty-pine furniture, this hotel is about two hundred meters from the lifts. Considered to have one of the better restaurants in town.

Bucaneve (tel. 949-119) L. 490,000 (L. 595,000)—Center-of-town location.

Planet (tel. 949-426) L. 455,000 (L. 560.000)—Plain and with little atmosphere, this hotel is, however, relatively modern and very convenient to the slopes.

Lyskamm (tel. 949-074) L. 364,000 (L. 448,000)— Small; perhaps the closest to the slopes.

Mignon (tel. 949-344) L. 350,000 (L. 455,000)—Very small and cozy, just minutes from the slopes. Its rooms have recently been renovated and its restaurant has a good reputation.

Perruquet (tel.949-043) L. 224,000 (L. 238,000)—Bed-and-breakfast only. In the center of town; clean and roomy.

Dining

Cervinia's best and most typical restaurants, such as the Cime Bianche and Les Clochards, are located on the slopes just outside town. Have your hotel call arrange for a van or jeep to pick you up free of charge. Both restaurants mentioned above serve excellent food, so even if your hotel arrangement includes meals, make an effort to eat out at least one night in one of the two.

Try *bagna cauda*: vegetables covered with an anchovy sauce; *tomino*, a type of delicate riccota, normally covered with parsley or peppers; *brisaula*, cured ham from the mountain regions; *larde d'Arnaz*, lard that has been cured in a secret mountain concoction.

Other recommended restaurants: Matterhorn, Serenella, Nuovo KL and Les Neiges d'Atan, a bit out of town but with a menu well worth the taxi ride. The Cave des Guides and the

Copa Pan were recommended by plenty of tourists but not by one Italian.

Nightlife

There is not a lot from which to choose; however, there is a growing English-speaking clientele at the few spots in town.

The town's disco is La Chimera with a younger crowd. The Etoile attracts an older crowd. The two most popular bars are the Yetti and the Dragon Pub. All the bars are within a five-minute walk of each other in the center of town.

Child care

Baby-sitting services and special ski classes for children are available. Contact the tourist office for more information; tel. 949-135 or 949-086.

Getting there

Drive to Cervinia easily from either the Geneva or Milano airport. From Geneva come through the Mont Blanc tunnel from Milano and Torino take the autostrada. then take the Cervinia exit and wind the last 20 miles up to the resort. Buses make the trip between Aosta and Milan but the connections with the local busses in the mountains to Cervinia are useless. Anyone attempting to catch a plane leaving at noon or even 1 p.m. will be forced to take a 6 a.m. bus to Chatillon, then a bus to the superhighway toll booth at Novara, then phone the radio taxi for the Lire 60.000 ride to Malpensa airport. If you have any luggage or can not speak Italian fluently enough to let the taxi dispatcher know where you are standing forget this experience. I hate to think of the trip in the rain as well. There is no other way. The entire Val d'Aosta does not have any international car rental service, which would be wonderful.

Other activities

An Olympic-sized pool is located in the Hotel Cristallo and is open to the public.

Cervinia has a bobsleigh run, an ice-skating rink, and bowling alleys. Day-trips can be made to Geneva, Lausanne, Milano or Torino.

The ski trip over the Alps to Zermatt is a "must-do" side trip.

Fenis Castle and Issogne Palace are less than an hour away and well worth the trip.

The valley's capital city, Aosta, has several excellent Roman ruins. The valley also features Europe's most popular casino in St. Vincent, only 30 kilometers from Cervinia, where rubbing shoulders with the elegant upper crust is fun. Some tour packages offer an overnight at the Grand Hotel Billia adjacent to the casino for one last night of gambling and cabarets.

During the last weekend in January, the Feast of Sant'Orso, one of the largest craft fairs in Italy, takes place in Aosta. Fantastic woodcarvings and other crafts can be purchased at great savings.

During *Carnevale*, the town of Ivrea is one of the wildest places to be in Italy. Costumed residents and a "Battle of the Oranges," in which a castle that's defended by "bad guys" is besieged by "good guys" hurling more than a ton of oranges, make for pre-Lenten fun.

Tourist information

In Cervinia: Via J.A. Carrel, 11021 Cervinia; tel. (0166) 949136 or 949086; telex: 211822 ASTCER I.

Courmayeur

Located at the Italian end of the Mont Blanc tunnel. Courmayeur enjoys one of the best ski resort locations in Europe. Mont Blanc, the highest mountain in Europe guarantees snow, the Alps in the region are among the most spectacular in Europe and Courmayeur lies at the junction of Switzerland, France and Italy. If a skier tires of skiing the slopes of Courmayeur, Cervinia and La Thuile in Italy are within striking distance, Chamonix in France and Verbier in Switzerland can also be reached for a full day of skiing

Where to ski

The major ski area is on the opposite side of the valley from Mont Blanc. This area is centered around the **Plan Checrouit**. The Plan Checrouit is a transfer point for the cable cars which carry skiers up to a ski area serviced by 24 lifts and covering terrain which will keep both the expert, intermediate and beginner happy.

The highest lift arrives at Cresta Arp at 2755 meters (8954 ft.) however the skiing from that point is for experts only, and at that only with guides. The highest skiable point for the run-of-the-mill skier is the Cresta Youla at 2624 meters (8528 ft.). From here you can ski a good, tough intermediate run finishing at Zerotta at 1520 meters (4940 ft.).

The second major skiing area at Courmayeur is Mont Blanc itself. Here a cable car carries skiers in two stages to 3375 meters (almost 11,000 ft.) where they can ski back down towards Courmayeur or over the mountain to Chamonix or take some time skiing on the glacier. This side of the mountain is connected to Chamonix by a cable car which makes getting back to Courmayeur fast and easy. If for some reason a skier manages to arrive at Chamonix after the lifts have closed, it is

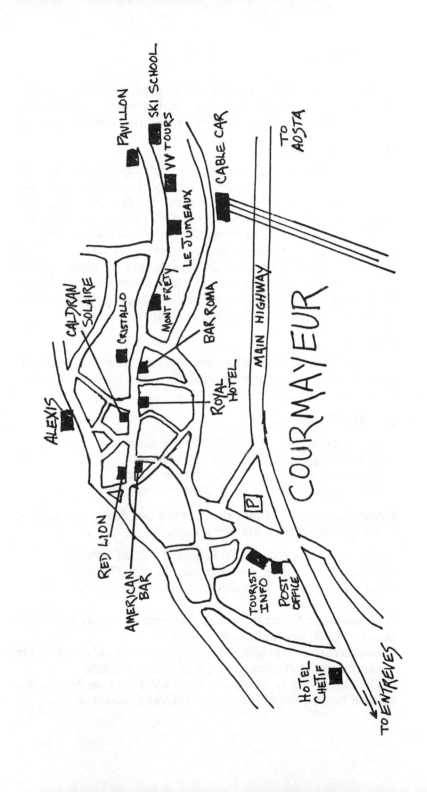

relatively inexpensive to take a taxi through the tunnel back to Courmayeur. Normally there are small groups of skiers with the same problem. Team up and save some Francs.

Mountain rating

If you an absolute beginner, this is probably a mountain you should avoid. Although there are some beginners' areas the terrain is steep enough to take the fun out of skiing if you are over your head. For the intermediate this is heaven. There are plenty of semi-steeps to make the intermediate feel like an expert and enough moguls to keep one's head from swelling. The expert can find some challenging slopes off-piste. The ski instructors can take expert skiers down slopes which will keep them coming back for more. Even the normally marked slopes are good enough for a good day of cruising.

Ski school

The ski school of Mont Blanc has over 100 instructors. Many speak English. Make sure you ask for one who does. Lessons are given every day.

Individual Lessons

one person	L. 24.000 per hour
two people	L. 28.000 per hour
three people	L. 32.000 per hour
four people	L. 35.000 per hour

Group Lessons (includes three hours per day of instruction with about 6-10 skiers per group).

one day:	L. 28.000 (low); L. 30.000 (high)
three days:	L. 64.000 (low); L. 68,000 (high)
six days:	L. 96.000 (low); L. 103,000 (high)

A ski instructor for an entire day costs approximately L. 175.000 plus L. 15,000 per additional person.

Lessons are also available for cross-country, ski competition (6-day course), off-piste skiing and summer skiing.

The ski school is located next to VV Tours on Strada Regionale just up the hill from the Val Veny cable car.

Lift tickets

	low season	high season
for a half day	L. 21.000	L. 21.000
for one day	L. 30.000	L. 30.000
for two days	L. 55.000	L. 55.000
for three days	L. 73.000	L. 82.000
for six days	L. 129.000	L. 152.000
for seven days	L. 146.000	L. 172.000
for 14 days	L. 232.000	L. 288.000

Low season is 8 Jan. to 4 Feb. and 2-30 April 1989.
Lift tickets valid for more than five days include one day of skiing in Cervinia and Chamonix, France.

Accommodation

These hotels and pensions have been visited by a representative of Ski Europe and are recommended. The prices unless otherwise noted are for seven days/half pension, which means breakfast and one meal (normally dinner). High season costs are in parenthesis. There is also a shoulder season between the lowest cost period and the high season with prices between these two ranges. This normally come into effect for the week between low and high season, or for spring skiing.

Hotel Pavilion (telex: 210541; tel: 842420) L. 700.000 (L. 875,000). The best in Courmayeur, with indoor pool, sauna, garage and TV. Only 100 yards to the lifts and the ski school.

Hotel Jumeaux (telex: 214261; tel. 844040) L. 658.000 (L. 826,000). A first category hotel, brand new, and closest to the lifts. Sauna, TV and exercise room.

Hotel Palace Bron (tel: 842545) L. 525.00 (L. 665,000)

Hotel Cresta Duc (tel: 842585) L. 420.000 (L. 539,000)

Hotel Cristallo (tel: 842015) L. 385.000 (L. 490,000)

Hotel Lo Scoiattalo (tel: 842274) L. 310.000 (L. 340,000)
For bed and breakfasts try the Buton d'Or, Croux or the Vittoria. Avoid the Etoile des Neiges about which I only heard complaints.

Dining

Most of the hotel restaurants are good. If you want to get out and explore the local restaurants follow the rule: if it is crowded with locals then it must be good.

Special restaurants in town are the expensive Caldran Solaire on the main street (0165-844609) reservations are suggested and very reasonable Mont Fréty at 21 Strada Regionale, just down from Hotel La Jumeaux (tel. 0165-84.17.86). The Mont Fréty food is every bit as good as the Caldran Solaire and it is perhaps the best place in town to try the regional specialties.

Outside of town is the famous Maison de Filippo (0165-89968) in Entrèves where for a fixed price of Lire 35.000 you are served some 40 courses. The stream of food seems never to end with servings of pasta, antipasti, sausages, contorni, salads, various meats, and baskets of nuts and breads. Another enjoyable restaurant is next to the cross-country area "La Ferret," and known locally as La Floriana (tel. 0165-89947). The owner rightfully prides himself on his local specialties of "Bouden"—blood sausage with beets, fontina cheese, marinated lard and excellent wines.

The local red wines are excellent. Try Donnaz—a strong heavy dry wine; and Enfer d'Avvere—lighter and fruitier. A good Grappa or Genepy finished off the meal in proper Val d'Aosta style.

Apartments

This is a relatively new development for Courmayeur. There are two areas where apartments can be rented for a week.

Residence Les Jumeaux includes two beds, TV/Radio, and maid service. Low season price is approximately L. 630.000 per week. In high season the same room will cost L. 840,000. Additional beds cost another 25%. These are located in the center of Courmayeur next to the main lift. (tel: 844040; telex: 214261).

Residence Universo features several types of rooms including a studio for two or three persons and two room apartments for up to five people. All are equipped with TV and complete kitchen equipment. A free shuttle bus takes guests to the ski lifts in the town. Low season rates range from L. 316.000 per week for a two-person studio to L. 650.000 for a two room apartment for four or five persons. In high season prices will be L. 440.000 for the two-person studio and L. 800,000 for the two-room apartment for up to five. Cleaning will cost a maximum of L. 60.000 for the week. Make reservations through VV Tours, Strada Regionale, 47, Courmayeur, telephone (0165) 842061 or telex: 210260.

Nightlife

The English-speaking crowd hangs outs in the Bar Roma on the main street. A few can be found in the American Bar and the Red Lion. The main street is the best place to wander. Keep an ear and eye alert for the sounds of a good bar and go on in. The most popular discos are Le Abatjour and Le Trou, which also has a good restaurant. The Clochard, a bit outside of town in Dolonne, is also an excellent disco.

Child care

The ski school runs an all-day ski course which starts at 9 a.m. at the ski school and lasts until 4 p.m. The cost for one-day is L. 36.000, and for six consecutive days is L. 170.000. These prices include a snack at lunch for the children.

Getting there

The closest airports are Geneva and Milan. Both are within a two-hour drive of Courmayeur. Train and bus service connects Milan with Courmayeur. Bus service connects Courmayeur with Geneva. Car rentals are available from both airports.

Other activities

Geneva, Milan and Torino offer excellent sightseeing and museums. The Val d'Aosta is spectacular in itself and features one of the best collections of castles in Italy as well as excellent Roman ruins in Aosta, the capital city. During the last weekend in January the "Feast of St. Orso" is held in Aosta. It is one of the largest crafts fairs in Italy featuring fantastic woodcarvings and other mountain crafts. During *carnevale* time, the town of Ivrea is one of the wildest places to be in Italy. The residents are decked out in costumes reminiscent of "Star Wars." They participate in the "Battle of the Oranges" which features a castle defended by the bad guys being assaulted by the good guys who hurl over a ton of oranges during the seige. The valley also boasts a casino in St. Vincent. Milan in addition to its sights features the La Scala opera house, the largest in Italy and one of the best opera companies in the world.

Tourist information

Courmayeur is as much as any place in the world a one-tourist agency town. In fact the tourist agency doubles in many cases as the tourist office. They also happen to own the lift system in Courmayeur. For any additional information contact: VV Tours, Strada Regionale, 47, tel. (0165) 842061 or 844161, or telex: 210260.

La Thuile

Once merely a small collection of older second-class hotels—
served by even fewer lifts—La Thuile has become one of Europe's ski bargains during the past few years. The reason: the addition of an all-purpose resort, coupled with a link-up of the ski-lift system to slopes served by neighboring French resort, La Rosière.

La Thuile lies at the end of the road that leads to the Little St. Bernard Pass. The pass is normally closed during the winter, thus the resort can be reached then from the Italian side of the valley only. This Alpine region is one of Europe's most spectacular and, if wanderlust strikes, within easy reach of other major resorts such as Cervinia, Courmayeur and Chamonix.

Where to ski

La Thuile's slopes face north and northeast, crisscrossed by 80 kilometers of prepared ski runs. These range from the easiest—nicknamed the *"Autostrada"* due to its wide, gentle run—to expert slopes that drop from the first cable car station back to the town below.

Expert skiers looking for the steeps can bypass La Thuile. But for those want a good, all-around vacation at a reasonable price, La Thuile may be just what the doctor ordered.

The French side

La Rosière's slopes are neither as challenging nor as extensive as those on the Italian side. With about 40 kilometers of prepared runs, the area is currently undergoing a lift-extension program, which is designed to double the skiing terrain over the next two to three years.

The fascinating change in culture and the chance to alternate French cooking with Italian cuisine makes a trip to La Rosière a real pleasure.

The combined areas, La Thuile and La Rosière, boast 120 kilometers of prepared runs, serviced by 27 ski lifts that range from cable cars to chairlifts, T-bars and poma lifts.

La Thuile's elevation is 1441 meters and the highest point reachable by lift has an elevation of 2642 meters. La Rosière lies at a higher elevation than La Thuile (1850 meters), but does not have as great a vertical drop.

Mountain rating

This area has something for everyone. Beginners can look forward to plenty of cruising along what the Italians call the *Autostrada*.

Intermediates will also find runs galore to keep themselves happy but, unfortunately, experts may become disappointed after about a day on the slopes. The area is just not extensive nor challenging enough for this level of skier. However, nearby Courmayeur and some excellent off-piste areas will provide some good challenges for experts.

Ski school

The ski school employs approximately 26 instructors. Ask for one who speaks English and, since these are limited Do not wait until the last minute to make lesson arrangements if you want to have hope of an English-speaking instructor.

Lessons are conducted daily at the approximate rates listed below:

Individual lessons

	high season	low season
for one person	L. 24,000	L. 22,000
for two persons	L. 28,000	L. 25,000
for three persons	L. 32,000	L. 28,000
for four persons	L. 35,000	L. 31,000

Group lessons are given three hours each day.

three days	L. 55,000
six days (a.m.)	L. 85,000
six days (p.m.)	L. 60,000
	(with White Week)
twelve days	L. 140,000

An instructor's fee for the entire day is normally between L.140,000–175,000.

Lift tickets

Many hotels include lift tickets with the weekly "White-Week" packages. If purchased separately, tickets are priced as follows:

	low season	high season
half day	L. 16,500	L. 19,000
one day	L. 24,500	L. 27,500
three days	L. 63,000	L. 73,000
six days	L. 110,000	L. 130,000
seven days	L. 125,000	L. 150,000

A photo is required for lift passes valid for three or more days. Tickets include use of all lifts in La Thuile and in La Rosière. A pass valid for six non-consecutive days of skiing can be purchased for L. 150,000.

Accommodation

The soul of La Thuile is the Planibel holiday center. This center sparked the area's growth and is one of the driving forces behind the linking of La Thuile With La Rosière. True, there are other hotels and pensions, but for all intents and purposes, Planibel *is* La Thuile for accommodation, dining, recreation and nightlife.

Featured are restaurants, two swimming pools, squash courts, a disco-ice-skating rink, exercise room, steam bath, sauna, bowling, a game room that offers billiards and video games, and the area's hottest disco.

A cable car provides direct connections to the hotel and cars can be parked underground.

The low-season rate for half-pension—including access to the facilities—is L. 345,000 per person per week, when two share a double room. During the Christmas vacation period the price jumps to L. 645.000 per week half-pension.

Apartments

The Planibel Residences are apartments within the Planibel complex. Each apartment accommodates two to six people and features a kitchen, a balcony overlooking the slopes, ski-storage area and Scandinavian pine furnishings.

The rate for a studio apartment that can easily accommodate four people during low season, is L. 798,000; during February and high season is L.1,000,000; during Christmas vacation is L. 1,500,000.

Prices include cleaning service, all bedding and electricity. There are TV, radio and phone connections in each apartment. The rates do not include meals. However, there is a well-stocked supermarket in the complex, several excellent restaurants in the hotel itself and several other restaurants in town.

Child care

Supervised activities for young children can be arranged with the hotel. Special beginning ski lessons are offered for children, normally running from 9:30 a.m. until 4 p.m.

Other activities

An extensive cross-country ski course has been laid out in town. The hotel extras, such as pool, sauna, steam bath and exercise room, cost L.5000; squash courts cost L.10,000; and the ice skating rink, including skate rental, costs L.5000.

Getting there

By car, La Thuile is about a half hour south of Courmayeur; within two and a half hours from either the Geneva or Milan airport. Bus service connects La Thuile with Courmayeur and with Aosta, with further connections to the airports. Rental cars are available at both airports.

Tourist information

The Azienda di Soggiorno e Turismo can send information on the region, restaurants and hotels. Contact it at 11016 La Thuile (Val d'Aosta); tel. (0165) 884179. Or, contact Planibel Hotel and Residences,11016 La Thuile (Val d'Aosta); tel. (0165) 884541; telex: 215016 PLANIB.

Madonna di Campiglio

One of the jewels of the Brenta Dolomites in Trento is Madonna di Campiglio. The elegant resort is packed with hotels and is situated at 1550 meters amid beautiful, easy-going ski terrain. Long before Madonna di Campiglio became famous as a winter playground, it was the favorite summer vacation spot of Austrian royalty, providing a stunning backdrop of brilliant mountain flowers and crystal clear lakes.

Where to ski

The skiing areas literally surround the town. Start at one end of town and ski around the village—only a short walk is needed in order to complete the circle. Most of the hotels are at the base of the slopes, making them convenient for both lunch breaks and quitting time.

The immediate area is linked with two others, Folgarida and Marilleva. The area has thirty-four lifts and more than one hundred kilometers of prepared runs. The Folgarida and Marilleva areas add another twenty lifts and fifty kilometers of prepared slopes.

The highest point accessible by lift is Groste at 2510 meters.

Cross-country skiers will discover that this region is a mecca for the sport. Pinzolo, about twenty minutes away, hosts the 24-hour endurance race and the Campo Carlo Magno boasts one of the world's best expert cross-country courses.

Mountain rating

The area is good for beginning and intermediate skiers. While the 3 Tre, Fortini and Spinale will give experts some good exercise, all in all, the area is mellow. During the Spring, when

helicopter skiing is possible, experts can ski off-piste and adventurous types can try ski mountaineering.

Ski school

Check with your hotel or in town for recommendations for the
best English-speaking ski instructors. There are eight competitive ski schools, with a total of140 instructors, that offer lessons; the prices, however, have been stabilized.

Individual lessons (per hour)

for one person	L. 29,000
for two persons	L. 33,000
for three persons	L. 39,000
for four persons	L. 44,000
for five persons	L. 50,000

Group lessons are given two hours each day for six days. Prices
below are per person:

for six persons	L. 99,000
for eight persons	L. 87,000

Children's lessons are given three hours each day for six days.
There is a maximum limit of ten per group. Cost: 113,000

Lift tickets

Tickets for six or seven days are often included in "White-Week"
packages. They do not include skiing in Folgarida and Marilleva, but you can purchase these Skirama passes separately for
L. 26,000 a day.

These prices are for high season. Low season prices are approximately ten percent less.

one day	L. 27,000
six days	L. 154,000
seven days	L. 175,000

Note: six- and seven-day tickets require a photograph.

Accommodation

Madonna's hotels, for the most part, are modern. The ones
listed here have been selected on the criterion of price and

were visited by a Ski Europe representative. The prices listed below include seven days' stay during low season, full pension (breakfast, lunch and dinner).

A six-day ski pass, seven-day pass for the town's swimming pool, free Wednesday ice skating, and free shuttle bus service to the lifts will costs L. 142,000 during low season and L. 154,000 in high season.

High-season prices are given in parentheses.

Hotel Des Alpes (tel. 40000) L. 924,000 (L. 1,267,000)—Perhaps the town's best hotel; a beautiful hotel built around the former hunting lodge of the Austrian emperors. The Milva restaurant is excellent.

Hotel Golf and Hotel Savoy Palace L. 707,000 (L. 987,000)— Excellent high quality, elegant hotels with all the amenities.

Miramonti (tel. 41021) L. 625,000 (L. 825,000)

Hotel Palu (tel. 41280) L. 504,000 (L. 672,000)—Town's best value; a beautiful hotel.

Majestic (tel. 41080) L. 469,000 (L. 630,000)

Touring (tel. 41051) L. 420,000 (L. 553,000)

Laura (tel. 41246) L. 441,000 (L. 581,000)

Detassis (tel. 41102) L. 343,000 (L. 462,000)

Apartments

Residence Roch has apartments for three, four or five people. During low season expect to pay approximately L. 140,000-200,000 per person a week during low season; during high season—L. 220,000-250,000. The price includes daily maid service (except kitchen clean-up). Rent garage space for L. 55,000. Both sauna and solarium are available.

The tourist board can provide additional listings of apartments in the same approximate price range and help with all arrangements.

Dining

Probably the best restaurant in town, Mildas, which is located in the Des Alpes, offers dining as good as can be found in any

European ski resort. The atmosphere is elegant and the service is excellent. You will pay a premium price but this is a highly recommended splurge. For reservations, call 42877.

Other recommended restaurants are: Artini (tel. 40122), La Cucina della Streghe (tel. 42388) and Pappagallo (tel. 42717). Perhaps the most typical restaurant in town is Malga Montagnoli (tel. 42670). Two good pizzerias are Le Roi (tel. 42670) and Zodiaco (tel. 41686).

Nightlife

The Grand Hotel Des Alpes has a pricey disco, as well as a very cozy piano bar, where you can nurse a drink for as long as you want. Each evening a cabaret is presented in the restored Hapsburg ballroom. Less refined and more of a blast is the Stork Club, which features a country bar upstairs and both a pizzeria and full-blown disco downstairs. Find English-speaking tourists and Scandinavians here.

Child care

Both children's ski classes and a special kindergarten are available. Contact the tourist office for details.

Getting there

By car, Madonna di Campiglio is two hours north of Verona. The closest airports are in Milan and Venice. Both offer rental car services. If driving from Milan, take the Brescia exit and follow the signs for Idro Lake, Tione, then Campiglio.

To reach Madonna di Campiglio by train, go to Trento and then transfer to a bus (the stop is about fifty yards from the Trento train station), which runs on a regular schedule during the day.

Other activities

Once you are in Madonna, it is not an easy task to get out. But, if one insists, Venice can be reached in about three and a half hours. Verona, with its giant Roman amphitheater and Romeo and Juliet legends, is about two hours away.

During *carnevale* , Madonna di Campiglio hosts many costume balls and special events.

Tourist information

The tourist information office, or Azienda Autonoma Soggiorno, in Madonna di Campiglio is located in the center of the resort in the Centro Rainalter. They are well organized with information and a capability to make reservations in hotels and pensiones. To write address to Tourist Office, Centro Rainalter, 38084 Madonna di Campiglio (Trento). Telephone is (0465) 41026 or 42000. Telex is 400882 CARUPI.

Sauze d'Oulx

Sauze d'Oulx is part of the Italo-Franch "Milky Way system." The "system" has been undergoing political maneuvers worthy of any entangled bureacracies. Where once all resorts in the area were interconnected and shared lift passes, now the future us cloudy. As originally organized, the "Milky Way" was a consortium of ski areas that had interconnected their ski-lift systems and sold ski tickets that were valid for the entire region. Nine towns made up the "galaxy"; however, of the nine, only four serve as ski area hubs. These are: Sauze d'Oulx, Sestrière, San Sicario, and Mont Genèvre. The other five towns have ski lifts that link Up with the larger areas but offer little skiing in their own right. As of press time the "system" was being pieced together again, but it needs a lot of repairing and I don't expect to see the total interconnection of the resorts for another few years. In the meantime, Sauze d'Oulx is the best destination for English-speaking skiers.

Sestrière, packed with spanking new condos, is perhaps the best known. It was one of the first single-theme resorts in Europe. Today, it hosts a Club Med village. Chic and somewhat pretentious, it's not the type of resort an American or Englishman will feel comfortable in unless he is fluent in Italian.

Mont-genèvre is actually in France and a bit out of the way for the main skiing action. Sauze d'Oulx, though, manages to combine good skiing with a fantastic, easy-going atmosphere. Curiously, the mix of tourists virtually guarantees that any English-speaking visitor will make friends and have a great time. Excellent pubs and inexpensive hotels make Sauze d'Oulx come highly recommended as your home base.

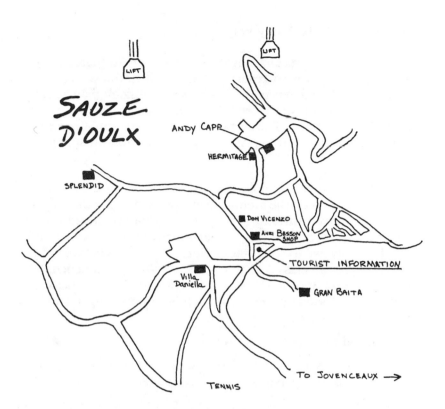

Skiing Sauze d'Oulx and Sestrière

Sauze d'Oulx has more than one hundred kilometers of prepared ski runs, serviced by twenty-six lifts. However, the resort's ski pass is also valid for Sestrière, which lies just over the mountain and offers another twenty-two lifts and more than one hundred kilometers of runs. Sestrière also boasts the largest and most modern snow making equipment in Europe. Sauze d'Oulx' runs wind through deep forests, while those in Sestrière are, for the most part, above the tree line. The Sauze d'Oulx runs are asprout with small restaurants and cafes where thirsty, hungry skiers can relax. Sestrière, on the other hand, has limited facilities on the slopes.

Mountain ratings

Elevations in Sauze d'Oulx that are accessible by lift range from 1500 to 2700 meters. Sestrière is a bit higher, with lifts running from 2035 to 2823 meters. Sauze, together with Sestrière, makes for a good, all-around resort. Experts will find few thrills in Sestrière, although it is perhaps a bit more difficult than Sauze.

Intermediate and advanced intermediate skiers will find plenty to do in both areas. The terrain is good for beginners and a cruiser's dream when the snow is good and the sun shines.

Ski schools

Sauze has two ski schools: the traditional "Sauze Sportina" school is located on the mountain at Sportina and is the largest with eighty-five instructors; the second, more non-traditional "Sauze d'Oulx" school has its headquarters in the town and employs only twenty instructors. Both schools offer a full range of classes for all classes of skiers, plus off-piste and helicopter skiing. "Sauze Sportina" has relatively fewer English-speaking instructors. "Sauze d'Oulx" staff tends to be younger and its teaching methods more modern.

Individual lessons (per hour)

for one person	L. 24,000
for two to five persons	L. 29,000

Group lessons are given three hours each day for six days:

low season	high season
L. 77,000	L. 97,000

Lift tickets

	low season	high season
one day	L. 31,000	L. 35,000
two days	L. 55,000	L. 62,000
six days* (M-Sat)	L. 95,000	L. 125,000
seven days*	L. 110,000	L. 140,000

These prices apply to hotel guests in Sauze d'Oulx. Prices are about twenty-five percent higher for those staying outside of town.

Accommodation

These hotels have been visited by a Ski Europe representative and are listed in descending order of comfort. The hotels are not luxury class but all are good value, are comfortable and have friendly proprietors.

Prices are for seven days during low season at full pension (breakfast, lunch and dinner). High-season prices are given in parentheses.

Il Capricorno (tel. 85273) L. 600,000 (L.700,000)— Perhaps one of the all-time hotel finds in Europe; beautiful rooms, excellent food and fantastic owners. One of our favorites in all the Alps. The kitchen rates a Michelin star, which means that a guest staying at full pension gets prize-winning meals three times a day. Take a ski lift to reach the hotel. Half-pension.

Villa Daniella (tel. 85196) L. 350,000 (L.440,000)— Its small rooms are well appointed and were recently renovated; has the second-best restaurant in town.

Hermitage (tel. 85385) L.350,000 (440,000).

Gran Baita (tel. 85183) L.350,000 (L.440,000)

Splendid (tel.85172) L. 350,000 (L.440,000)

Dining

Be sure to visit Il Capricorno at least once. The lunch is fabulous and the restaurant's right on the slopes. Villa Daniella serves exceptional meat dishes. Don Vicenzo has great antipasti and atmosphere. Old Inn is good for steaks. La Griglia is the place for pizza.

Apartments

The Tourist Office's English-speaking staff can recommend apartments. Expect to pay between L.120,000 and L.180,000 per person a week, depending on the size of the apartment.

Nightlife

The town is not very big. Most discos were recently closed, but new ones are opening. Try Babaiaga, Charlie Brown, and VIP for dancing. Andy Capp is the place to be when the lifts close.

Child care

A kindergarten ski school is available for children three years and older. Cost is L.225,00 for seven full days. For younger children, 6 to 8 months, there is a full-service kindergarten that is staffed with nurses. Cost is about L.5500 an hour.

Getting there

The closest airports are Turin (93 kms/1.5 hours), Milan (230 kms/3 hours) and Geneva (190 kms/3 hours). Rental cars are available at all three airports.

The main Rome-Paris train line stops in Oulx, just fifteen minutes by bus from Sauze d'Oulx. Trains leave for Turin and Milan twelve times a day.

Other activities

Sauze has a public sauna and covered tennis courts. A ski shuttle bus runs through The town every fifteen minutes and provides easy access to the lifts.

For a group of people, an organized evening at the Hotel Monte Triplex, complete with snow cats and torchlight skiing, is worth looking into.

Tourist information

The local tourist office has been organized to deal with English-speaking visitors. Call or write for information and reservations: Tourist Office, Piazza Assietta 18, 10050 Sauze d'Oulx (TO); tel. (0122) 85009; telex: 214321A ABI.

Val Gardena

While a trip through the spectacular Italian Dolomite mountain range is worthwhile in itself, when combined with the experience of skiing the largest and most extensive ski-lift system in the world, a vacation in the Dolomites rates as tops. And Val Gardena, with some of the lowest prices in Europe, is hard to beat.

The valley is a stronghold of the Ladin culture and its residents speak "Ladin," a Latin derivative, as their first language. They also speak German and Italian. The Ladin culture is centered in the four main Dolomite valleys, in eastern Switzerland and in Italy's far northeast.

The Gardena valley has three towns. The first and the largest coming from Bolzano is Ortisei. The second is St. Cristina, and the third, just at the start of the Gardena Pass, is Selva. St. Cristina is spread out along the highway and does not have much of a town center in which to congregate after skiing. For this reason, book accommodation in Ortisei or Selva if you want to have a good time. Ortisei, further away from the interconnected ski areas, has a more active nightlife. Selva, smaller and closer to the other Dolomiti slopes, is quiet but you can still have a good time. The atmosphere is more German than Italian with a beer-hall flavor.

Where to ski

The interconnected Super Ski Dolomite lift system, with 440 lifts, reaches more than 1050 kilometers of prepared slopes, plus hundreds of kilometers of off-piste skiing through rocky crags and spectacular mountain scenery. Seceda is the highest elevation reached by the lift system in the Ortisei/Selva region at 2498 meters directly above Ortisei.

Perhaps the biggest drawing card for the region besides the

panorama is the Sella Ronda, a 26-kilometer section of inter-connected runs with 20 kilometers of ski lifts, allowing skiing around the Sella mountain group. This full-day expedition involves visiting eight different ski areas. The runs are well marked and the Sella Ronda can be skied either clockwise or counter-clockwise. Any advanced beginner can complete the basic circuit. Better skiers will find many opportunities for adventurous detours.

The major requirement for doing the entire Sella Ronda in one day is stamina. Intermediates should allow about five and a half to six and a half hours of skiing time and should start early enough to get back over the final passes before the lifts close at 5 p.m. If you are planning to do the Sella Ronda, do it on a Tuesday or Wednesday. During the end of the week many ski classes tackle the circuit for their final project; during the weekend lift lines are at least twice as long and can add another hour to an hour and a half to the total time necessary to complete the runs.

Mountain rating

If judged solely on the extensiveness of its skiing opportunities, this area might be considered one of the best. However, expert skiers will have to go off-piste for real excitement. While there are some hair-raising runs above Arabba, Selva and St. Christina, expert skiers in search of off-piste action should hire the services of a good guide. Try the Langkofel-Gap or the Pordoi-Gap at your own risk. If you decide to go without a guide, be sure to check in with the ski school for a briefing on your proposed route with regard to snow conditions and avalanche warnings.

The intermediate and the beginning skier will find ample suitable terrain. When a skier tires of one area, he just heads over to another for variety. The Alpi di Siusi above Ortisei is a beginners' paradise.

Ski school

The Ortisei Ski School has 60 instructors and is located in the public swimming pool building. St. Cristina and Selva also have ski schools. Prices are uniform throughout the valley. Most ski instructors speak a little English, but make sure yours does by asking for an English-language instructor.

Individual lessons (per hour)

one person	L. 27,000
two persons	L. 34,000
three persons	L. 40,000

Group lessons

Four-day course (14 hours)	L. 95,000
five to six days (21 hours)	L. 125,000

Childrens' Ski School Prices (4-12)

One day	L. 50,000
Five days	L. 210,000
Six days	L. 230,000

Lift tickets

Local area lift tickets can be purchased. However, the difference in price between these tickets and the "Super Ski Dolomite" pass is small. The prices listed below are for the Super Ski Dolomite lift pass.

	low season	high season
for one day	L. 26,500	L. 31,900
for two days	L. 52,800	L. 63,400
for three days	L. 75,700	L. 91,000
for six days	L. 132,500	L. 159,400
for seven days	L. 140,400	L. 169,000
for fourteen days	L. 238,000	L. 286,600

Note: Children born after January 1, 1975, and seniors born before Decemeber 31, 1928, get 20 percent discounts. Make sure you have proper identification and be sure to ask for the discount.

Ski passes for eight days or more will require a photograph. Long lines are the norm for obtaining these passes on Saturday. You'll get your pass quicker on Sunday afternoon and Monday morning.

Accommodation

The following hotels and pensions come recommended by locals who have also traveled extensively in the United States. Except where noted, accommodations are in Ortisei, the valley's largest town. They are listed in descending order of "luxury." Prices are for "white-week" packages, which include seven days at half pension (breakfast, with either lunch or dinner) and room with bath (confirm when making reservations). The low-season price is given first, with the high-season fee in parentheses. The prices do not include lift tickets.
Note: the telephone prefix for Ortisei is 0471.

Hotels

Aquila-Adler (tel. 76203) No white week. One of the best, in the center of town. Normal daily rate 78,000 LS (90,000 HS).

La Perla (tel. 76421) L. 310,000 (L.340,000) Via Digon—Our favorite in the area. Beautiful; a bit out of town, however, there's bus service to the lifts and a pool.

Grien (tel. 76340) L.450,000 (L.546,000)

Hell (tel. 76785) L. 415,000 (L. 491,000) Via Promenada. This was formerly only a pension and now is a four-star hotel.

Gardena (tel. 76315) L. 346,500 (L.385,000) Via Vidalong— Has a good restaurant.

Posta (tel. 76392) No white week. Via Rezia—Right in the middle of town. Normal rate: L.50,000 LS (L.60,000 HS).

Cosmea (tel. 76464) L.305,000 No white week during high season.) Via Setil—Has a good restaurant.

Note: In Selva, try the Antares, Gran Baita, and Aritz which are among the best. Des Alpes, is a bit less expensive.

In Corvara, the La Perla is at the top of the heap mainly due to an excellent restaurant.

Apartments

The tourist office has an extensive listing of vacation apartments that can be rented for a minimum period of one week. General descriptions included in its brochure indicate TV, garage, balcony, etc. The apartments all have fully furnished kitchens, but not all provide bedding, which may entail a small extra cost. Prices listed below vary according to the level of furnishing and apartment location (Christmas-New Year's rates are higher and require a minimum two-week stay):

	low season	high season
two beds	L. 170-250,000	L. 220-390,000
four beds	L. 250-430,000	L. 350-550,000
six beds	L. 330-550,000	L. 440-800,000

Private rooms

A great chance to save money and get to know the natives awaits skiers who speak either German or Italian. Rooms rented in private homes include breakfast. Once again, the prices vary depending on the room. The price ranges for a room with bath (per person, per day) are:

Low season	L. 12,500 to L. 17,500
Middle season	L. 13,000 to L. 19,000
High season	L. 15,000 to L. 21,000

Dining

For an authentic "Ladin" meal, head off to the Stua Catores on Sacunstr. 47. This restaurant is where the President of Italy comes when he is in the region. The food is hearty and the atmosphere rustic and unpretentious. Don't be afraid to ask among the restaurant patrons for someone who speaks English and can help you with the menu selection.

Other recommended restaurants:

Concordia Romstr. 41; tel.76276
Ramoser Bahnhofstr. 4; tel. 76460
Waldrand Furdenanstr. 9; tel. 76385
Hotel Adler Stuben Reziastr.; tel. 76203
Hotel Gardena Vidalongstr.; tel. 76315
Sarteur (for great pizza), Bahnhofstr. 60; tel. 77663.

If you can manage to be in Corvara for lunch, splurge at the Hotel La Perla. The food is excellent and the setting is memorable.

Nightlife

Nightlife in Val Gardena is rather tame, but there is a collection of good bars that offer some local music.

Try the Traube (very rustic); also, the piano bar, L'Chamin, and the Cianel, both on Vidalongstraße, are excellent, especially at ski-lift closing time. Sneton features good local music. Cafe Haiti serves the best coffee and cakes.

Child care

A ski school accepts children from about the age of five and offers a course that runs from 9:30 a.m. until 4 p.m. with midday supervision. Ski-school prices are the same as those for adults. Register at the ski school office.

A ski kindergarten is available for children who either are under four or five or not interested in learning to ski. It opens at 8 a.m. and accepts children from the ages of two and a half to eight years old. Half-day and full-day programs are available. Reservations are not necessary. Call 76153 after 10 a.m.

full day (with lunch)	L. 25,000
half day (with lunch)	L. 19,000
half day (without lunch)	L. 15,000

Getting there

The closest airports are in Venice (about three hours' drive), Milan (about four hours' drive) and Munich (about three hours' drive). Major rental car companies have offices in Ortisei and at the airports.

Trains reach Bolzano, which is connected to Ortisei by five buses daily. A taxi to Ortisei from Bolzano will cost about L.50,000 but will require some negotiating.

Other activities

Ortisei is a woodcarving capital. Take time to browse through the stores and, if the urge strikes, enjoy a short introductory woodcarving course that is given Tuesday through Thursday in the evenings.

The music society schedules concerts during the winter. Horse-drawn sleigh rides are given on the Alpe di Siusi. There is a swimming pool and a new public sauna and steam bath.

The tourist office or your hotel will provide a free schedule of events, including folk nights, band concerts, film evenings, ice hockey games and toboggan races.

As in the rest of the Alps, *Carnevale* season hosts parades, costume balls and crazy ski races.

Tourist information

Tourist Information Office, Reziastrasse 1, 39046 Ortisei/St. Ulrich; tel: (0471) 76328 or 76749; telex: 400305.

France

The French have skied for decades. Resorts like Chamonix, Megève and Val d'Isère were at the forefront of the development of alpine skiing. But many of the modern French resorts have only recently been "purpose-built" for skiing. This means entire villages, such as Avoriaz, Tignes, Courchevel 1800 and Flaine, have been created with skiing uppermost in the designers' minds. The result has been thousands of low-priced apartments and hotels that combine the convenience of walking outside your door, stepping into your skis and starting to ski on some of the most extensive ski slopes in the world. For a skier, it's only a short step into heaven—one that is affordable. The après-ski life is great and the food and wine is France at its best.

A note on prices

The prices in this section are valid for the 1987/1988 winter season. You can expect them to increase approximately five to seven percent during the 1988/1989 winter season. Use the prices as a guide.

All prices are given in French francs (FFR). Information for the book was gathered when the franc was at an exchange rate of FFR 6 to $1. Any subsequent change in the exchange rate will be the biggest factor affecting the prices.

The seasons

High season—21 December 88 - 5 January 89, 28 January to 11 March, and 25 March to 9 April.

Low season—5-28 January then 11-25 March.

Use these as general guidelines since some resorts may have slightly adjusted seasons due to local school holidays. Check with the resort you choose to get the exact dates if you are planning your trip on a season borderline.

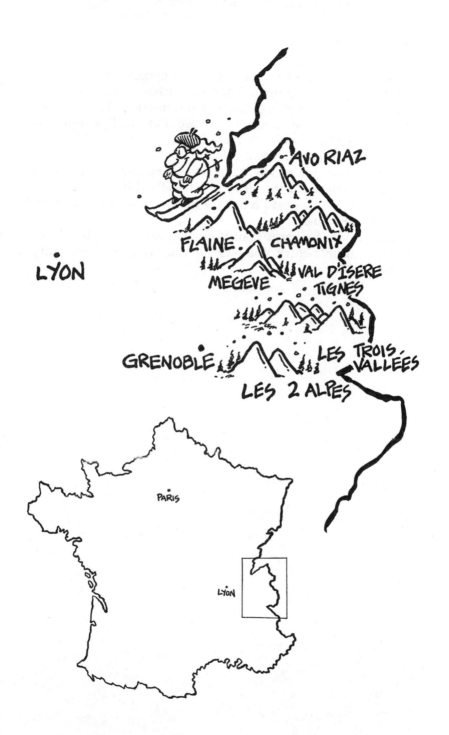

NOTE: The French Government has imposed a visa requirement for all non-Common Market tourists. Check with the nearest French Consulate for visa information. French Consulates are located in Boston, Chicago, Detroit, Houston, Los Angeles, Miami, New York, New Orleans, San Juan P.R., San Francisco and Washington, D.C.

Visas can be obtained by mail. Send your passport, a passport photo and check for the visa fee with self-addressed stamped envelope to the nearest French Consulate with proper visa application filled out.

Current visa fees are: Transit visa (72 hours)—$3.00; Three month multiple-entry visa—$9.00; One Year multiple-entry visa—$15.00.

Avoriaz

Avoriaz was the first purpose-built ski resort in France and is still considered the most pleasant. Jean Vuarnet, yes the same Vuarnet of sunglasses fame, upon returning from the 1960 Olympics in Squaw Valley with a silver medal on his chest managed to convince investors to build Avoriaz. For all intents and purposes this was also the birth of the Portes du Soleil concept. The setting of Avoriaz in the midst of mountains with skiing in virtually every direction, no cars and a world-famous child care facility can make claims on being one of Europe's most complete resorts.

Avoriaz together with Torgon and Champoussin in Switzerland are the only purpose-built resorts in the Portes du Soleil circuit. The other towns have long histories, ruined monasteries, cloisters, and thermal baths. Avoriaz is clearly the glitzy capital of the region. It's in Avoriaz that movie stars gather, Michelin-star restaurants are clustered, dancers can shift discos hourly, and in Avoriaz the annual "Festival of Fantasy Films" is held. For the skier coming from the virtual farm community of Champéry arrival in Avoriaz has the same impact as unexpectantly stepping into Las Vegas.

Where to ski

If you have come to really ski, Avoriaz is perhaps the best base from which to explore the Portes du Soleil area. As well as easy access to the Le Crosets/Champoussin sector reached over the "Swiss wall of death," Avoriaz has easy access to Plaine Dranse with perhaps the most enjoyable and varied skiing of the region. The slopes directly above Avoriaz will challange every level of skier and the nearby section of Morzine and Les Gets

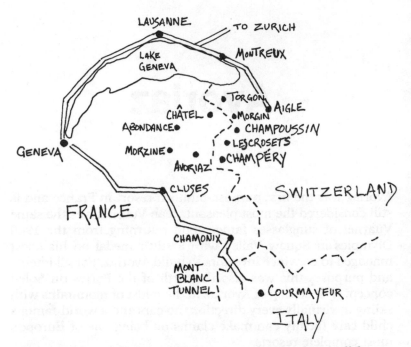

offers another full day of skiing. Any skier's plate will be overflowing for a one-week stay here. (See also the Portes du Soleil description in the Swiss Portes du Soleil section).

Mountain Rating
Avoriaz has some of the best beginner facilities in the Portes du Soleil region. For experts—hold your hat. For intermediates—you'll never have to ski the same run twice. (See Mountain rating section in Swiss Portes du Soleil section.)

Ski school
The French Ski School office and meeting place is the Place du Téléphérique. Lessons sign up can also be taken care of in the Tourist Office and in the Cap-Neige building near the Fontaines Blanches.

Group lessons: six days, from 10 am to noon and from 2 pm to 5 pm—FF640 for adults (FF 450 for children). one morning lesson from 10 am to noon—FF 53 for adults (FF 41 for children). one afternoon lesson from 2 pm to 5 pm—FF82 for adults (FF 62 for children).

Private lessons: one hour—FF120; one day (7 hours)—FF 900; half-day (3 1/2 hours—FF495.

Monoski, surf and competition lessons cost FF 130 for a morning or FF 650 for six consecutive morning lessons.

Ski passes are not included in the lesson prices.

Lift tickets

A skipass for the entire Portes du Soleil will cost: one day— FFR 130; three days—FFR 390; six days—FFR 655; 13 days— FFR 1145.

The pass for only the Avoriaz section of the Portes du Soleil costs: one day—FFR 100; six days—FFR 525; seven days—FFR 600.

Children under 12 years of age receive approximately a 20% discount.

Accommodation

Avoriaz has been developed primarily as a resort of apartments. There are two hotels, neither of which will take groups. The prices are per person, per night, half-board, based on double occupancy in normal season. High season rates are approximately 15% higher. The Fantasy Film Festival normally takes place during the third week of January. Check for exact dates, since that period is treated as high season. Normal season will be January the after mid-March.

Hotel Les Dromonts (tel. 50.74.08.11) If a movie or rock star comes to Avoriaz and doesn't already own a private suite, this is where you'll find them. Les Dromonts' restaurant boasts four stars. Rate: FF660.

Hotel des Hauts Forts (tel. 50.74.09.11) Slightly more rooms than Les Dromonts without the hype. Rate: FF 560 (for a south facing room), FF 500 (north facing room).

Apartments

This is what Avoriaz is all about. Write to the tourist board and they will send you a list of agencies who will be overjoyed to make reservations for you. Note that studio normally means one large room, 2 *pieces* translates to "two rooms" or one bedroom with one living room with sleeping facilities therein, 3 *pieces* is three rooms which translates to two bedrooms plus a living room which can sleep another two people.

Here are some sample prices:

During January except for festival week expect to pay, for a luxury studio considered large enough for four persons, FF 1600 per week.

For a luxury three-room apartment during January the price will be FF 2500 per week.

During Springtime (after mid-March) the same studio will cost FF 2100 and the same three room apartment will run FF 2750.

These are the major agencies in Avoriaz:

Pierre & Vacances, 54 Avenue Marceau, 75008 Paris, Tel. (1)47.20.70.87, telex: 613778.

Maeva-Locarev, 30 rue d'Orleans, 92200 Neuilly-sur-Sein, tel. 47.45.17.66. or in Avoriaz as tel. 50.74.28.00.

Avoriaz-Location, place des Ruches, 74110 Avoriaz, tel. 50.74.04.53; telex: 385773.

Place Centrale, Immeuble "Portes du Soleil," 74110 Avoriaz, tel. 50.74.16.08.

Or contact the tourist office directly at telephone: 50.74.02.11; telex: 385578.

Child care

Avoriaz is world-famous for its excellent child care program organized by Annie Famose. Located directly in the center of Avoriaz, the "Village des Enfants" is open from 9 am until 5:30 pm. It accepts children from three to 14 years of age. Telephone: 50.74.04.46. Children can play in a snow playground or take ski lessons. Half-day—FF 57 (without lunch); full-day—FF165 (FF 140 w/o lunch); six days—FF 820 (FF 675 w/o lunch).

Dining

Next to Courchevel, Avoriaz has perhaps the best collection of gourmet restaurants in any French resort. Here's a suggested lineup for the gourmand. Try the restaurant in the Hotel Dromonts, then try La Grignotte and for Tunisian specialties eat at Princesse d'Haroun. Crépy owned by the former director of tourism has excellent meals in a middle price range and try Kinkerne at the foot of Avoriaz.

Though the Portes du Soleil is not known for good mountain restaurants a stop in the Savoy village of Les Lindarets provides what some food conoisseurs call heaven on earth. The restaurants "Marmottes," "L'Eau Vive" and Braize are each special. On the Swiss side try Télécabine des Mossettes restaurant in Les Crosets and then try a fondue Chez Cocoz at Planachaux above Champéry.

Late at night head for Mama's Pizza or Lapon for cold fare.

Nightlife

Avoriaz has plenty of action but as in all French resorts the discos "The Manhattan" and "Le Roc-Club" begin filling up after midnight.

Other activities

If you aren't here for the skiing you are probably in the wrong place. Geneva is within an hour and a half drive, but that means taking the car out of the garage and a winding drive down the mountain. There are no swimming pools, no covered tennis courts, no town streets through which to wander, no skating rinks. . . only snow—lots of it.

Getting there

The nearest airport is Geneva. From the airport a special bus runs each Saturday and Sunday leaving at 10:30 am and arriving in Avoriaz at 12:50 pm. The return trip leaves Avoriaz at 1:30 pm and arrives at the airport at 4:20 pm.

Avoriaz can be reached by a train/bus combination. The train from Paris arrives at Thonon and then a bus makes the hour and fifteen minute climb to the resort.

For those driving, take the Autopiste from Geneva to Mont Blanc and leave at the exit marked Morzine/Avoriaz. It is only 80 kms from Geneva. A free parking lot is located 600 meters from the town with 24-hour transfers between the parking and the town center available for between FF 35-60 for 3/4 persons with baggage. Closer covered parking places are available for a weekly fee.

Tourist information

L'Office du tourisme d'Avoriaz, Place Centrale, 74110 Avoriaz-Morzine, tel. 50.74.02.11; telex: 385578.

Chamonix

To fully enjoy Chamonix, one of Europe's greatest ski resorts, you need a car to get to its slopes: These are spread out for miles along the valley floor in the shadow of 4807-meter (15,767-foot) Mont Blanc. Shuttle buses are slow and sometimes crowded. It can take more than a half hour, for example, to get from Les Houches to the far end of Argentiere. Top that off with the fact that some of the best skiing is done at the top of the lifts and waiting time to get up can stretch to an hour or more.

There have been significant improvements in the lift system during the past year. The lift capacity in the popular Argentiere sector has been doubled and there is now virtually no waiting, where only two years ago, an hour in the lift line was not uncommon. Some of the hotels in town have also started to provide shuttle buses for their clients which makes starting out in the morning and returning much more pleasant.

Where to ski

Let's move on to the reasons Chamonix is fabulous for skiing. From the slopes of Les Houches to Chamonix and on to Argentiere and finally La Tour, a string of lifts takes skiers up both sides of the valley. On the Mont Blanc side, you ascend above outcroppings and slopes of this magnificent peak while on the opposite side, you enjoy the Mont Blanc panorama as the lifts take you to outstanding runs.

There are six different ski areas. The first good one you'll encounter entering the valley is Les Houches. This is intermediate-level country with a cable car taking you to Le Prarion at 1966 meters (6453 feet).

The two-mile-long blue-rated trail from Col de Voza below Le Prarion is ideal for a warmup. Our favorite trail in Les

Houches is the shorter (about 1.5 miles long) red trail descending from the Bellevue summit (1812 meters—5943 feet). You'll need advanced-intermediate skills in order to get down comfortably.

An additional opportunity offered in Chamonix is the chance to travel through the Mont Blanc tunnel into Courmayeur, Italy, on the opposite side of the massif where skiing is very good. There's often good weather here when Chamonix is shrouded with clouds. The toll charge is about Lire 30,000.

In Chamonix most skiers choose the challenges of Le Brévent (2525 meters—8288 feet). Try the black run from the back of Le Brévent in the company of another experienced skier. If, after the first few hundred feet, you're not confident of your turns, branch to the left and take the red intermediate trail down instead of the expert slope!

Intermediate skiers may prefer the midstation slopes at Planpraz, especially the two chairlifts that reach the 2000-meter (6560-foot) level. In addition, work your way to the right and take the chair up to the 2283-meter (7488-foot) level for a good intermediate run.

Ten minutes away by car is Les Praz, ground station for the cable car to the La Flégère midstation. From here, a gondola takes you to L'Index at 2385 meters (7822 feet) where the skiing is outstanding for intermediates. Take the combination red-and-blue run all the way down to the chair at La Trappe at 1751 meters (5743 feet).

In good weather you'll probably continue to ski this fifteen-minute run until your thighs ache. The entire run from L'Index to Les Praz ground station lasts thirty minutes, a challenging advanced-intermediate romp. However, during high season expect to wait as long as forty-five minutes at the bottom in order to get back on the cable car. You'll want to stay on the mountain unless you're moving to another slope or making the last run of the day.

From L'Index, look across the valley to the rocky crags of Aiguille du Dru and, below it, Les Grande Montets, the 3233-meter (10,604-foot) end station for the two-section cable car from the valley. For our money, this is the best skiing in the valley. Come off the right side and take the black trail down a vertical drop of 4200 feet, cross the Argentière glacier to Croix de Lognan and you've experienced some of the finest skiing Europe has to offer. The red-rated trail beneath the cable car to the La Herse chairlift is often as much a challenge as intermediates want to handle.

There is a system of one gondola and five other lifts at the valley end in La Tour, but after skiing Brévent and Les Grande Montets it will probably not interest you.

The most talked about—not necessarily the most challenging—skiing adventure in Chamonix is the 18-kilometer (eleven-mile) glacier run from the Aiguille du Midi (3842 meters—12,601 feet). You must take a guide. The scenery is magnificent and the memory of the run down the Vallée Blanche and over the Mer de Glace will remain forever. The run is usually not open until February. Guides will cost about FF 840 for one to four persons then add FF 70 for each additional person.

Mountain rating

Beginning skiers should look elsewhere for lots of easy slopes; there are not that many blue trails here.

Intermediates choose Chamonix year after year as an ideal area to increase their skills on challenging terrain.

Experts need never worry that there may not be a bigger challenge over the mountain. Because in Chamonix there always is.

Ski school

Chamonix hosted the first Winter Olympic Games in 1924 and the French Ski School based its instruction manual on lessons given on these slopes. A total of 300 instructors offer courses through Chamonix (tel. 50.53.22.57) and Argentière (tel. 50.54.00.12) ski schools.

Private lessons (one or two people) cost FFR 130 an hour. A day of private instruction runs approximately FFR 960 (high season) and FFR 850 (low season).

Group lessons for a half day (two hours) cost FFR 58. A six-day course, consisting of morning and afternoon instruction daily (four hours per day), is FFR 475.

Out of bounds ski guides for groups of up to five skiers can be hired for FFR 940 (full day) or FFR 540 (half day).

Lift tickets

The Mont Blanc ski pass is valid for the entire Chamonix valley, plus Megève, St. Gervais and eight other resorts for a total of 300 miles of trails served by 180 lifts. Free bus and ski shuttle bus services in the areas are included as well as a day of skiing in Courmayeur, Italy with the purchase of a six-day or 13 day pass..

two consecutive days	FFR 250
four consecutive days	FFR 470
six consecutive days	FFR 670
13 conseictive days	FFR 1200

Day tickets are also available. For example, Les Houches costs FFR 71 for a half day, FFR 94 for one day and FFR 450 a week. But the Mont Blanc pass is the best bargain.

Accommodation

The Chamonix reservation service (it also has listings for Argentièrer and Les Houches) is centralized at the Tourist Office, place de L'Eglise; tel. 50.53.00.24. Nearly 90 hotels provide a range of accommodation from luxury suites to dormitory-like rooms. Because of the many restaurants and snack bars, don't hesitate to book a hotel without a half-pension plan. Accommodations are available starting at the weekly prices below:

Four-star hotels will cost FFR 4900—full pension during the high season. Low season rates are FFR 3970—half pension; FFR 4800—full pension.

Three-star hotels cost FFR 3580—half pension and FFR 4200—full pension during high season. Low season costs are FFR 2280—half pension and FFR 2980—full pension.

Two-star hotels cost FFR 2180—half pension and FFR 2645—full pension during high season. Low season costs are FFR 2025—half pension and FFR 2600—full pension.

The best hotels in town are Mont-Blanc (tel. 50.53.05.64) and Auberge du Bois Prin (tel. 50.53.33.51). The Alpina, next on the list, (tel. 50.53.47.77) is excellent and in the center of the action. It can bee booked through Best Western in USA 1-800-528-1234. Try Hotel Roma (tel. 50.53.00.62), Au Bon Coin (tel. 50.53.15.67), Croix Blanche (tel. 530011), Arveyron (tel.

50.53.18.29), Simond et Golf (tel. 50.53.06.08), Sapiniere-Montana (tel. 50.53.07.63) for lower-cost acommodations.

Dining

Meals in Chamonix can be exciting. Try the Hotel Albert I and Monsu; and in Argentièrer try Dahu.

Try the 190-franc menu in the Matafan restaurant (tel. 50.53.05.64) at the Mont Blanc hotel. We also liked the Eden restaurant (tel. 50.53.06.40) below the Mont Blanc tunnel entrance for cheap eats.

Handle pizza cravings (including take-away service) at La Pizza (tel. 50.53.15.51) in Chamonix-Sud.

Lunchtime restaurants on the slopes are uniform, although you might try the midday meal at Le Blanchot (tel. 50.53.30.80) at the foot of the cable car to Aiguille du Midi. The menu is about FFR 60, including beverage.

Apartments

Better known as a hotel town, Chamonix does have some furnished chalets and apartments that are offered through several area agencies. Prices for a studio with sleeping arrangements for two to four—FFR 2610 during high season; FFR 1390 during low season. For a two-room apartment housing four to five people costs will be FFR 4120 during high season; FFR 1785 in low season. The tourist office offers a special folder with info on how to rent (*see address below*).

Nightlife

This is home to one of France's major casinos. Nightlife devotees have plenty of opportunity here besides gambling. In contrast to the limited fare in Flaine, there are seven discos, several nightclubs and several dozen hotel bars for the après-ski crowd. We've heard that "Le Pele" is the current hot spot. Remember, nothing really starts cooking until midnight.

Camp de Base (tel. 50.55.90.68), a bar-disco in Chamonix-Sud, is lively with an international crowd.

Better still, try the Driver (tel. 50.53.02.43), with piano bar, in the center of town.

Child care

Argentière offers ski nursery for (tel. 50540476) children two and older. Costs are FFR 105 for a half day; FFR 875 for six consecitive days plus an additional FFR 200 for six days of lunch.

The Chamonix school (50531224) will take children from 18 months to six years. A half day for children costs FFR 76 and a full day costs FFR 99Meals are not included.

The Panda Club in Chamonix (50558612) takes children from 18 months to 14 years. A full day of skiing and playing costs FFR 175 plus FFR 35 for lunch.

Child-care services are available at the larger hotels and baby sitters are available for FFR 65 (half-day) or FFR 110 (full day). For more information, contact the tourist office.

Getting there

Nearly everyone arrives via the autoroute or by train from Geneva. However, Chamonix—with Courmayeur on the other side of Mont Blanc—is ideal for visitors who have skied in Italy and who want to work their way up through Switzerland and France.

The TGV leaves Paris at around 8 a.m. and arrives in Sallaches at about 1 p.m. There is also a special train bus combination with the train departing from Paris a little after 7 a.m. then with a change to bus in Annecy and arrival in Chamonix before 1 p.m.

Taxi from the Geneva airport will cost around FFR 600 and a bus from the airport to the resort costs around FFR 150.

Other activities

More than any other area you may visit, consider taking an aerial tour here. The Mont Blanc massif and the stunning series of peaks surrounding you are best seen from the air. Choose from among four different trips ranging from FFR 100 to FFR 400 per person. Call Air Mont Blanc at 50.58.13.31.

The casino has long been a center of action while the swimming center has three pools, all heated.

We recommend going to Courmayeur for at least one day to enjoy lunch and a day of skiing.

Tourist information

Tourist Office, place de l'Eglise, F-74400 Chamonix; telex: 385022
OFITOUR CHAMX; tel. 50.53.00.24.
Office du Tourisme, F-74310 Les Houches (tel. 50.55.50.62).

Megève

Expert skiers should get to know Megève as this winter-sport center offers more black-rated runs than any other along the rim of the Mont Blanc massif. Megève's skiing area includes the neighboring slopes of Saint-Gervais-les Bains, Le Fayet, St. Nicolas de Véroce and Combloux. The towns are linked by a lift circuit that opens up about one hundred miles of trails.

Where to ski

Though Megève's slopes are not of the caliber of Val d'Isere or as extensive as the Trois Vall'agees, get ready for some of the best and most varied intermediate skiing you can find in Europe. Numbers one and two on your list should be Mont Joly and Mont Joux. The two peaks above Megève are lined with black- and red-rated runs. A favorite here is the chairlift run, which starts halfway up the Mont Joly slope at 1960 meters (6107 feet). You have one real choice coming down and it's black all the way. Nearby, a shorter run that descends from the Epaule lift is also rated black. From atop the Mount Joux lift you can pick out some part of ten black trails in the immediate area. There are a half-dozen runs down to St. Nicolas that shift from steep to mellow, starting from the wide-open snowfields and ending through tree-lined pistes.

Down the mountain, the Mt. d'Arbois summit above St. Gervais was our favorite because there was a mix of black, red and blue runs. One of the longest and best for intermediate skiers parallels the lifts past Le Bettex—all the way to St. Gervais.

Across the Plateau Mt. d'Arbois and above Megève are Rochebrune and Cote 2000, summits which both offer exciting black trails. Best is a descent from the Rochebrune summit through the trees and back to the valley staton.

Across the valley, advanced beginning and lower intermediate skiers will find Le Jaillet, at 1700 meters (5576 feet), ideal. There are, however, four black-rated runs on this mountain; as skills (and courage) increase, you don't have to go far to try something new.

Most scenic of the black runs is the one-mile-long trail (1870 meters—6133 feet) from Christomet. Our favorite on this side is the run through the woods along the Creve Coeur lifts just below Le Jaillet summit.

Mountain rating

Taken together, Megève's mountains offer several challenges and make the area an acceptable destination for the expert skier. Intermediate skiers and those trying to push to the advanced-intermediate level should find this a great place to improve and test skills.

The area of Les Contamines, included in the Mont Blanc skipass, offers excellent wide-open skiing. It will soon be interconnected with Megève, but for now skiing it requires about a 45 minute drive or a short hike along the ridge from Mont Joly with a guide. It's worth a daytrip to ski the area. I'm sure you'll return for more once you sample the great skiing.

Beginners should go to Megève without hesitation: there's enough good skiing at the lower ability level to keep them going until the improvements come. Then it's on up the mountain with the big boys.

Ski school

About 200 teachers are registerd in the Megève area. Large ski classes are conducted by schools in Megève (tel. 50.21.00.97), St. Gervais (tel. 78.21.00) and Combloux (tel. 58.60.49). Note: English is very limited—make sure you get a good English-speaking instructor.

Average price per person:

one hour (private instruction)	FFR 130
six days (half-day)	FFR 265
twelve days	FFR 375

Lift tickets

Mont Blanc's ski pass also includes this area. It is by far the best lift-ticket bargain. In addition to Megève it covers Chamonix, St. Gervais, St. Nicolas, Les Contamines plus eight other resorts around Mont Blanc. It includes 150 lifts and covers over 360 miles of prepared runs.

four consecutive days	FFR 470
six consecutive days	FFR 670
13 consecutive days	FFR 1200

Day tickets are available for all areas. A full day in Megève is FFR 126 and six days will cost FFR 650.

Accommodation

Megève's tourist office offers an accommodation service (tel. 50.21.29.52) which will book a room, apartment or chalet for you. Altogether, there are 63 hotels and pensions in town, although not all are open year round. The wealth of restaurants and the liveliness of Megève's night scene may cause you to opt for a hotel without restaurant. Accommodation is available starting at the weekly prices below. These are low season prices available during most of January and late-March. They include seven full consecutive days with half board, taxes and services per person in a double room occupied by two people, with bath or shower.

Four Star	FFR 4480
Three Star	FFR 2625
Two Star	FFR 1970

During high season the rates are approximately 20 percent higher

The best hotels are the Mont Blanc (tel. 50.21.20.02) and Chalet Mont-d'Arbois (tel. 50.21.25.03). Two of the best three-star hotels (however both without restaurants) are Au Coin du Feu (tel. 50.21.04.94) and Fer à Cheval (tel. 50.21.30.39). An excellent two-star hotel is Ferme-hotel Duvillard (50.21.14.62) another two-star without restaurant is the Week-End (50.21.26.49).

Saint Gervais

Just over the mountain from Megève is the town of St. Gervais. It is somewhat closer to the autoroute and provides an excellent central location for visiting the other resorts included on the Mont Blanc skipass. The best hotel in town is the Carlina (tel. 50.93.41.10). The hotel has a small indoor swimming pool and is not too far from the lifts. The best bet is to stay up on the side of the mountain in the village of Le Bettex. Three-star accommodation is available in the Arbois-Bettex (tel. 50.93.12.22). Le Flèche d'Or is a two-star hotel (tel. 50.93.11.54).

The town of St. Nicolas which is a part of the St. Gervais area has a reduced January week package. The tourist office will provide forms and other information.

Dining

An excellent restaurant highly recommended to us by French friends is Chez Nano (tel. 50.21.02.18)—this is perhaps the best restaurant in town. Megève is one town where you won't have problems getting excellent food—there are seven Michelin-rated and five Gault et Millau-rated restaurants.

Other highly praised medium-price restaurants are Le Prieuré (tel. 50.21.01.79) which has the best atmosphere of any restaurant in town, and Le Chalet Dan Les Arbes (50.21.39.36). Perhaps the best value meals are served at le Tire-Bouchon (tel. 50.21.14.73). For down-to-earth fare, try something light at Trattoria Madona (tel. 50.21.04.59) or the Brasserie (tel. 50.21.02.60).

If you are in St. Gervais, try Lou Granani (tel. 50.78.05.51), Val d'Este (tel. 50.93.65.91), and Le Four (tel. 50.78.14.16).

For eating on the mountain, the best is Le Relais des Communailles between Le Bettex and St. Nicolas (tel. 50.93.10.15). La Petite Coterie in Le Bettex (tel. 50.93.11.74) is also excellent. For snacks try La Cote 2000 (tel. 50.21.31.84) on Mont D'Arbois, Auberge du Christomet (tel. 50.21.11.34) at Le Jaillet, and Snack le Denieu (tel. 50.21.14.62) at the foot of the d'Abois lifts.

Apartments

Write to the Megève tourist office (tel. 50.21.25.92) who will contact the major rental organizations in town. You will hear from several agencies. Just choose the apartment you want and send back the paperwork.

In St. Gervais the apartments are best in Le Bettex. Write to the tourist office and specifically ask for an apartment in Le Bettex. They will send several selections. Make your pick and let the agencies know your decision. In January expect to pay approximately FFR 2490 per week for an apartment for four persons. During Christmas and in February the price will be around FFR 4505 per week. Linen will cost an additional FFR 110 per week.

Nightlife

La Nuit, c'est Megève!, roughly translates as "the night belongs to, or is, Megève." Despite the rustic, chalet-style buildings and the old-atmosphere resort, Megève is modern in all aspects. Megève is trendy, discos are light and bright, the entertainment live and continuous until morning. The nightlife abounds, but discos don't get rolling until midnight or later, so don't race out in the early evening to find the action.

We were partial to the music and frantic group at Enfants Terribles (tel. 50.21.20.02), but our traveling companion preferred L'Esquinade (tel. 50.21.27.06) because she saw someone who "looked" like a movie star. It really doesn't matter because Megève sparkles for as long as you let it.

Child care

A kindergarten for children, 12 months-12 years old, costs FFR 154 for six days, FFR 260 for twelve days. Other daycare facilities are available for children from ages of 20 months to 12 Years of age. Les Bruyeres (tel. 50.21.20.12) and Montjoie (tel. 50.21.01.56) have English-speaking staff. Prices range from FFR 275 to FFR 150 for a full day and FFR 70-150 for a half-day. Hourly rates are approximately FFR 40. For details, call the tourist bureau at 50.21.27.28.

Getting there

Geneva is the main arrival airport; from there it is about an hour by car to Megève.

Trains run to Sallanches, 13 kilometers away, where bus and taxi services are available.

Other activities

Megève and the neighboring villages draw many non-skiers, who, as part of their entertainment, walk throughout the area. To help them, the walkways are better kept than any you'll probably encounter at other Alpine resorts. Megève's shops are outstanding for window shopping or purchasing the exclusive items that will threaten your budget. Day outings to Chamonix and Geneva are popular.

Tourist information

Office du Tourisme, rue de la Poste, F-74120 Megève; telex: 385532; tel. 50.21.27.28.
Office du Tourisme, F-74920 Combloux; telex: 385550; Tel. 50.58.60.49.
Office du Tourisme, F-74190 Le Fayet; telex: 385730; tel. 50.47.01.58.
Office du Tourisme de St. Gervais, F-74170 St. Gervais; telex 385607; tel. 50.78.22.43.

Flaine

Flaine is an all-or-nothing proposition: either you take to this "planned" concrete-and-steel French resort in the Haute Savoie region or you search deeper into the Alps for quaint chalets and sleighs to form the backdrop to your downhill adventures. You may dislike Flaine's soul, but its skiing, which is overwhelmingly intermediate, is bountiful and good.

Flaine was created on an empty mountain site a generation ago, another of the now-familiar "new" French high-rise resorts. The central complex, at 1580 meters (5182 feet), is linked to lifts above Samoens, Morillon and Les Carroz to form a ski circus of more than one hundred trails and a total length of 160 miles of downhill adventure. Snow is practically guaranteed from early December until April.

Where to ski

Head first to the 2480-meter (8134-foot) Les Grandes Platieres, which overlooks a treeless snow-covered landscape dotted with lift stanchions.

For a quick reading of your ski skills, take the black-rated run from Platieres. Descending beneath the cablecar route, the run has been dubbed Black Diamond (*Diamant Noir*); you'll either enjoy it tremendously or hastily make your way over to the red-rated runs by the Chalet de Sales chairlift.

A favorite run lies on the other side of Platieres at Tete des Lindars (2561 meters—8406 feet), where there's a delightful intermediate trail all the way through the trees to Flaine.

We also liked the powder skiing down to the lift at Gers. Les Carroz, Morillon and the valley town, Samoens, are Flaine's supporting cast but their attraction for thousands of skiers each year lies in their more traditional Alpine accommodation.

Of the runs above these towns, we liked the blue-rated trail from Cupoire summit (1880 meters—6166 feet) to the bottom of the chair near the parking lot in Morillon. With easy turns, a few moguls and trees for orientation, it's a fine cruise. The runs on this side are almost invariably of the intermediate level. One exception to try is the black trail from Plateau des Saix summit to the Vercland lift station.

Mountain rating

Beginners will like Flaine because of its training slopes and the quality of the ski instruction.

Intermediate skiers are in the majority here and the slopes are laid out with that in mind. Les Grand Platieres is practically an intermediate's mountain, offering at least fifteen different red-rated trail variations.

Expert skiers will find plenty of challenges, particularly if they enjoy off-trail skiing, which is permitted in most areas of Flaine.

Ski school

Flaine excels in ski instruction. There are two schools here: the French Ski School (*Ecole du Ski Français*, tel. 50.90.81.00) and the International Ski School (*Ski Ecole International*, tel. 50.90.74.41). Each has about 50 instructors.

Private lessons can be arranged for up to four people at one time. 2 hours will cost FFR 240 and a full day costs FFR 990.

Group lessons are a good bargain when class size is limited. The ESF guarantees a limit of not more than ten people per group.

Group lesson prices for six half-days of instruction are FFR 340 for adults and FFR 250 for children.

An extended ski school with four hours a day for eleven lessons costs FFR 480 for adults and FFR 340 for children.

Ski school prices are reduced during so-called "first-ski" times—periods outside the school holiday breaks when all facilities are jammed.

Prepared cross-country trails in the area total twenty miles and instruction is offered through the ski schools.

Cross-country lessons will cost for a full day—FFR 60 (adults) and FFR 55 (children); five days are FFR 285 (adults) and FFR

235 (children); and six days costs FFR 340 (adults) and FFR 250 (children).

Lift tickets

Flaine (includes 31 lifts) Children get approximately a 20 percent discount.

half day	FFR 80
one day	FFR 105
five days	FFR 455
six days	FFR 525
14 days	FFR 1050

Accommodation

Flaine primarily offers apartment accommodations, although you can choose from the following hotels near the Forum square. Hotel rates are generally: two-star hotels FFR 1540-2625 for full-pension and FFR 910-1855 for half-pension per person based on double occupancy; three-star hotels are FFR 2240-3360 for full pension.

Le Totem (tel. 50.90.80.64)

Les Gradins Gris (tel. 50.90.81.10)

Les Lindars (tel. 50.90.81.66) This, like Le Totem and Les Gradins Gris, is a pension hotel. Rooms come with bath.

The Aujon (tel.50.90.80.10) This hotel offers half pension or bed-and-breakfast.

The least expensive week to stay in Flaine is the one after New Year's. The remainder of January and the first few days of February are also less pricey.

Dining

Your choice of where to eat is limited because most hotel guests are on the full-pension plan, taking meals in their hotels, and apartment guests cook in their apartments. We recommend the fixed-price menu at the Totem dining room.

The Aujon offers a less expensive menu.

In the mountains the lunchtime fare is pretty much standardized, although you'll pay less on the Samoens-Morillon side. In Flaine, get a quick, tasty snack at Trattoria.

Apartments

Apartment complexes in Flaine have been built on three levels. Above the Forum on the hillside are the units of Flaine Foret. These are the better apartments, many privately owned. Apartment buildings are also clustered around the main Forum square and there are more below the Forum level at Front de Neige. The most convenient are those in the Forum area.

The least expensive studio apartment on the Forum level during middle season costs about FFR 1555 a week. The same apartment during high season costs about FFR 3110.

For rental bookings in all areas, call Agence Renand (tel. 50.90.81.40). In addition, the tourist office will mail a brochure and booking reservation information upon request. (*See address below.*)

Nightlife

Plan on staying in Flaine, since the road down the mountain can become treacherous, particularly after the sun goes down. Our ski instructor met with the class one evening in the lounge at the Hotel Aujon. And a friend from Liverpool took us to the very British (and nice) White Grouse Pub. Quadrium may seem like a disco to you.

Child care

A ski kindergarten is conducted daily from 9 a.m. until 6 p.m. The fee for a half day is FFR 70; six half days cost FFR 290. Full-day ski kindergarten runs FFR 130, or FFR 350 a week of half days and FFR 650 for a week of full days. Prices include instruction and a meal.

The baby-sitting services at Les Lindars Hotel are best. The hotel runs a nursery for children under two. Costs are FFR 140 for a full day; FFR 75, Half-day; and baby sitting for hotel guests is FFR 28 per hour. A kindergarten without ski course from 9 a.m. until 6 p.m. for children from two to seven is also available.

The children's Rabbit Culb ski school is another child-oriented program which costs FFR 850 for six days with lunch (FFR 680 without lunch) and FFR 180 for one day with lunch (FFR 150 without lunch).

Getting there

Geneva airport, about 45 miles away by the Geneva-Chamonix autoroute, is the closest. Take the Cluses exit.

You can also take the train to Cluses and then a bus (for information on Transport Alpbus, call 50.03.70.09) to Flaine.

Tourist information

Office du Tourisme Flaine, F-74300; telex: 385662 F; tel. 50.90.80.01.

Flaine-Information, 23 Rue Cambon, F-75001 Paris; telex: 670512 F; tel. 12.61.55.17.

Tignes

Tignes, Val d'Isère's sister resort, appears to be nothing more than a group of concrete apartment buildings huddled at the foot of one of Europe's largest glaciers. It is really a series of modern villages at altitudes that range from 1500 to 2100 meters. The main village, Tignes Lac, lies at 2100 meters. The highest village is Val Claret, and it is from here that the cablecar leaves for La Grande Motte. The other villages are Lavachet, Le Rosset and Les Almes.

The entire area is modern, having been built after the original village, at a lower altitude, was flooded in the early 1950's by a lake created when the Chevril dam was built. Tignes shares slopes with Val d'Isère through an interconnection project which was completed only a few years ago, culminating in "L'Espace Killy."

Where to ski

The skiing at Tignes is fantastic. The resort rates as one of the best in the world for intermediate cruisers, for experts, for beginners, for sun worshipers, for people who don't like to ski the same trail twice and for people who travel with children. What more is there?

Unlike Val d'Isère, Tignes has skiing opportunities on tap 365 days a year due to the glacier which dwarfs the town. The lift system offers 24 lifts linking different parts of town. This means you'll never have to walk very far to start skiing. The lift system peaks at La Grande Motte at 3656 meters, site of the year-round glacier skiing. In all, the system has 116 lifts serving almost 200 miles of prepared ski trails and 30,000 acres of open powder skiing.

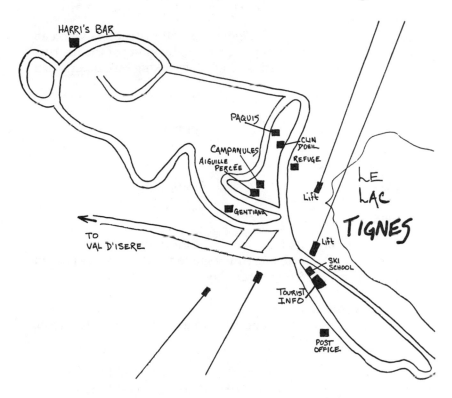

Mountain rating

It's easy to see why the area has been rated as tops in every category. Just the snow expanse is mind-boggling. With a vertical drop of more than a mile and a third, coupled with 30,000 acres of terrain, you can be sure that there is something for everyone. Beginners and intermediates can cruise all over the resort's upper reaches and experts can test themselves on extensive off-piste and powder skiing. It is best, at least for a day, to take a guide along who will show you the best places to test your skills. Before skiing off-piste, check with the ski school for the latest information on snow conditions.

Ski school

The French Ski School in Tignes has 150 instructors who can teach any level skier. English is spoken by many of the instructors, but say that you need an English-speaking instructor when signing up.

Individual lessons

for one hour (12:30-1:30 p.m.) (max. five skiers)	FFR 120
for a half day (9 a.m.-noon or 1:30-4:30 p.m.)	FFR 410
for a full day	FFR 850

Groups complete with a certified guide for the powder and off piste cost FFR 975 per full day.

Group lessons

Three-hour courses are conducted in the morning or afternoon. Prices are for one week.

	adults (with video)	children (4-12 yrs.)
for a half day	FFR 450	FFR 390
for a full day	FFR 840	FFR 700

Special courses in off-piste and powder skiing cost FFR 1000 per person a week. A six-day slalom racing course for FFR 1500 includes a ski pass. Freestyle, mogul and mono skiing courses with video tapes are available for FFR 1000 a week with a minimum of four students. More information is available from the tourist office.

The ski school has three offices: in Tignes Lac, call 79.06.30.28; in Val Claret, call 79.06.31.28; and in Lavachet, call 79.06.53.26.

Lift tickets

The prices below are for "L'Espace Killy," which includes both Val d'Isère and Tignes areas.

for one day	FFR 148
for two days	FFR 275
for three days	FFR 385
for six days	FFR 710
for seven days	FFR 810
for 14 days	FFR 1385

There are discount rates of about 30 percent available on some tickets for children 13 and under, for seniors over 60 years and for beginners. Check with the tourist office or at the ticket office when buying lift tickets.

Incidentally, the company that runs the lift system in the Tignes sector of "L'Espace Killy" is so confident in the efficiency of its lift system that it promises to refund a free coupon to any skier who can prove that he waited more than 17 minutes at the bottom of a lift. It's the only such guarantee in the world, and with a lift capacity of 52,580 skiers an hour, the company has had very few complaints. There are some limitations to the guarantee, based on weather, but the point is well taken: they aim to see you skiing, not waiting in line.

Accommodation

A special program has been organized by the tourist office and hoteliers. Check with the tourist office for exact dates. The program's cost is based on which category hotel and type of package (with or without ski lessons) is selected by the skier. Prices below are for a week's accommodations at half pension in a room with bath or shower. Included is a six-day ski pass, use of the pool and skiing insurance. All packages run from Saturday to Saturday. The prices are per person.

	Feb	Jan.
in apartments*	FFR 2345	FFR 1230
two stars	FFR 3420	FFR 2295
three stars	FFR 3720	FFR 2600

* no meals included, 2 people per apartment.

For bookings, contact the tourist office's service, 73320 Tignes, France; tel. 79.06.35.60; telex: 980030. The office will send more information and will require a 25 percent deposit to reserve your space.

The best hotel in town is the Ski D'Or (tel. 79.06.51.60). Ask for room 23 if you can. The Curling (tel. 79.06.34.34) across the street is considered the next best. In the two-star range we recommend Paquis (tel. 79.06.37.33), Aiguille Percée (tel. 79.06.52.22), Campanules (tel. 79.06.34.36) and Gentiana (tel. 79.06.52.46).

Apartments

When you learn that Tignes has only 1200 hotel beds but almost 15,000 in apartments, you realize the importance of the apartments. The French have a very well organized apartment rental system. The tourist office acts as an information clearinghouse, providing an extensive listing of individuals and agencies who will rent apartments at extremely low rates.

In many cases, linen is not included; but can be rented for from the apartment owners or agencies. Normal fee is FFR 90 per week.

A typical sample of apartment rates in Tignes is provided below. The centrally located units are only about 100 meters from the lifts.

	high season	low season
studio: two to four persons	FFR 4030	FFR 1510
for four to five persons	FFR 5200	FFR 1960
for six to seven persons	FFR 5550-7390	FFR 2105-2775

Most agencies and individual owners offer apartments within similar price ranges. Note the differences between low, and high season. But even during high season accommodation costs will range between $15 and $18 a day per person, based on four people sharing a two-bedroom apartment.

For more information and a complete listing of rental apartments, write to the tourist office. It will send lists of both agencies and individual owners, along with prices.

Dining

Outside dining is limited, but the best in town is Le Clin d'Oeil (tel. 79.06.59.10). Make reservations, as it is very small. The Refuge (tel. 79.06.36.64) and Le Caveau (tel. 79.06.52.32) are also excellent. There is a Japanese restaurant called Myako (tel. 79.06.34.79) which is fun for a change of pace.

Nightlife

Nightlife is almost non-existent since most people are either "there to ski" or are partying in their own apartments. Most English speakers seem to hang out at Harry's Bar or the American Bar. But there are several other discos and pubs in town where true aprés-skiers gather. The discos are "Le Palaf" in Tignes Lac, "Les Chandelles," the most popular in town, in Val Claret and "Playboy."

The best pubs are "Club 73," "Pub 2000," and "Why Not?" all in Val Claret.

Child care

This is a category in which Tignes excels. There are two kindergartens. The first, Les Marmottons in Tignes Lac, accepts children between two and a half and ten years. Children over four are taught to ski. For six consecutive days, with lunch and skiing included, the cost is FFR830.

The other kindergarten, La Rotonde, is in Val Claret adjacent to the ski school. Children from 18 months to three years are accepted in its "Baby Club." A special first-steps-on-skis program is organized for children between three and five years. And children between six and ten years take group lessons with the French Ski School. The costs are FFR 170 for a full day, including lunch, or FFR 860 for six consecutive days. Both kindergartens are normally open from 8:30 a.m. until 5 p.m.

Getting there

The closest international airports are Lyons and in Geneva. Geneva is about 140 kilometers (86 miles) and Lyons approximately 240 kilometers (150 miles) from the resort. A smaller airport that offers some domestic and international flights is Chambéry.

Rail transport is available to Tignes, but connections can become complicated. TVG trains run to Chambéry, then a normal train to Bourg St. Maurice, where a bus connections take you to Val d'Isère and to Tignes.

If you plan to drive, the best route from Geneva is autoroute A41 to Annecy and then N90 to Albertville. From there, follow the signs to Bourg St. Maurice and on to Val d'Isère or Col de l'Isèran. From Lyons, take autoroute A43 to Chambéry, then follow the signs to Albertville and on to Val d'Isère.

A daily regular bus service to Tignes from the Geneva, Lyons and Chambéry airports operates during the winter months.

Other activities

Tignes is relatively remote, so you will probably be content to keep your wanderings within the area's ski resorts, or try some of the activities in the town itself.

Areas that are close enough for a good day of skiing include Les Arcs, La Plagne, La Rosiere and Megève, among others.

Val d'Isère offers more shopping opportunities than Tignes and is only a short bus ride or drive away.

Hang-gliding lessons from the top of Toviere are offered for about FFR 400 a flight.

Special scuba diving courses, which are conducted beneath the ice in the lake, are organized in March and April.

There is a bowling alley with 12 lanes; FFR 30 a game.

Ice skating on the lake is on tap daily and at night twice a week, weather permitting.

Tourist information

Office du Tourisme, BP 51, 73320 Tignes, France; tel. 79.06.15.55; telex: 980030 F.

For hotel and apartment booking, call 79.06.35.60; address and telex the same as above.

Val d'Isère

Val d'Isère installed its first poma lift in 1934 and has retained its traditional ski-village atmosphere ever since. Many skiers refer to it as the "Mecca of Skiing," and for them it is well worth the pilgrimage for the chance to ski its wide-open, seemingly endless runs. Here, powder and off-piste skiing are king. If you can ski the deep and the steep in Val d'Isère, you can ski anywhere in the world.

Where to ski

In the Val d'Isère/Tignes area, which is called "l'Espace Killy," after the famous French skiing champion, 116 lifts carry skiers to more than 170 miles of marked runs. No matter where you stay the free shuttle bus system is very efficient and will move skiers from one end of the resort to the other with buses running at least every ten minutes.

Mountain rating

There is something for everyone; the upper reaches of the mountains are excellent for any range of skier. Experts can test themselves on the steeps that drop into town and on extensive off-piste and powder-skiing pockets. It's a good idea to take a guide along, at least for a day, so you can find the best places to test your limits. Also, if you plan to ski off-piste, check with the ski school before you leave for the latest information on snow conditions.

Ski school

Val d'Isère's French Ski School boasts having Jean-Claude Killy as its technical adviser. Its ski instructors are among the most qualified in the world: three former world champions and many members of the national ski team serve as instructors. In total,

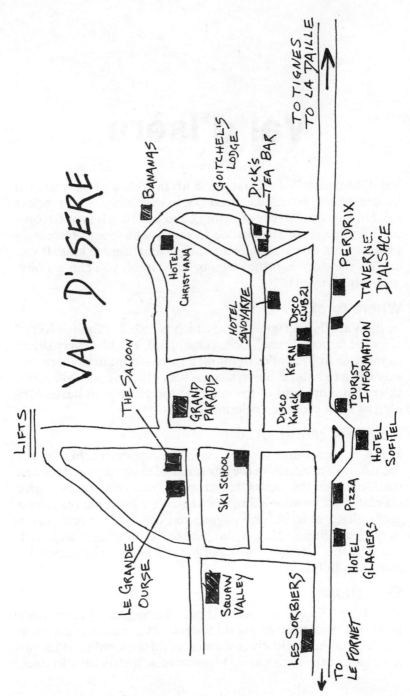

there are 120 instructors and 19 mountain guides who can teach any level of skier, from the basic beginner to the absolute best racer. English is spoken by many of the instructors. Be sure to specify that you need an English-speaking instructor.

Individual lessons

for one hour	FFR 125
(12:30 to 1:30 p.m.	
—max. five skiers)	
for a half day	FFR 425
(9 a.m. until noon or	
1:30 until 4:30 p.m.)	
for a full day	FFR 850

A certified guide for powder skiing costs FFR 975 per day.

Group lessons

Three-hour morning or afternoon courses are conducted. Prices are per week. These are high season prices—low season costs approximately FFR 65 less for each category.

	adults (with video)	children (4-12 yrs.)
for 5 half-days	FFR 410	FFR 330
for 5 full days	FFR 745	FFR 595

There are also off-piste courses and powder skiing lessons, which range in price from FFR 800 to FFR 960 a week per person.

Lift tickets

These prices are for the entire "L'Espace Killy," including the Val d'Isère/Tignes area pass. (88/89 prices)

for one day	FFR 148
for two days	FFR 275
for three days	FFR 385
for six days	FFR 710
for seven days	FFR 810
for 14 days	FFR 1385

There are discounted rates on some tickets for children 13 and under, seniors over 60 years and for beginners. Check with the tourist office or at the lift ticket office when purchasing your pass.

Children under five years go free. Photo is needed for all tickets two days and over. The ticket is valid for one day of your stay on La Plagne and Les Arcs skilifts.

Accommodation

The tourist office and the hoteliers have organized a special "blue-week/white-week" program, which is in effect only during the week before Christmas, during January, after New Year's and for two weeks in April. Check with the tourist office for exact dates. The costs for the program are based on the category of hotel chosen and the type of package the skier desires, with or without ski lessons. The "white-week" prices below are for seven days accommodations at half pension in a room with bath or shower. Included is a six-day ski pass and ski insurance. These are per person prices based on double occupancy.

hotel category	w/o lessons	with lessons
two stars	FFR 2415	FFR 3145
three stars	FFR 2790	FFR 3520
four stars	FFR 3875	FFR 4605

Recommended hotels are:

In the three-star category—Savoyarde (tel. 79.06.01.55), Grand Paradis (tel. 79.06.11.73) and Squaw Valley, bed and breakfast only, (tel. 79.06.02.72). The best two-star hotels are Les Sorbiers (tel. 97.06.23.77), Chamois d'Or (tel. 79.06.00.44), Glaciers (tel. 79.06.00.01), Lern, bed and breakfast, (tel. 79.06.06.06).

Apartments

In the French apartment rental system, the tourist office acts as an information clearinghouse. It maintains an extensive list of individuals and agencies who will rent apartments in the resort area at extremely low rates.

In many cases, linen is not included but can be rented for the week from the apartment owners or agencies.

A typical sample of the apartment costs in Val d'Isère is provided below. These centrally located units are about 100 meters from the lifts.

	high season	low season
for two to three persons	FFR 1615-2550	FFR 815-1410
for four to five persons	FFR 2480-4290	FFR 1280-2215
for six to seven persons	FFR 4820-6745	FFR 2415-4325

Most agencies and individual owners offer apartments within similar price ranges. Note the differences between low and high seasons. During high season, accommodation costs will range between FFR 100 and FFR 150 per person a day, based on four people sharing a typical two-bedroom unit. For more information and a complete list of rental apartments, write to the tourist office. It will send listings of both agencies and individual owners along with prices.

Dining

Two restaurants that have been recommended as the best by local residents are Le Grande Ourse (tel. 79.06.00.19) and Goitschel's Lodge (tel. 79.06.02.01). Other excellent eateries are White Ocean (tel. 79.06.20.02), L'Aventure (tel. 79.06.08.30), El Cortijo (tel. 79.06.03.25) and Taverne d'Alsace (tel. 79.06.02.39). Restaurants with excellent atmosphere are La Crech'Ouna (tel. 79.06.07.40) and Samovar, in La Daille, (tel. 79.06.13.51). Pizza can be found at Perdrix Blanche and Pacific Espace. Local specialties are best found in La Raclette (tel. 79.06.02.00) and Arolay, in Le Fornet, (tel. 79.06.11.68).

On the slopes the best food is at La Petite Folie at the La Daille mid-station. Other good lunches are at Cabaret des Neiges, the mid-station at Solaise; La Datcha at Solaise; Col de l'Iseran with great views and a peaceful setting and fast food; Le Crech'Ouna at the bottom of La Daille for a real restaurant.

You can be sure that locals will promote their favorites, so ask them for other recommendations. Tell them what you are looking for: low prices, meat specialties, fish dishes, atmosphere and so on.

Nightlife

Until recently, Val d'Isère was not known for wild nightlife. In fact, the resort was best known for its lack of it. Times are changing. In this skier's resort, though many people come to ski and are in bed after a hard day on the slopes, the nightlife is beginning to pop. Whenever thousands of skiers gather, a good time can't be far behind.

For drinking and dancing, Dick's Tea Bar and Playbach are the two main English language hangouts. For real French discos try Club 21 or the Knack in the Blizzard Hotel. Mephisto in the Grand Paradis Hotel hosts an older crowd, mainly French. Good bars are the Squaw Valley with videos and music, the Saloon in the Hotel Brussels which has a huge Swedish crowd, Bananas—a good local with many English speakers, Perdrix and Taverne d'Alsace.

Child care

There are many alternatives for child care in Val d'Isère. The hotels and the tourist office can put you in touch with private baby sitters.

In addition, there are three organized day-care facilities. Kindergarten Les 3 Pommes (tel. 79.06.17.66) takes children between the ages of three months and three years. Cost is FFR 31 per hour, FFR 120 for a morning until 2 p.m. with meal, and FFR 95 for the afternoon from 1-5:30 p.m. without meal.

Le Petit Poucet (tel. 79.06.13.97) is for children between three and ten years. Costs are FFR 34 per hour, FFR 160 per day, and FFR 980 for seven days. Both kindergartens are open from 9 a.m. until 5:30 p.m. and offer bus services that pick up the children from the hotels.

The third facility is the French Ski School, which has an

extensive children's program for four-year-olds up to 12. There is the "Children's Corner" with 30 instructors and the Snow School Solaise (tel. 79.06.11.79), which conducts a 30-hour program of English-language lessons. Other ski school opportunities are the Mini Champions club available for FFR 700 per week or FFR 130 per day (meals not included), or the Enterlou Club for more advanced children skiers which costs FFR 753 per week or FFR 130 per day without meals. More information from the ski school at telephone 79.06.02.34.

Getting there

The closest airports are in Lyon and Geneva. Geneva is about 140 kilometers (86 miles) and Lyon is approximately 240 kilometers (150 miles) from the resort. Rail transport is available from both cities but connections can become complicated. Trains also run to Bourg St. Maurice, where a bus connection takes you on to Val d'Isère.

The best autoroute from Geneva is A41 to Annecy; then take N90 to Albertville, where you should follow the signs to Bourg St. Maurice and on to Val d'Isère or Col de l'Isèran. From Lyons, take autoroute A43 to Chambéry, then follow the signs to Albertville and on to Val d'Isère. There is a daily direct bus service from both airports to Val d'Isère during the winter months.

Other activities

Val d'Isère is at the end of a long mountain road and once you get there it is doubtful that you will be anxious to leave on day-trips. The town offers good but limited activities for non-skiers. There is a covered, heated swimming pool open 3-8 p.m. with a daily entrance fee of FFR 18 for adults and FFR 12 for children (free to holders of seven-day ski passes). Week passes can be bought for FFR 75 (adults) and FFR 40 (children).

An outdoor natural ice rink is available for skaters from 10 a.m. to 7 p.m. Special dancing courses are given in the evenings and visitors interested in bubble-bath treatments, underwater seaweed massages, exercise rooms and regular massage can get the full treatment at Hotel Sofitel (tel. 79.06.08.30). The price for a six-day package is FFR 1850.

Tourist information

For more information, contact Office du Tourisme, BP n. 28, 73150 Val d'Isère, France; tel. 79.06.10.83; telex: 980077 OFI-TOUR.

For accommodation, contact Val Hôtel, BP n. 73, 73150, Val d'Isère, France; tel. 79.06.18.90; telex: 980077.

Les Trois Vallées

Welcome to the largest ski area in the world. Les Trois Vallées is the collective name for four separate villages in France's Savoie region which are connected by the most extensive lift system anywhere. The statistics are staggering: 175 lifts, 700 ski instructors, a 250-square-kilometer area boasting 280 miles of marked runs and a lift capacity of 130,000 skiers an hour.

The four villages comprising Les Trois Vallées are Courchevel, Méribel, Les Menuires and Val Thorens. Of the four, only Méribel is a truly traditional village; the others are "purpose-built," as the French say, and that purpose is skiing. This is an area that has been constructed for skiers with skiing as its number-one priority. Let's deal with each of the villages separately.

Courchevel

This is perhaps the most cosmopolitan of the four resorts. Courchevel itself is really a series of smaller villages whose names reflect their relative heights in meters; thus, Courchevel 1850, Courchevel 1650, Courchevel 1550 and so on. Every village features modern, massive apartment buildings and hotels.

The most prestigious of the villages is the highest, Courchevel 1850. Prices for everything are a bit higher than in the lower villages, but it's also where most trails run right outside the hotel or your apartment door. Built for ski in/ski out, Courchevel 1850 really works. Its lift system covers both sides of the valley. The world's largest cable car lift, heading up to La Saulire (2708 meters), connects Courchevel to the rest of the Les Trois Vallées area.

Méribel

Méribel has been developed into a first-rate ski resort but has taken pains to retain the traditional mountain architecture of the French Alps. The resort has two sections, Les Allues—traditional and very popular with the British, and Mottaret—purpose built and more French. Allues was virtually founded by the British, still retains much of its British trappings and English seems to be spoken almost everywhere.

Méribel is located in the central Valley of the Les Trois Vallées and is served by the smallest number of lifts. It makes up for this relative disadvantage, however, by providing the easiest connections to either of the other two valleys. Don't get the idea that you will have trouble finding a lift: there are 18 of them which originate in the village and link up with the other 175 lifts of the Les Trois Vallées system.

The lift to La Saulire provides the best access to the Courchevel valley and the lifts to either Roc des 3 Marches (2703 meters) or Mont de la Challe (2575 meters) provide the best connections To Val Thorens and Menuires.

Val Thorens

Val Thorens, at 2300 meters, is the highest resort in the Les Trois Vallées area. It has been adopted by the Scandinavian skiers and a sprinkling of Dutch. Little more than a cluster of modern high-rise apartment buildings and hotels, Val Thorens' real claim to fame is a cable car that takes skiers to the summit of Cîme de Caron at 3200 meters. From here, the skiing sweeps around the valley to the Thorens glacier and then to the west-facing slopes below Mont de la Chambre descending into Les Menuires. A new detachable four-seater chair and a high speed button lift have opened a new Boismint area for skiing. In the summer this is one of the best places to ski in Europe.

Les Menuires

Les Menuires is also a modern resort with only a few hotels and lots of apartments. From a distance the original section of the resort looks like a misplaced spaceship resting on the snow. The newer sections have concentrated on smaller buildings built in community clusters which seem cozy after walking through the massive original complexes. Here you will find skiers traveling with families and those looking for the steeps. The skiing is wide open on the west-facing slope with lifts running up toward Val Thorens. The east-facing side of the valley offers more challenging skiing from Pointe de la Masse (2808 meters), which can be reached by riding a combination of two lifts. The off-piste skiing from this point and from Cîme de Caron are exceptional, especially during the Spring when skiers can drop over the back side of the mountains with certified guides. Cîme de Caron, towering over Val Thorens, is also easily accessible and offers good runs.

The lifts taking skiers to the Roc des 3 Marches and to Mont de la Challe provide the best connections to Méribel and the rest of the Les Trois Vallées area.

Mountain rating

This area is so vast and varied that no skier should have trouble finding the perfect slope for his level of ability.

The best expert skiing is in the Val Thorens/Les Menuires valley. Here, on the Cîme de Caron and descending from Pointe de la Masse, experts can find the best steeps, the best powder and the smallest crowds. There are also good expert runs dropping from the ridge separating this valley from that of Méribel. Méribel has few expert runs, the only one of note being a straight shot from La Saulire into town. Courchevel is not known for expert terrain. The best you can find in that region is under La Vizelle, running from Col de la Loze (2280 meters) into Courchevel 1300, or try the runs dropping from Col de Chanrossa which will test any expert.

Intermediates can ski almost anywhere since all expert trails have good escape routes. The area around Courchevel is wide open and good for intermediates.

Beginners will find plenty of trails for learning and will probably leave feeling that they have conquered the entire Les Trois Vallées area.

Ski school

All of the area's resorts have excellent instructors. There are over 400 instructors in Courchevel (the largest ski school in the world; tel. 79.08.07.72), 130 instructors in Les Menuires (79.00.61.43), 100 in Val Thorens (79.00.02.86) and 70 in Méribel. The prices vary by resort—these are for Les Menuires.

Individual lessons

for one hour (1-2 skiers)	FFR 122
for one hour (3-4 skiers)	FFR 155

Group lessons

for six	FFR 650
consecutive lessons	
children's group	FFR 540

Mlaaeribel: six-day group lesson—FFR 500; private hour—FFR120. **Val Thorens:** five-day group—FFR620; private hour—FFR135.

Special lessons for powder skiing, mono skiing, ski ballet and free-style skiing are offered. There are also racing clinics and a ski kindergarten. A special accompanied ski adventure through the Les Trois Vallées and another tour through the 12 valleys of the Tarentaise—including the resorts of Val Thorens, La Plagne, Les Arcs, Val d'Isère and Tignes—are also offered. For more ski school information, call 79.00.02.86; for special courses, call 79.00.08.08.

Lift tickets

Each area offers three lift-ticket combinations: one covers only the lifts in the resort area, the second covers lifts in the entire valley; and a third is a full Les Trois Vallées lift ticket. Skiers who are staying for a week or more will want to purchase the Les Trois Vallées combination ticket. The difference between a local pass and the combination pass for a seven-day period is less than FFR 130.

Prices for the Les Trois Vallées combination pass during high season are:

for one day	FFR 158
for six days	FFR 790

for seven days FFR 650
for fourteen days FFR 1506
for each extra day FFR 110

During low season prices drop by about 15 Percent. For children under 13 and seniors over 60, day passes cost FFR 126 and low-season prices are in effect throughout the ski year.

Accommodation

This is one of the most expensive areas in Europe. Accommodations in the villages all fall within the same price range, except for Courchevel 1850 which is slightly higher. But even though its prices are 15 to 20 percent higher than the other resorts, Courchevel 1850 still offers extremely reasonably-priced accommodation in luxury surroundings, but you must be very careful about making arrangements during the low season.

Most hotels are modern and were built during the same period. However, the rooms are small, even by French standards.

The hotels listed below are only identified as to category and phone number to help when making reservations; all normally feature special "white-week" prices. The tourist office will send a complete list of hotels with information about "white week" periods and details of making reservations.

Val Thorens
Le Val Thorens***tel. 79.00.04.33
Novotel***tel. 79.00.04.04
Le Corotel** tel. 79.00.02.70
La Marmotte** tel. 79.00.00.07
Le Sherpa** tel. 79.00.00.70
Les Trois Vallées** tel. 79.00.01.86

Les Menuires
Hotel Pelvoux***tel. 79.00.61.09
Hotel Skilt***tel. 79.00.61.00
Hotel Edelweiss**tel. 79.00.66.17

Méribel
Hotel Le Roc**tel. 79.08.64.16
La Chaudanne** tel. 79.08.61.76

Le Belvédere**tel. 79.08.65.53
Mont Vallon****Ltel. 79.00.44.00 in Mottaret
Mottaret***tel. 79.00.47.47 in Mottaret
Le Ruitor***tel. 79.00.48.48 in Mottaret

Courchevel

Bellecote****(Lux) tel. 79.08.12.12
Grand Hotel**** tel.79.08.02.69
Des Neiges**** tel. 79.08.03.77
Airelles*** tel. 79.08.02.11
Aiglon** tel.79.08.02.66
Poitniere** tel. 79.08.00.16
Flocons** tel.79.08.02.70 in "1550"
Peupliers**tel. 79.08.11.61 in "1300"

Apartments

Apartments are the French choice for accommodation. In fact, apartment beds outnumber hotel beds by at least five to one. What you get is the ability to schedule off-slope life at your own pace. Apartment rates are slightly higher in Courchevel 1850. In general, for a one-week stay expect to pay:

	low season	**high season**
for two to three persons	FFR 1000-2000	FFR 1740-3090
for four to five persons	FFR 1400-2000	FFR 2800-3800
for five to six persons	FFR 1800-2500	FFR 3500-4900

Even at the high end of low-season prices, an apartment shared by four people costs less than FFR 75 a night per person.

During "white-week" periods, in Les Menuires, for example, apartments come with a six-day ski pass for the three valleys and cost FFR 1200 per person a week when sharing a two person apartment. For a four person apartment the costs drop to FFR 1010 per person. That's FFR 150 a day.

The tourist office will send more information and a registration card, and will help make reservations.

Dining

The area has excellent restaurants both on and off the slopes and in surrounding small mountain villages. Enjoy a great meal with good wine for around FFR 100 per person. If you go overboard, the price may creep up to FFR 175. Normally, a restaurant packed with Frenchmen can't be bad.

I have only had the opportunity to sample food around Le Menuires and Val Thorens. La Bouitte in St. Marcel is probably the best restaurant in the valley. The restaurant in the Hotel Val Thorens, Chalet de Glacier and Galoubet all in Val Thorens are excellent. "La Loubine" in Meribel has been recommended and Hotel Belvedere on the mountain serves a great lunch. Courchevel boasts four Michelin-star restaurants.

Nightlife

Courchevel is considered to have one of the best balances between nightlife and skiing of any European resort. While not as glitzy as Mégeve, Gstaad or St. Moritz, après-ski entertainment here is varied and you will be sure to find a bar or disco to your taste. Be prepared to fork over lots of money—this is some of the most expensive nightlife to be found in the Alps.

If you are looking for wild nightlife, the rest of the three valleys is not the place to be. Méribel has no discos that we've discovered! Nightlife consists of a few night clubs, a piano bar, a jazz bar and whatever you can organize on your own. Try "The Pub"—it seems to be the best in town. Les Menuires has four small discos, packed with the very young, tucked into the basement of the massive apartment buildings and in Val Thorens the nightlife is centered around the hotel bars.

Child care

The tourist office, your hotel or apartment manager can put you in touch with qualified private baby sitters who provide child-care services at any time of the day or night. Each resort also offers child-care programs. Here's a resort-by-resort rundown.

Val Thorens has a "Baby Club" at Tourotel for children from three months to three and a half years (tel. 79.00.03.63). The "Mini-Club" kindergarten for children from three and a half to

12 years is at Le Roc de Péclet and features ski lessons for children over five and snow activities for younger kids. Ask about discounts for three children or more from the same family. The costs are FFR 60 for a half day, FFR 105 for a full day and FFR 525 for a six-day program. Meals are extra; closed Sunday (tel. 79.00.00.47). Marielle Goitschel, former world champion skier has started a children's program in Val Thorens (tel. 79.00.00.47). Mornings cost FFR 91 without meals or FFR 120 with meal. A full day costs FFR 181 without meal and FFR 205 with meal.

Les Menuires has three possibilities for children. The Schtroumpfs' Village is divided into two sections: three months to two and a half years; two and a half to ten years. An intro to skiing is provided for children from four years; different programs are offered to each group. Reservations are recommended (tel. 79.00.63.79). A second kindergarten, called "Scoubidou," is located in the "Les Fontanettes" area. It serves children between two and eight years (tel. 79.00.67.75).

The ski school also runs special programs for youngsters from 5 years old. The lessons are coordinated with The Schtroumpfs' Village to allow children to spend the remaining time after and before lessons at the child care facility.

Méribel has a highly respected child care program. "Le Club Saturnin" accepts children between two and eight years. It is associated with the ski school and ski lessons are offered to children ready to ski (tel. 79.08.66.90). The second possibility for children is in Méribel-Mottaret. "Les Pingouins" accepts children between three and eight years (tel. 79.00.46.46).

Courchevel 1850 has a ski school for children from four years. Call 79.08.07.72 or 081459. There are also two kindergartens, one in 1850 and another in 1650. Both take children between the ages of two and five years. Call (for "1850") 79.08.31.54, or (for "1650") 79.08.03.29.

Getting there

The closest airports are Geneva (152 kilometers), Lyons (190 kilometers) and Chambéry (110 kilometers). There are daily connections from the airport to the resorts. The rail service takes skiers as far as Moutiers, 36 kilometers away, a one-hour drive, from the resorts. Bus and taxi services are available from the station.

If driving, follow the signs to Chambéry, and then take route N90 to Moutiers and up to the Les Trois Vallées. Some distances: Paris, 657 kilometers; Brussels, 921 kilometers; and Strasbourg, 555 kilometers.

Other activities

Val Thorens —Facilities include an indoor swimming pool, whirlpool baths, saunas, squash courts, six indoor tennis courts, a gymnasium and an outdoor skating rink. Hang-gliding and aerobics are offered.

Méribel.—Facilities include an indoor swimming pool, indoor golf practice range and an ice skating rink. Mountain flying lessons are offered.

Courchevel —Facilities include indoor swimming pools, saunas and an Olympic-sized skating rink. Hang-gliding, ski jumping, parachuting and mountain flying courses are taught. Special language courses are organized for foreigners, allowing participants to combine skiing with language lessons. On Wednesday there is a musical evening with concerts and recitals.

Tourist information

Courchevel —Office du Tourisme, La Croisette, 73120 Courchevel 1850, France; tel. 79.08.00.29; telex: 980083

Méribel —Office du Tourisme, 73550 Méribel, France; tel. (79) 086001; telex: 980001

Val Thorens —Office du Tourisme, 73440 Val Thorens, France; tel. 79.00.08.08; telex: 980572

Les Menuires —Office du Tourisme, 73440 Les Menuires, France; tel. 79.08.20.12; telex: 980084

Garmisch, Germany

Garmisch, at the base of the Zugspitze (2964 meters—9721 feet) the country's highest mountain, is less than an hour's drive from Munich. As Germany's most famous and best ski resort it attracts an international group of ski enthusiasts. The resort consists of the twin towns of Garmisch-Partenkirchen and ranks as one of Europe's friendliest and best-organized, with activities for visitors of every age. When considered along with neighboring slopes in Mittenwald and those across Germany's border with Austria on the other side of the Zugspitze, Garmisch is an excellent ski-vacation destination. ($1.00 = DM 1.7)

Where to ski

Garmisch offers nearly 75 miles of runs, but the rugged Alpine landscape prevents any sort of continuous ski circuit between the seven different slopes. You'll ski in one of two large areas. One is on the high slopes of the Zugspitze plateau. You'll reach the top via cable car from Lake Eibsee above Garmisch or from the Zugspitze cogwheel train; the cable is more scenic, the train more direct. Skiing here is at its best in early November and December, and in spring—April-May—when other resorts are closing. Best of the trails is the two-mile-long run from the Schneefernerkopf at 2874 meters (9427 feet).

The Wank, at 1779 meters (5835 feet), joins the adjacent, lower Eckbauer (1238 meters) as the two most limited slopes in the area. We liked the Wank more, particularly after taking a deep-snow excursion with a guide on the trail from the summit down towards the Esterbergalm.

The Eckbauer is more popular for sentimental reasons. At its base is the Olympic Ski Stadium and the ski jumps where the greatest ski fliers in the world perform each year.

Garmisch hosted the Winter Olympic Games in 1932 and 1936 and its facilities are well maintained. The World-Cup runs on the Eckbauer and the neighboring Hausberg provide several difficult turns but, overall, it's perfect terrain for intermediates.

Our favorite runs are from the Osterfelderkopf. From here you can make the only real skiing circuit runs in Garmisch, linking up with lifts from the Hausberg below.

For Zugspitze fans there is a new double-chair lift to the glacier at 2800 meters. A new tunnel for the cogwheel train eliminates walking, and now allows direct access to the slopes.

One more suggestion: for interesting skiing and sometimes shorter lift lines, take the border highway past Grainau into Austria. Here, on the other side of the Zugspitze and less than a 30-minute drive away, try the slopes of Ehrwald. Occasionally, when Garmisch's weather is bad the sun will be shining in Ehrwald. Neighboring Lermoos and Biberwier, also in Austria, are popular with local skiers.

In the other direction, at Mittenwald, the Damkarr run from the 2385-meter (7822-foot) Karwendel summit is interesting and the mountain panorama superb.

Mountain rating

Garmisch is intermediate country. Despite challenging parts of red runs that might be considered black, and difficult World-Cup sections on the Eckbauer and Hausberg, the intermediate and advanced beginner will find it the place to be. Beginners could not come to a better place for outstanding ski instruction and a large number of lifts.

We gave Garmisch an excellent rating for its cross-country trails. There are 35 miles of maintained trails in the area.

Ski School

Garmisch's ski school program includes off-trail touring instruction and an outstanding climbing school. Eight schools offer instruction in the area. Rates for the various schools are within a few Marks of each other.

Individual lessons

for one hour	DM 45
for each additional person	DM 10
for two hours	DM 90
for one day	DM 200
(four hours)	

Group lessons

for one day	DM 30
(three hours)	
for three days	DM 80
for five days	DM 110
for a five day tour	DM 150
(includes lessons in a	
different area each day)	

All schools have good reputations. However, their locations may play a role in your choice. The schools also offer cross-country instruction. For more information, contact:

Skischule Hohenleitner (tel. 50610) Located near the Zugspitze railway station.

Skischule Woerndle (tel. 58300) At the Hausberg cable car station.

Olympia Skischule (tel. 4600) Near the Osterfelder station.

Skilanglaufschule (tel. 1516) Cross-country school at the Olympic stadium.

Skischule Garmisch-Partenkirchen (tel. 4931) At the Hausberg slope.

Bergsteigerschule Zugspitze (tel. 3040) Mountain climbing and ski touring instruction.

Cross-country

Garmisch, unlike many resorts, has a separate school for cross-country fans. The school at the Olympic stadium (tel. 1516) offers private and group lessons.

Individual lessons

for one hour	DM 40
for each additional	DM 5
for one day	DM 210
(four hours)	

Group lessons

for one day	DM 25
(two hours)	
for three days	DM 65
for five days	DM 95

Lift tickets

The least attractive aspect of Garmisch skiing is the mishmash of tickets you may need if you're moving around the area. The best general ticket to purchase is the Garmisch V ticket, good on lifts of the Wank, Eckbauer, Hausberg, Kreuzeck and Osterfelder areas.

for a half day	DM 26
(from noon)	
for one day	DM 34

A day-ticket for the Wank area (*W Tageskarte*) costs DM 25; for the Eckbauer area (*E Tageskarte*) DM 19.

If you want to ski the Zugspitze, you need the *Z Tageskarte*, which costs DM 42 daily.

In addition, there is a special ticket for the V area which offers a price reduction if you use it less than four hours.

The closest thing to a regional pass is the M card, good for a minimum of three days. It can be used at any of the area slopes, but you can't mix your skiing on any given day. For instance, if you choose The Zugspitze, then the ticket is good only there for the day. If you choose the V area, then the Zugspitze is out of bounds that day.

M card

for three days	DM 100
for four days	DM 130
for five days	DM 154
for six days	DM 176
for seven days	DM 196

Accommodation

The lift-ticket confusion is not carried over into accommodation. You can quickly find a place to stay, whether a farmhouse or an ultra luxurious hotel.

Garmisch has an outstanding selection of all-in plans and especially caters to families or couples with one non-skier. There are at least a dozen other organized sports and free-time pursuits set up for non-skiers in week-long packages.

The best ski plan is SLI1, a tourist-office special offered during middle season and priced from approximately DM 450 to DM 750. The price includes half-pension accommodation in several excellent hotels, including the famed Schneefernerhaus on the Zugspitze, plus five days ski intruction and lift tickets for the Zugspitze.

The SLI2 plan is even more outstanding for the budget-minded. Bed-and-breakfast in a private home, plus a week's ski course starts at about DM 250.

Additional plans are: SLI3 for cross-country, also beginning at approximately DM 260; EL for figure skating, beginning at about DM 285; and CL curling, from DM 250.

Listed below are hotels and guesthouses which a Ski Europe representative found to provide comfortable, reasonably priced rooms. These prices are per person per week based on double occupancy in high season unless noted otherwise. Telephone prefix for Garmisch is (08821).

Hotel Sonnenbichel (tel. 7020; telex: 59632) DM 140-165 per person per night with half pension. This is considered by many to be the best hotel in the town.

Best Western Hotel Obermühle (tel. 7040; telex: 59609) DM 125-165 per person per night with breakfast. It has what many feel is the best restaurant in town.

Hotel Boddenberg (tel. 51089) DM 65 per person per night Bed and Breakfast.

Hotel Forsthaus Graseck (tel. 54006; telex: 59653) DM 64-104 half pension per person per night.

Aschenbrenner (tel. 58029) DM 55-80 Bed and breakfast.

Hotel Hilleprandt (tel. 2861) DM 54-81—Quiet, family-run hotel within walking distance of the Hausberg ski school. Lower-priced rooms begin at approximately DM 350 a week. A good choice for the budget plan.

Hotel Pension Therese (tel. 2773) DM 35-56—Bed-and-breakfast. Near the center of town, about five minutes by foot from the railway station.

Haus Hamburg (tel. 3003) DM 34-45—Small bed-and-breakfast guesthouse with 26 beds, located near the middle of town. Particularly quiet location.

Schneefernerhaus (tel. 58011) DM 78-97—On the Zugspitze slope, Germany's highest hotel at 2650 meters (8692 feet). Unequalled for the skier; otherwise, extremely isolated.

Haus Schell (tel. 2989) DM 42-60—half-board. No bath in rooms, go down the hall. Located very close to the station.

Apartments

The popularity of apartments has increased in Garmisch in recent years and many hotels now offer them. The Garmisch

Tourist Office provides an 85-page accommodation booklet, which not only lists available apartments but also includes pictures of some of them. Most interesting of those we saw were the apartments in the Husar section (tel. Alpina Hausbau 50084) with furnished apartments for two to six persons. Prices begin at approximately DM 65-85 a day.

Child care

Larger hotels provide baby-sitting services. In addition, check with the tourist office for a listing of baby sitters in the area. Ski kindergarten and ski courses for youths are offered. Ski kindergarten prices:

for a half day (9 a.m. until 12 or 1 until 4:30 p.m.)	DM 8
for one day (9 a.m. until 4:30 p.m.)	DM 17 (includes lunch)

A five-day children's ski course with four hours of instruction daily, including lunch, is approximately DM 160.

Dining

The Obermühle in the Hotel of the same name where they serve excellent Bavarian specialties and suprisingly good fish.

The Post Hotel in Partenkirchen on Ludwigstr. 49 also serves excellent fare.

We were partial to the bountiful, tasty dishes at another Hotel Post (tel. 08825-211) in Wallgau, about 12 miles from Garmisch. Traditional Alpine decorations, massive wooden tables and chairs and extra-friendly service complement the food.

Of course, you need walk only as far as yet another Post Hotel (tel. 58071) in Garmisch's Marienplatz for excellent dining in the Poststüberl.

You can eat less expensively, surrounded by an international group, in La Fattoria (tel. 58445) or at the Chapeau Claque bistro (tel. 71300).

For a typical Bavarian evening, go to Gasthof Fraundorfer (tel. 2176) at Ludwigstrasse 24.

Nightlife

Young and old, continental rich and ski-bum poor. That's the usual mix of people at Juergen's Pilsbar on the Marienplatz.

Chapeau Claque, where the food is also good, is a popular meeting spot.

If you want to dance, we suggest the Baccarat (tel. 1626) on Bahnhofstrasse. Try Clausings Casino in the former casino on Marienplatz for dancing or try the Peacock Bar in the Sonnenbischel on Friday and Saturday nights.

Getting there

Riem airport on the outskirts of Munich is only an hour away via autobahn. Innsbruck is less than two hours away by car. Rail travelers will find connections to Garmisch excellent.

Other activities

Garmisch is ideal for the visitor who does not want to ski during his entire vacation. Within an hour's drive are world-famous attractions. Chief among them is Munich, the Bavarian capital and Germany's number-one museum city. Above all, visit the Deutsches Museum, the German technical museum, which rivals the Smithsonian.

Central Munich, around the Marienplatz, should be included on any tour. Best view of the city is from the nearly 1000-foot-high television tower on the 1972 Olympics grounds.

Oberammergau, site of the famed passion play, is about a half-hour away by bus or car. Here you can visit dozens of wood-carving shops displaying the work of artisans, many of them trained in Oberammergau's national woodcarving school.

Along the road to Oberammergau, take a side trip up the Graswang valley to Schloss Linderhof, the ornate palace built by Ludwig II, the Mad King of Bavaria.

Nearby Mittenwald is famous for its violin makers and Innsbruck, capital of the Austrian Tyrol, is one of the most culturally rich cities in Europe.

Also consider a full-day trip to Neuschwanstein, the most famous of Ludwig's castles (near Füssen) and to Berchtesgaden.

One of Garmisch's most exciting events is the international

ski jumping competition at the Olympic stadium on New Year's day.

Tourist information

Verkehrsamt Garmisch-Partenkirchen, D-8100 Garmisch-Partenkirchen; tel. 08821-5355.

Baqueira/Beret
The Spanish
Pyrenees

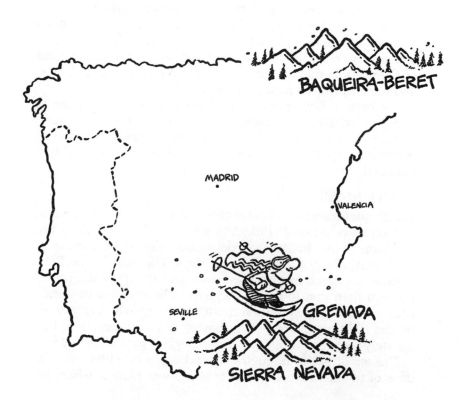

The remote Valle de Aran lies tucked hard against the French border in Spain's rugged Pyrenees mountains midway between the tempestuous Atlantic Ocean and the balmy Mediterranean Sea. This Spanish valley, virtually cut off from the rest of the country by jagged mountains, is accessible only by bus or car along a winding mountain road dwarfed by waterfalls and narrow canyons, and watched over by grazing mountain goats and shaggy cattle. Though the drive is arduous, beauty unfolds with every turn as you pass a string of timeless villages presided over by Romanesque churches. From the far eastern section of the valley rises a modern cluster of apartment buildings, Banqueira/Beret. Though over a dozen ski resorts have sprouted up in the Pyrenees, Baqueira/Beret is the largest. In fact, it is the most extensive of any European resort outside of the Alps.

This resort has a rather complex season structure. Expect the Christmas/New Year period to be super high season as it is everywhere, but in Spain the week after New Year normally remains high season. The middle two weeks of January list as low season, then the last week of January and the first week of February is middle season and the remainder of February and most of March is high season.

The bottom line on Baqueira/Beret is that the snow can be very patchy. The best skiing is normally in January and early February. Though there have been years where snow has remained for Easter, planning a vacation on that possibility is foolhardy.

Where to ski

The Baqueira and the Beret sections of this resort are in reality two separate ski areas linked by one lift. The network of lifts and runs above Baqueira is dense and should keep most intermediates busy for a couple of days. The runs in the Beret section are much more widespread, and the lift system more modern than that found in Baqueira. The runs are extremely poorly-marked. It is more a matter guessing whether you are on the right piste rather than having any real direction. Fortunately the area is not extensive enough to get hopelessly lost.

The sector above Baqueira is reached by two lifts from the edge of town. This brings skiers to a lower plateau where beginners learn on what are called the "pastures" and four more lifts drag skiers to the upper reaches of the mountain. Head to the left of the restaurant and take the Mirador 1 or 2 lift. This allows experts and good intermediates the option of dropping down to the Cap de Baqueira single chair to return to the summit, or of dropping down to the "Luis Arias" lift to head up to the Cap de Baqueira peak. Intermediates can enjoy the Isards and Perdix Blanca runs back to the lower plateau or all the way into the valley to the De la Choza chairlift. Beginners can stay to the right side of the restaurant where there are a chair lift and a drag lift opening plenty of practice area.

The Beret area is served by only four lifts but its terrain allows skiers to venture virtually anywhere and choose from expert to beginner difficulties. The link with Beret from Baqueira is made in the valley by either a drag lift or a new chairlift. The run from the top of either of these lifts is colored red on the piste map but should probably be catagorized as blue. Once arriving in Beret get ready to cruise. Two triple-chair lifts bracket the restaurant. The one to the right reaches intermediate terrain and that to the left serves long beginner slopes, and also allows a link up to the most exciting part of Beret, the bowl under Tuc de Dossal (2510 m). Most of the skiing in Beret is rather straightforward but the mountain beneath Tuc de Dossal opens itself to infinite possibilities. There are intermediate drops directly below the chair or just to the

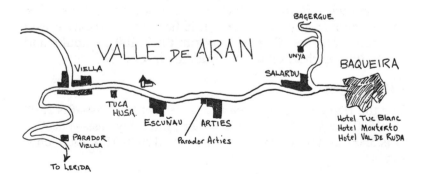

right of the lift; an adventurous skier can traverse along the ridge and choose steeps that will keep any expert happy. For those who get cold skis at the last minute, the traverse turns into an enjoyable beginner cruising piste back into Beret. All in all, this part of the mountain is fun for every skier.

Mountain rating

This resort is not easy enough to reach to be considered a weekend trip, unless you live in Barcelona, Zaragoza or Lerida in Spain or in one of the French cities lining the Pyrenees. For an intermediate there is plenty of skiing and enough challenge to leave one feeling pushed beyond one's normal limits. Absolute beginners have plenty of area to begin their stem-christies then strike out for excellent long easy slopes. Experts will find enough to keep them busy for about two days: then will probably get itchy for new slopes to conquor. However, if there is a good snowfall the powder below the Tuc de Dossal is hard to beat.

Ski school

Here Baquiera has a problem with English-speaking instructors. When I checked last year only four of the 25 instructors were capable of conversing in English. Make sure to request one of the English-speaking instructors and do it the day before, if at all possible, to make sure you are not forgotten.

The prices for private lessons, per hour, during high season are Pts. 2500 for one or two persons; and Pts. 3200 for three or four persons. Six days of group instruction will cost Pts. 9000 per week for adults during middle season and Pts. 8000 for children (5-11years) during middle season. Weekly lesson arrangements including ski pass run Pts.20100 for adults and Pts.18300 for children during middle season.

Lift tickets

For the Baquiera/Beret area the rates are: full day—Pts.2300 (Pts1500 children 11 years and under); three-day pass—Pts.6000 (Pts.3900 children); six-day pass—Pts.12000 (Pts.7900 children).

Accommodation

The accommodation is spread throughout the valley. When first informed of this situation it seemed very inconvenient, but after spending several days driving through the valley, hotel accommodation outside Baqueira is not extremely inconvenient, especially if you arrived by car. With plenty of parking near the lifts, the best restaurants spread along the entire length of the valley, and two relatively luxurious paradors ten minutes outside the resort town itself, an automobile is a real asset in the Valle de Aran rather than an unwanted problem it might be in other resorts.

For those coming with a group, having a hotel in Baqueira means being able to ski when you want, not when your bus heads in that direction. Don't make the mistake of missing your group bus to the lifts since the public transportation is woefully inadequate making only two scheduled runs from Viella to Baqueira and back each day.

Baqueira/Beret's accommodation has been organized weekly ski prices which include bed and breakfast, based on double occupancy, plus lift tickets from Monday to Saturday. These weekly prices for the medium season are noted for each hotel. Prices increase approximately 12% during the high season and drop 15% during the low season. The normal daily rates are quoted for bed and breakfast. You must remember to add 6% value added tax (VAT) to these prices.

There are two paradors in the Valle de Aran. Most Americans and British confer an aura of luxury on these lodgings. Here in the Valle de Aran the paradors are the most luxurious.

Parador Nacional Don Gaspar de Portola, Arties tel. (973) 640801. This is a new four-star parador located in Arties seven kilometers from the slopes. The town of Arties is the gourmet center of the valley with some of Spain's top restaurants within a five-minute walk of the parador. Special weekly rate: Pts.32,000.

Paradors Nacional Valle de Aran, Viella tel. (973) 640100. An impressive building overlooking Viella at the entrance to the tunnel leading south from the valley. The relatively modern parador is a three-star hotel and is located 14 kilometers from the Baqueira/Beret lifts. There is local bus service twice a day to the lifts and back. Unlike the other parador this one is a long walk from the town. Special weekly rate: Pts.30,100.

There are three hotels in the resort of Baqueira. All three are clustered at the base of the runs and the lifts. The most sought after rooms are in the **Val de Ruda** a small, new three-star hotel. Special weekly rate: Pts.35,000. Normal daily rate: Pts.5,225. **Tuc Blanc** is a big modren hotel which is closest to the lifts. Special weekly rate: Pts.35,000. Normal daily rate: Pts.4,050. **Montarto** is the classiest hotel according to reputation among the Spanish however, the facilities are not particularly better than any of the other establishmsnts. Special weekly rate: Pts.38,400. Normal daily rate: Pts.4,450.

The only other relatively upscale hotel in the valley is the **Hotel HUSA Tuca** located at the base of the smaller ski area of Tuca. This hotel is convenient to Viella and 13 kilometers from the Baqueira slopes. Special weekly rate: Pts.29,000. Normal daily rate: Pts.1,550. The **Hotel Aran** which does blockbusting business with British tour groups is in the middle of Viella. Hotel Aran is very simple lodging located right in the middle of town and very convenient to any nightlife which might be percolating. For almost an identical rate I would head for the HUSA Tuca just up the road. Special weekly rate: Pts27,600.

Apartments

Baqueira/Beret has thousands of beds in apartments (or condos for the Americans). For the special weekly rate in middle season including lift passes for the week expect to pay the following: two-person apartment—Pts.38,200 per person; three-person apartment—Pts29,000 per person; four-person apartment—Pts.24,400 per person.

For reservations call the tourist office in Baqueira/Beret, tel. (973) 645025 or 645050 between 9 am and 1 pm or from 3 pm to 7 pm. There are also reservation offices in Barcelona and Madrid.

Child care

The resort has two child care centers accepting children from three to eight years of age. One is at the 1500 meter level in town which will also take infants from three months and there is a children's snow park with supervisory personnel at the 1800 meter level near the restaurant. Children can learn to ski or just play in the snow and watch movies. Expect to pay (including lunch) Pts.2000-2200 per day; and Pts.11,000 per week.

Dining

The restaurants in this valley are perhaps the best collection of eateries surrounding any ski resort in Europe. This assessment is made not based on snooty, high-class gourmets and guidebook stars, but on overall excellent affordable restaurants which range from some considered the best in Spain to others hidden in high mountain villages reachable only after long drives over barely-paved roads. The blend of French and Spanish cooking together with the mountain basics of the Valle de Aran has resulted in a unique cuisine which has been praised across Europe. Even without the skiing at Baqueira/Beret the trip to this valley would be worth any effort for the peace and the "comida."

Once again the restaurants are spread throughout the valley. The town of Arties is considered the cuisine capital of this region. Here you will find "Casa Irene" (640900) where the King and Queen of Spain often dine. It is obviously considered one of the premier restaurants in Spain. Around the corner is the almost equally legendary and royally visited "Patxiku Quintana" (641613) which is famous for its fish dishes. Even if the King and Queen are not coming to dinner the restaurants are usually full. Call for reservations. Expect to pay Pts. 5000 per person with house wine.

In the resort of Baqueira itself you'll find three excellent high-priced restaurants, "La Borda Lobato" (645708), "La Perdui Blanca" (645075), and "Ticolet" ((645477). These are not quite as popular but every bit as expensive.

If you are in Viella try to enjoy a meal at "Era Mola" (640868) once blessed with a royal visit, or "Neguri" (640211) where chef and owner José Antonio creates new dishes each night.

My favorite restaurants are those enjoyed by the locals. The top ranking in this category goes to "Carmela's" (645751) in the tiny dorf of Unha huddled above the town of Salardú. If you are looking for the name of the restaurant in the guide which theoretically lists every restaurant in the valley, you will find it listed as "Restaurant Es de Don Juan." If you are trying to find it ask the locals for "Carmela's." Make reservations. This place is every bit as crowded as any restaurant ever visited by the King and Queen down in the valley. One night after threading my way up the narrow road to "Carmela's" I was greeted with those famous words, "no room at the inn." After spirited begging and appropriate groans which did not secure a place Carmela sent me to another restaurant she personally recommended. This was another few miles up the mountain in the tiny town of Baguergue. In Carmela's word's, "See that church lit up on the mountain. . . go there and look for Casa Peru." After heading up from Salardu, pass the left-hand fork heading to Unha and continue up the mountain. The next town you reach is Baguergue. Park in the church parking lot and walk down the only street in town to "Casa Peru" (645437). There are normally tables.

Other recommended restaurants for good typical "Aranese" food are "Casa Turnay" and "Casa Estampa" in Escunhau, the next town up the road from Viella; "Et Restrille" in Garòs; and "Borda de Benjamin" in Salardú.

Here, as in the rest of Spain, dinner is served late by English/American standards but not as late as in Andalusia. Restaurants open around 8 pm and most patrons show up between 9 and 10 pm.

Nightlife

There is just not much from which to choose. The major disco in the valley is the "Tiffany" in Baqueira. It attracts an older crowd than the "Viella" disco in Viella. No one really shows up until midnight and the gyrations continue until three or four in the morning. The Pub in the Hotel Aran serves as a smokey local meeting place in the center of Viella, but is nothing to get excited about. Score this valley as very dead at night.

Getting there

Valle de Aran is not one of the easier spots on the earth to reach. There are no trains and no planes. That means bus or automobile. If you are arriving by plane in Zaragoza or Barcelona, the nearest airports, and then have a bus transfer arranged, be ready for approximately a four-hour ride. If you aren't with a group I would suggest you arrange car rental. The drive from Barcelona takes four hours, though natives claim that they can easily make the run in three. The resort is just over 300 kilometers from Barcelona and from San Sebastian and 290 kms. from Zaragoza

The scheduled buses leave Barcelona at 8 am and 3 pm arriving in the valley at 2:30 pm and 9:30 pm. There are also two return trips to Barcelona leaving at 4:30 pm and 4:55 am and arriving at 11 pm and 11:30 am respectively. Buses also run between Madrid and Baqueira. Leave Madrid at 8 am and arrive in Baqueira at 7:30 pm. The return from Baqueira leaves at 10:30 am and arrives in Madrid at 9:30 pm. Bus fare: Barcelona to Baqueira—Pts 2900; Madrid to Baqueira—Pts 4000.

Other activities

No swimming pools. No tennis courts. No bowling. No saunas. No major towns within easy striking distance. You can enjoy testing restaurants until you have waddle home. You can tune up your card playing. You can bring a lover.

Tourist information

Officina de Turismo de Baqueira/Beret, Apartado 60, Viella, Valle de Aran, tel. (973) 645050 or 645025; telex: 57707. Snow information in Spanish: (973) 645052.

Sierra Nevada, Spain

It's hard to believe, but there is skiing in southern Spain, less than an hour from Granada. The Sierra Nevada resort has skiing at an altitude of over 3000 meters (almost 10,000 feet) and brilliant sunshine most of the winter. The resort town itself is modern, basically a sparse cluster of hotels and apartments at the base of the first series of lifts. It is not a traditionally Spanish enclave, nor does it appear in any sense apline. But if you want to find snow in southern Spain, this is the place to be. ($1.00 = Pts 110)

Where to ski

To be honest it would be hard to get lost on this mountain unless faced with white-out conditions. The skiing range is not that extensive but the skiing is wide-open and the runs are long enough and gentle enough to bring smiles to most skiers' faces. The resort is undergoing a major series of improvements which has added four new lifts. The first of these new lifts opens the upper reaches of the mountain which required a change of lifts to reach. The other lifts add capacity to the slopes below the Veleta peak. Previously, the lifts went to the top of Veleta at 3470 meters, but the wind was so strong that they rarely remained open.

Borreguiles is the hub of the mountain. Here, at the midstation of the cable car rising from the town, restaurants are grouped together with the ski school.

If you take the Veleta II lift and traverse a little to your right you will enter the Laguna Yeguas, a wide bowl which offers some more testing intermediate terrain. When the snow is good, better skiers can drop down the Loma Dilar section of the resort and find some acceptable steeps.

Mountain rating

Don't even think that you will find anything terribly expert. There are testing sections of the resort, especially when skiing off-piste, but for the most part this is a mellow beginner/intermediate paradise. Lay back and enjoy the sun. The object here is sheer enjoyment. It is not hard.

High season in Spain is Christmas and Easter plus Saturdays, Sundays and holidays.

Ski school

There are few places which are such a perfect place to learn to ski. The Spanish tempcament makes for great initial instruction and most of the mountain can be handled by beginners after three or four days of instruction. The Spanish Ski School (tel. 48.01.68 or 48.05.11) has offices in the main square of the town and at Borreguiles near the middle station of the cable car. The ski school has 125 instructors. Approximately 30 speak English.

Individual lessons during high season, cost Pts. 2400 per hour for one or two students; and Pts. 2900 per hour for three or four students. During middle and low season the prices are Pts. 2000 for one or two, and Pts.2500 for three or four skiers.

Group lessons during high season, run Pts. 10000 for one week of three-hour classes each day. During low season the rates drop to Pts. 6900 for the one-week class. Children's classes are Pts. 8000 in high season; and Pts. 5500 during low season.

Lift tickets

These are the high season prices. Low season is about 12 percent less expensive. Children with birthdays in 1975 or later get about a 30 percent reduction.

One day	Pts. 1850
Two days	Pts. 3700
Six days	Pts. 10500

Accommodation

All the hotels are relatively new. Add 12% value added tax to each of these rates.

The telephone prefix for the resort is 958 from Spain and 58 from outside Spain.

Hotel Melia, Sierra Nevada (tel.48.04.00; telex: 78507)—Daily room rates of Pts. 13,550 per double room with breakfast.

Hotel Melia Solynieve (tel. 48.03.00)—Daily rate for double is Pts. 8200-8550.

Hotel Nevasur (tel. 48.03.65)—Normal rate: Pts.5050-5350 with breakfast.

Hotel Telecabina (tel. 48.03.65)—Normal rate: Pts.4800 (B&B).

Apartments

A typical apartment per week for two persons will cost Pts. 31,900 during the middle season. A four-person apartment will cost Pts. 53,500 and a six person apartment will run Pts. 70750.

Dining

This tiny village has plenty of restaurants. That's an indication of the importance the Spanish put on a good meal. Pradollano, Antorcha, Carinvela, Alcazaba and Pepe Reyes all serve traditional Spanish fare. For French food try Pourquios Pas. Cunini has excellent fish dishes and Mama Rosa and Fromagerie serve up Italian cooking.

On the slopes the best place to head for lunch is Restaurant Nevasol near the middle station at Borreguiles.

Nightlife

This is a small place. You should be able to find out if anything is going on rather quickly. For checking out the scene after skiing, McClarens has a pub atmosphere and live music. Or try Lemon, Don Paco or Crescendo. The leading disco in town is La Chimenea—it usually has a good crowd every night.

Child care

The Hotel Melia has a kindergarten and there is another on the mountain. The mountain kindergarten is open from 10 a.m.

to 4 p.m. and costs Pts. 650 per hour or Pts. 3700 per day. The ski school will take children from six years to twelve for classes.

Getting there

From Granada there is only one road. By car there is no problem and that is the recommended transport. Buses leave Granada each morning at 9 a.m. and return at 5 p.m.—the fare is Pts. 300. On Friday, Saturday and Sunday for visitors who want to see beautiful Granada, there are buses from Sierra Nevada to Granada at 11 a.m. and return busses to the mountain at 4 p.m.

A taxi from Granada to the resort will cost about Pts. 3500.

Other activities

The location is what makes this resort so special. Within an hour you can reach Granada and have a chance to see the fabulous Alhambra and the old center of the city. Malaga is only about two hours away and the actual Costa del Sol, with white towns, such as Salobrena, clutching small hilltops, is even closer. Excursions can be made to Jaen with its massive cathedral and Moorish baths, or Gaudix and Purullena with their troglodyte villages and nearby Lacalahorra castle where you will have to find the gate keeper in the town below the castle before heading up the hill.

Tourist information

The reservation center and information office has a 24-hour telephone line: (958) 48.01.53.

The provincial tourist office in Granada has responsibility for the resort. Write Patronato Provincial de Turismo de Granada, Pl. Mariana Pineda, 8- 3, 18009 Granada, Spain (tel. 958-22.35.27).

In the USA contact the National Tourist Office of Spain, 665 Fifth Avenue, New York, NY 10022; tel. (212) 759-8822.

Andorra

The 1000-year-old principality of Andorra offers an awesome adventure of natural scenery set in a range of the fabled Pyrenees Mountains. A side benefit of the mountain landscape is good intermediate skiing which awaits the visitor with the time and the driving nerve to get to it.

Andorra is a first class excursion, a trip through the mountains which is nearly as exciting as the actual skiing you'll do once you get there. The country is about 90 square miles or 1.5 times larger than England's Isle of Wight. It is ringed by 65 peaks reaching to 10,000-feet. These snow-capped summits isolate the principality from France and Spain and from the pressing uncertainties of the 20th century. Andorra has no standing army and only a small police force.

Andorra is a long way from anywhere, about four hours drive from Barcelona and 15 hours (1,285 kilometers) from central Germany. Getting there is the rub although it's only the last three hours plus of driving which is difficult. Once you have negotiated the climb up into 3000 meter range, crossed Col de Puymont, at 2,400 meters, the highest pass in the Pyrenees and come down into Andorra La Vella, capital of the country, there is a feeling of accomplishment, as if you've reached a place where few travel in winter. Expectations are to see something unique, a blend of 1000 years of Spanish and Franch culture in a landlocked little place that time brushes only gently while elsewhere it rushes at a headlong pace.

Forget that thought. It disappears as soon as you get stuck in a traffic jam that would do Frankfurt or Madrid proud. Perhaps the drivers who never made it to La Vella, those whose crashed vehicles you passed in ravines, or over the side of hairpin curves and in rocky river bottoms, had a bit of good luck mixed with the bad. They didn't have to drive into the city expecting Pyrenees exotica, only to find the golden arches casting a dark shadow across the valley. Not only is there a Big Mac waiting for the traveler, but Best of Buck Owens cassettes and 30-minute A-Team segments of Mr. T and Murdoch swapping insults in Catalan, the local language.

There is a seemingly endless line of rather dirty looking shops, competing for the dollars of tourists, primarily Spanish, who fuel the economy of this mountain-rich, land-poor country. Skiing is the major winter sports activity and the five resorts are somewhere between average and good compared to the better Swiss, French or Austrian alpine stations. It's better skiing than Garmisch, inferior to St. Anton, hopelessly outclassed by Verbier.

Where to ski

The best skiing is at El Tarter/Soldeu and Pal. Both are within 25 minutes of downtown Andorra La Vella. El Tarter and Soldeu interconnect so park your car in the big lot at El Tarter and ride the chair up. In either place lock your car and keep valuables out of sight. Andorra seems to have a deserved reputation for sticky fingered thieves who prey on visitors.

El Tarter-Soldeu is intermediate with a touch of black. The finest runs are the linked mogul fields which seem to go on for miles down to the El Tartar chair.

Pal is the most picturesque of the three, situated above the tiny village of the same name. Everyone skis from the central station, a beautiful stone complex with chairs and poma lifts leading in. On top there are fine runs and two superior mogul fields from the Pic del Cubil summit.

A word of warning about the poma lifts, particularly those at Pal: They are brutal, literally snatching you off the ground when they startup. Take the chairlift when possible. Grau Roig/Pas de la Casa, is the most distant of the slopes, over half an hour by car. The runs are good and the lift system rivals Soldeu/El Tartar for number of ways up the mountain. All areas are subject to extremely high winds.

Mountain rating

Slopes are overwhelmingly intermediate. Soldeu has an excellent beginner area at the top of the first chair, but it is inconvenient to go up from Soldeu because there's a minimun 10-minute walk in ski boots before you reach the first chair.

Ski school

The school does a booming business with French, English and Spanish the three most popular languages for instruction. Pal is the best place for lessons because of the central station where all beginners start and where most of the lifts feed, thus ensuring that everyone in a group will come back together several times during the day.

Soldeu has over 75 instructors in high season and Pal and Grau Roig have about 50 each.

Individual lessons

for 1 hours 92 French francs FF
for each additonal person 20 FF
for 1 day 400 FF

Group lessons

for one day 96 FF
for three days 230 FF
for our days 275 FF
for five days 362 FF

Lift tickets

Despite the closeness of the resorts there is no combined lift ticket, a definite weakness for such a small skiing resort.

Prices at Soldeu are average for the region and are listed for high season. Low season is approximately 10 percent less. All weekend days are considered high season.

one-half day (from 1 p.m.) 62 FF
one day 86 FF
two days 156 FF
three days 234 FF
four days 296 FF

For each additional day add 74 FF. A passport-size photo is required for four or more days.

Accommodations

The city has good hotels but the streets are clogged with traffic, filled with stifling exhaust fumes and generally dirty. Look for a place out of the city on the way to the mountains. The Guillem, in Encamp, about 10 minutes from La Vella and 15 minutes from Soldeu, is modern and clean and quiet, one minute from the main road to the mountain. Daily rates are FF 188.The staff members speak almost no English. Tel. 32133.

To get on the mountain quickly, Parador Canaro at 1,700 meters in Soldeu, tel. 51046, will meet your needs. Daily rate is about 185 FF. For half pension add approximately 160 FF daily. The best mountain hotel we visited was Hostel St. Pere (tel. 51087), a superb little place across from the lifts in El Tartar. They only have half a dozen rooms from about 300 FF per day.

In La Vella the Andorra Palace (tel. 21072) and Andorra Center (tel. 24999) are full-service hotels with daily rates starting at 250 FF. The Eden Roc (tel. 21000), at FF425 for a double, is the most expensive of the group. The President (tel. 22922) has a less central location for shopping. Rates start at 240 FF. The annex to the President is not as well decorated but quieter, one block off the main street of Andorra.

The City Tourist Office, located one level below the main square, the Place of the People, will assist with directions and provide a map showing the location and telephone number of the local hotels. There is also a free guide to hotels and restaurants available from the Tourist Office.

Apartments

There are a substantial number of apartments available in the city and in towns near the slopes. The Tourist Office maintains a lot of apartments. In addition, the agencies listed below can book an apartment for you at a daily rate substantially below hotel prices.

Dining

Spanish customs apply with late meal hours in most places. To dine before 8 p.m. is boorish and around 10 p.m. is best. The best place to get true Catalan specialties is Hostel Calones (tel. 21312). They also have 26 rooms. The finest restaurant in the country is 1900, a deluxe establishment at the end of La Valla where the town meets Escaldes.

Nightlife

The base après-ski atmosphere is right on the slopes in the pubs that dot the ski towns. The biggest favorite with the English-speaking groups, especially the British, is El Duc, in Solde.

After the sun goes down, the action is in La Vella where Feelings, a disco adjacent to the President Hotel, is usually filled. Another is Pacha, near the Place of the People. Festa, nearer the river, is also a popular evening spot. But the best of the discos is Ambit, at Erts, about 20 minutes away near La Massala.

Because of the late closing and meal hours Andorra La Vella hardly springs into action before 10:30 or 11.

Child care

Both ski lessons and kindergarten are offered for children at the resorts. At Soldeu, for example, a five-day ski program for children under 10 is 331 FF. The kindergarten is 48 FF for one three-hour morning or afternoon session.

Five days of kindergarten care for 6 hours daily is 315 FF.

Getting There

Most convenient is to fly to Barcelona and take a special mountain taxi which will cost about $25 per person. If you are driving from Barcelona the trip is about 3 ½ hours. Coming in by car from Perpignan in France, the time is about the same through the other side of the Pyrenees. If you are squeamish about mountain driving on ice and snow, don't bring a car.

Other Activities

Andorra in winter is limited. Shopping is the chief attraction because of its customs free status. Prices on electronic items and clothing are often marked down substantially. But shop carefully because there's a lot of junk crowding the store windows.

The Pyrenees department store, associated with the Printemps stores in France, is a great place to start your shopping. It's near the center of town about a block from the tourist office.

Tourist Information

The Tourist Office (tel. 29345) is in the municipal center one level below the Place of the People. Coming in to town keep following the signs for Andorra La Vella city center.

Yugoslavia

Yugoslavia has for years had a strong skiing tradition. But, it was only with the 1984 Winter Olympics that the country became known as a real skier's destination.

In the north the Alps spill over from Italy and Austria. It is this part of Yugoslavia which has the real skiing tradition. Sarajevo, the site of the 1984 Winter Olympics, was virtually non-existent as a ski resort before the Olympic Games. Since then facilities have been developed at an accelerating pace. And three hours south of Belgrade, the Yugoslavs are developing a new resort Kopaonik virtually from scratch.

Ski Europe traveled Yugoslavia to see what has developed in this budget holiday ski arena. We cover Kranjska Gora and the resorts of Sarajevo in detail and offer some observations on the still developing resort of Kopaonik.

Note: Prices are not consistently in Yugoslav Dinars—Most are in German Marks (DM) or in dollars and sterling since Yugoslavia's pricing for non-Yugoslavs has been formulated in foreign currencies.

Observations on Kopaonik
Accommodation

This resort set in a natural forest in the rolling hills of southern Yugoslavia has been created where only pine trees stood watch. Five new hotels have been built. The Baciste and the Srebrnac are at either end of the area. Both are a long walk from the center of Kopaonik. They both have good facilities and both have self-contained evening entertainment with dancing and snacks. The "center" of Kopaonik is a group of very new tourist apartments and three hotels. When visiting the resort last year the apartments were still under construction but looked very promising. This tourist complex will feature an open market in the courtyard and dozens of small stores will ring the courtyard as well. The Hotel Karavan is perhaps the best and most centrally located in the resort.

The Skiing

Some 20 lifts open lots of ski area. The accent is on beginner and intermediate. Though there is a section suitable for experts, the offerings are meagre. Beginners should have a field day and intermediates will have lots of room to cruise.

The Verdict

A good resort for groups that get along well with each other. There is no life outside the hotels and apartment complex. Beginners will be happy, intermediates should leave smiling, experts will wonder why they didn't spend the extra money and go to really ski.

Kranjska Gora

This is the largest ski resort in the northern Yugoslavian republic of Slovenija. Tucked tightly against the Italian border to the west and the Austrian border to the north, Kranjska Gora is an alpine resort in every sense of the word.

The town, clustered around the old onion-domed Cerkev church, is small—a ten-minute walk is all it takes to wander from one end to the other. Every year this resort hosts one of the first World Cup races of the circuit. Though its altitude is low (1215-1825 meters) and most of the runs relatively short, skiing can be enjoyable, demanding and far-ranging with an interconnected lift system stretching from the town center to nearby Podkoren and Planica.

Where to ski

The ski area of Kranjska Gora easily breaks into beginner, intermediate and expert sections. The only difficulty for those in advanced-beginner levels or lower-intermediate status is the shift from the mild, beginner slopes outside the Kranjska Gora hotels to the true intermediate slopes in the Planica section. Between these two sides of the ski area lie the FIS Slalom and Giant Slalom courses. Any traverse requires negotiating several steep drops which will either offer a good test of skiing skills or of the waterproofing of your ski suits. Perhaps the best solution is to take the free shuttle bus from Kranjska Gora to the base of the Podkoren/Planica lifts.

For experts the trails are very limited but testing. The slalom and giant slalom courses drop through the center of the area. Off-piste there is some very tight, very steep tree skiing. The championship runs are served by a very slow single-chairlift (promised to be upgraded by a double-chair this season), an-

KRANJSKA GORA

HOTEL LEK
YUGOTOURS Holiday Club
ALPINA HOTEL
DISCO CLUB
#1 CAFE
Café Pinki
RESTAURANT BOR
SKI SCHOOL
RESTAURANT PINO
HOTEL PRISANK
HOTEL LARIX
PIZZERIA
KOMPAS Office
MIKI Rest.
MARKET
POST OFFICE PIZZA
SKI RENTALS
APPARTMENTS FLATS
KOMPAS HOTEL

← LJUBLIANA

TO AUSTRIA →
TO ITALY

other single chairlift linking central Kranjska Gora with the FIS, and a button-life. The lifts are slow, but with almost no waiting time in the area during weekdays the total time to get up to the starting point of the slalom run is just over ten minutes.

Mountain rating

Kranjska Gora has the potential to be an excellent overall resort with some new lift construction. But for the moment, tour operators bill Kranjska Gora as one of the best places to learn to ski. The mild slopes are just outside most of the hotels. The ski school, according to reports from legions of beginners, is very good with good English-speaking instructors.

The beginner lifts are extensive and crowded with ski school students. The absolute baby slopes are cordoned off to all except budding skiers learning the basics in peace. Tourist officials estimate that over 70% of the current visitors are beginners.

The most challenging sections of the mountain are empty. But, unfortunately, other than for the FIS slalom and giant slalom, it is poorly developed and poorly serviced by lifts. There are plans to extend the area and replace all single-chairs with double-or triple-chairlifts. But, I make no promises. Unless you hear differently, plan on the same slow lifts.

Experts might be tempted to stay in Podkoren within easy reach of the expert slopes. However, the nightlife is non-existant and facilities relatively underdeveloped.

Ski school

The ski school specializes in teaching beginners. If you are an expert and want a lesson in off-piste or racing on the FIS runs, the instructors almost fight to get out and ski hard.

There are two ski schools in town with similar prices: Gorenjks and Kompas. Kompas seems to do more work with English-speakers.

Group lessons for five days (2 hours/day) cost DM 62. Private lessons (one hour): one person—DM 25/person; two persons —DM 20/person; three persons—DM 15/person; four persons—DM 10/person.

Sign up in your hotel or with your tour guides. The school

assembly area is located behind the Hotel Prisank and Hotel Larix. Currently there is no children's ski school.

Lift tickets

If you come with a group tour contact the group leader to get tickets. Some tickets require photos, some require payment in foreign currency, some you can only buy with a Yugoslav ID card. Current rates for non-Yugoslavs are: one day—Dinars 6000; three days—DM 54; six days—DM 106; seven days—DM 120; 13 days—DM 203; 14 days—DM 215.

For those with a car there is also the possibility to purchase a special "Ski 3 Regions" international ski pass covering lifts in Italy and Austria as well as Yogoslavia. The pass is only sold by the week for DM 140 per six skiing days out of seven, allowing a day for bad weather or rest. This ticket offers 76 drag lifts, 23 chairlifts and six cablecars in nine different resorts. It's only available from hotels in Yugoslavia.

The three-country pass sounds appealing and makes a good souvenir but skiers are limited to only two days of skiing outside Yugoslavia. It may be less expensive to buy a four-day pass for Kranjska Gora, then purchase a day pass for the other resorts you visit. Buying your lift passes in this way offers more flexibility and insurance against bad weather.

Accommodation

Kranjska Gora has a strong tradition of hoteliers and tourism which shows in their hotel organization and staff. In almost all cases the least expensive lodging arrangements are made through a tour agency such as Yugotours. These arrangements can be made for "ground-only" eliminating the need to include airfare in the price.

The hotels are listed below with the current DM prices per person per day for half-board based on double occupancy from early January to mid-March

Kompas—DM 69; **Larix**—DM 68; **Hotel Lek**—DM 68. These three hotels have the best facilities in town including pool, sauna, discos, bars and bowling alleys. The Larix is a bit closer to the slopes, but the Kompas has better après ski and the Lek has the Holiday Club.

Hotel Alpina—DM 57. Almost as good as the Kompas and Larix but is a bit of a walk from the town center.

Prisank—DM 53. Excellent rooms and food, also the closest hotel to the ski school. Its only limitation is no pool or sauna.

The **Kranjska Gora** and **Pension Zrenjanin** are not in most tour programs. They offer good lodging for budget-conscious skiers who come into town on their own. Expect to pay around DM 50 per night.

If you arrive or plan to arrive without a group call Kompas Agency (064) 88437 to make reservations.

Apartments

These are a new addition to Kranjska Gora. The main new apartments in town are the "Apartments Gorenjka." These apartments are located in the center of town. Each apartment sleeps from four to six very comfortably. Expect to pay DM 120 per day per apartment.

The tiny dorf of Podkoren is just two kilometers from Kranjska Gora. Here the Family Sedej has restored an old farmhouse and turned it into apartments. The house name is "Apartment Serc." Expect to pay about DM 21/person per day. This small family-run operation makes an extra effort to provide a traditional Slovenjan experience for their guests. Homemade "Ustek," a herbal schnapps is served in the bar to fight the chills when the guests come back from the slopes. Reservations can be made by calling Andrej or Irena Sedej directly at (064) 88161 (they both speak excellent English or call Kompas Agency at (064) 88437.

Dining

Even with half-board arrangements, make an effort to experience the Yugoslavian cuisine. Kranjska Gora offers a wide range of restaurants.

Restaurant Miki is best known for fish dishes. **Restaurant Milka**, about a 15-minute walk into the mountains has good steaks. Next door on a tiny lake is **Restaurant Jasna**. **Restaurant Bor** offers traditional food and is located just behind Hotel Prisank.

For my money the best pizza in town is from **Pizzeria Kom-**

pas adjacent to the hotel of the same name. Others rave about pizza from **Pizzeria Pino** in the center of town.

The restaurant at the top of Vitranc is not noted for its food, but does provide a beautiful view and great spring sunbathing when the weather is clear.

Nightlife

Kranjska Gora is not in the running for nightlife capital of Europe, but it does provide a healthy environment for night entertainment.

The main hotels all have discos or live bands which play music until at least 2 a.m. Then, if people are still dancing the bars find a way to stay open a bit longer. The Kompas Nightbar can be fun. Only a few children hang out early in the evening. The disco in the Larix gets overrun with kids early in the night and they seem to linger until midnight and often later.

The only independent disco is the "Club" down in the center of town. It normally has the best action beginning at about eleven p.m.

For an earlier rendevous try the Cafe No. 1 near the Prisank.

Yugotours has organized a Holiday Club in the basement of the Hotel Lek. It offers a good English-speaking crowd, relatively inexpensive beer, no cover charge, and an English DJ called Anthony responsible for making sure the guests have fun. This means plenty of contests and games which force people to meet one another.

Child care

Here Kranjska Gora fails. There is no organized children's kindergarten, nor is there an organized nursery. If tourists are in a group of six or more, special arrangements will be made for children.

Other activities

There are numerous organized tours to surrounding areas. Tours to Nassfeld in Austria for a day of good intermediate/advanced skiing are organized for DM 23; and into Italy to Sella Nevea for DM 28. Ski passes are not included in these prices.

Venice is three and a half hours away and day tours cost DM 83. Tarvisio tours, also in Italy, cost DM 20.

Visits to the Caves of Postojna and the city of Ljubljana take a full day and cost DM 65.

Tourits information

There is an official tourist office in the shopping center across from the Larix Hotel. Telephone is (064) 88768.

The best information is from the tour representatives and from the tourist information boards set up in the hotel lobbies.

Sarajevo

This city has long been one of the major cultural crossroads —between Turkish and Austrian Empires, between Eastern and Western Roman Empires, and between Moslem, Jewish and Christian religions. Only since the 1984 Winter Olympics has it been considered a ski resort. Virtually all its resort facilities have been constructed in the last four years. Sarajevo, the city itself, is not a resort—the skiing is done at two centers both about 30 kilometers from the town. Jahorina at an altitude of 5478 feet was the venue of the women's downhill 1984 Olympic events. Bjelasnica, 27 kms to the northwest with an altitude of 4134 feet, was the site of the men's downhill events.

Jahorina has been better developed in terms of hotels and lifts than Bjelasnica. It has four excellent hotels and normally enjoys good weather.

Bjelasnica faces much more severe weather and in January and early-February is often partially closed due to storms and high winds. The skiing here is best planned in late February or March if at all possible. The one international-level hotel is located approximately four kilometers from the slopes. Frequent bus service shuttles skiers to the lifts.

Where to ski

Jahorina, with eleven lifts, offers about two dozen short runs. This is not a cruiser's paradise. With the main hotels to your back, the most challenging and the longest runs are to the far left.

Bjelasnica which looks smaller on the few brochure lift maps is actually a far more challenging mountain for intermediate and expert skiers. The runs are much longer and the verticle drop significantly greater than Jahorina. If you enjoy a challenging cruise, when the weather is good, this is a beautiful mountain.

All in all though, Jahorina has the best support facilities and far better overall weather. Plan to stay in Jahorina and take a couple of daytrips to Bjelasnica for more demanding skiing.

Cross-country—Mt. Igman, attached to the Bjelasnica area, has over 50 kms of prepared trails. Jahorina has none.

Mountain rating

Jahorina will keep any intermediate or beginner happy for a week. The expert can find some real challenges, but they are short and limited. Beginners have no choice—head for Jahorina.

Bjelasnica is a great mountain but with limited facilities and the drawback that it really isn't suitable for beginners or lower-intermediates.

Ski school and Lift tickets

Ski school for five days, 2 hrs/day, will cost about $55 according to the U.S. brochure and £22.50 according to the British brochure. Lift tickets good for both Jahorina and Bjelasnica for six days cost $30 or £21.

Accommodation

The best single hotel is the Hotel Igman in Bjelasnica. It is isolated and is therefore forced to be self-contained. In Jahorina the three main hotels are close to each other. The Bistrica offers the most facilities including a pool and bowling alley. The Jahorina and the Kosuta are also nice but with no pool. The Jahorina does boast the only after-midnight disco and a mediocre pizzeria. The Hotel Vucko about three kilometers down the mountain has only 24 beds and was the lodge of the King of Sweden during the Olympic Games. It offers a quiet, exclusive hotel with great restaurant and lifts only a few steps from the lodge. All hotels in Jahorina are very convenient to the lifts.

Nightlife

After nine, music with a live band starts in the Hotel Bistrica. This is the place to be until midnight when the disco in the Hotel Jahorina revs up.

The Bistrica is a good time with dance contests and plenty of room to move. The disco is smokey and packed shoulder to shoulder most of the time . . . but it is the only late night game in the resort. The Jahorina also has a small casino where you may win or lose big money.

Child care

Jahorina has a children's ski school and a kindergarten. Bjelasnica has no facilities for child care.

Other activities

There is a bobsled run available on the Olympic course on which amateurs can ride. Your hotel can make arrangements.

Try the pool and kegelbahn (bowling alley) in the Hotel Bistrica.

The major non-skiing activity is a visit to Sarajevo which is a fascinating city. Buses depart both resorts four times a day for Sarajevo and tour groups make the city tour regularly. A walk through the old town is a step into a middle-eastern world. The dozens of mosques are leftovers from the days of Turkish rule when it was decreed that there should be one mosque for every 40 houses. Adjacent, the Turkish bazaar and the imperial buildings of the Austrians rise in stark contrast.

Visit the corner where the Archduke was assassinated, starting the first world war. Then head for the covered market which has been restored with traditional stalls. Around the corner visit the Gazi-Husrevbeg Mosque and then head down the walking street to Baśćarśija. Just off Marshall Tito street make sure to visit the Old Serbian Orthodox church with its priceless icons.

If you want a snack, try Cevapćići with drinkable yoghurt at "Cevapćiniza Ismet Kapitanović" on Prote Bakovića 12. For a more substantial meal try "Morića-han" on Saraći 77, or "Daire" at Halsći 5. Both are in restored buildings in the center of the old town.

Tourist information

The Tourist Office is located on Marshall Tito street next to the Catholic church.

In the resorts check the tour group information boards for all other information, or ask your group leader.

Bulgaria Pamporovo and Borovets

In the far south of Eastern Europe tucked between the Romania, the Black Sea, Greece and Yugoslavia lies Bulgaria. For years considered the most secretive and xenophobic nation in Europe, Bulgaria has surprisingly pursued a steady increase in tourism and has developed one of Eastern Europe's best tourism infrastructures. Though individual tourism is difficult and infrequent, the group business is well-organized, with ever-improving hotels, excellent guides and efficient bus transfers. Bulgaria has two well-developed ski centers—Borovets and Pamporovo. Though some speak of Vitosha as a resort, it really is only a weekend ski mountain within a 20-minute drive of Sofia. If someone is looking for only skiing and lots of it, Bulgaria can not really be recommended. Though the slopes are adequate for day or weekend skiing, there is not enough to justify a week-long ski vacation for other than lower intermediates and beginners. But, if one is searching for a total experience, Bulgaria offers a vacation which will not be soon forgotten. Besides the "experience," Bulgaria does have one of the best ski packages for beginners with most instructors speaking excellent English, and Bulgaria is the absolute bargain capital of European skiing. There may be no better place to learn how to ski on the cheap.

Bulgarian tourism is also phenomenally international with a mix of cultures seldom found in Western Europe. During my first night in Borovets, there were groups from Britain, Germany, Spain, and Holland, plus from Leningrad and Murmansk and well as Bulgarians. There was no common language, but the dancing, laughter and smiles were contagious. The Bulgarians also keep you busy day and night. If you claim boredom on this vacation, it is only because you didn't take advantage of the opportunities. One night might be packed with Bulgarian folklore, the next spent sampling fifty or sixty Bulgarian dishes at a special cuisine night. Then head out by horse-drawn sleigh to a hunter's lodge where lamb is roasted on a spit, or visit a family where tourists in small groups can enjoy real Bulgarian home-cooked meals. If the skiing is not overly demanding, break for a day and visit the famous Rila Monastery, Sofia or Plovdiv. These "extras" normally cost $10-12 or $7-8.

Within Bulgaria the tourist world contrasts boldly with everyday lifestyles. The cities seem stuck in the mid-1960's timewarp—car models haven't changed, trucks look like throwbacks to the 50's, and clothing is functional. The new hotels in the resorts, however, are firmly planted in the 1980's—restaurants top TV towers, bowling alleys bustle, guests splash in indoor swimming pools, and bright ski fashions, even worn by Soviet visitors, adorn the slopes. In the towns there is not much person to person contact, but in resorts, where many Bulgarians speak English, the locals and tourists interact.

NOTE: The black market for currency is widespread in Bulgarian resorts with rates up to four times better than the official exchange. You will be approached to exchange money by the chambermaids, elevator attendants, waiters, ski instructors, bus drivers and others. Though I have heard no recent horror stories about tourists being carried off to prison for illegal money exchange, the possiblity is real. If you do get caught, there is little that can be done. **BE CAREFUL.**

The amount of money any tourist needs to exchange during a group tour is limited. The excursions and purchases at the "Corecom" stores must be paid for in sterling, dollars, travellers cheques, any other convertible currency or credit cards. Changing money through Balkan-Tourist will allow an exchange bonus designed to limit the black market. When your money is exchanged you will receive a receipt. Keep it. You will need it to change your money back before you leave Bulgaria.

One other note: The duty-free store in the Sofia airport is perhaps the least expensive I have visited.

Passports and Visas

Passports are necessary. Anyone ariving with a group of six or more, does not need a visa. If you plan to travel individually contact the Bulgarian Embassy in Washington D.C., Toronto, Canada or London. Balkan-Tourist will also assist.

You will be given a white visa card which you must keep with you during your travels through Bulgaria. This card is, in effect, an internal passport for Bulgaria and must be stamped by each hotel you visit. It then serves as your exit card when ready to leave the country.

Borovets

Borovets is only about 50 miles south of Sofia. The skiing in Borovets is split between Sitnjakovo sector rising directly in front of the new Hotel Rila, and the Jastrebets area, reached by a 20 minute ride on a three-plus-mile-long gondola. Sitnjakovo's runs are for lower intermediates and beginners. Be prepared to do a bit of pushing to make it from one valley to the next. The last quarter of the run splits into four. The area is great for beginners looking for confidence or for lower intermediates who are practicing technique, but any expert will make two runs and probably have little interest in repeating the experience unless with a good-time group.

The Jastrebets sector provides the longest runs and is reached by a very long gondola. The distance is over three miles and the ride takes 20 minutes. The gondola is about a three minute walk from the Hotel Rila and next to the Ela Hotel. The transfer to the five parallel lifts serving the slope behind Jastrebets requires a bit of a walk. These five parallel button lifts offer a series of short intermediate runs which have been cut through tough mountain brush. The furthest lift is naturally the least crowded. The only way to reach it is by working across all lifts, but a skier can ski down the ridge past the five lifts to return to the gondola upperstation. A climb over the peak is necessary before heading down the main slope into town. The long, three- and four-mile runs back into the resort are the highpoint of Borovets.

Accommodation The French-built Rila, Borovets' newest hotel, is close to the lifts but has no disco or pool. Hotel Breza, Hotel Bor and Hotel Ela all get good comments from guests. The Bor is the most desirable after the Rila, it is also the best from a nightlife point of view. The Hotel Sarnokov, being built by a Polish group, has been "almost finished" for several years. I would suggest that if it shows up in a tourist brochure it should be avoided. Give at least a year to get really finished and to get the problems worked out.

The major difference between Borovets and Pamporovo is that the former is much more spread out. This is true of the ski runs and the hotels. From the Rila to the Hotel Bor is a good ten-minute walk, while in Pamporovo all hotels are clustered together and connected by underground passageways. Pamporovo also has major resort-wide get togethers which are not duplicated in Borovets where the tours groups remain more autonomous.

Nightlife There are discos in the Hotel Mura and Hotel Mousala. There is also a live band playing everything from rock and roll to polka music in the basement of the Hotel Bor. After the discos close head to the wine bar under the tourist information office across the parking lot from the Hotel Bor.

Pamporovo

Pamporovo is a more tightly knit resort than Borovets. In Borovets there are woods for walking between the hotels and even the skiing is somewhat spread out. In Pamporovo the hotels are clustered and the skiing area is compact but, the hotels are about a 20-minute walk from the slopes. Shuttle buses run skiers back and forth between the hotels and lifts. There is also a ski storage area at the base of the lift system which means no one need carry equipment back to the hotel.

Pamporovo is an excellent resort for an intermediate who wants to have time to practice and improve on more challanging steeps. It also has excellent nursery slopes for the beginners and plenty of slopes for the average skier to make major improvements during a week of lessons. There are some challanges for experts. Once again, as in Borovets, this is not a resort for advanced intermediates and experts who expect to cruise.

There is a beautiful view from the TV tower at the top of the mountain. The entrance fee is redeemable against purchases in the cafe.

Accommodation

The lead hotel especially for English-speaking groups, is the Perelik. Pamporovo has more tourist facilities completed than Borovets with an indoor pool in the Perelik and another in the nearby Hotel Smolyan, plus a bowling alley in the Perelik. The underground connections between the hotels also make the nightlife circuit more accessible.

Ski school, Lift tickets, etc.

Ski School

For beginners and lower level intermediates this is an excellent school. The instructors speak excellent English and the slopes lend themselves to beginners and lower intermediates. The prices for ski lessons are in the range of $35 or $24 per week, or $66 (£44) per two-week period. Children's lessons cost $22 (£15) per week and $45 (£29).

Lift tickets: Six days—$27 (£18); 13 days—$48 (£35). For children prices are $22 (£15) for six days and $44 (£29) for 13 days.

Equipment rentals

The equipment provided by the Bulgarian resorts is actually excellent. But, make sure the ski shop prepares your skis before you walk off with them. I made that mistake, arriving at the top of the lift and found that my skis refused to slide. The bottoms looked as if they had been spread with a hair-growing elixer. It turned out to be a very unpleasant and difficult run down the mountain before I could get the skis tuned. I also suggest that you do a self-test to insure that you can twist out of your binding—there is virtually no binding check unless you ask specifically for one.

Both resorts have excellent **child care facilities.** Check with your group leader for specifics.

Tourist information

All tours into Bulgaria are controlled through Balkan-Tourist. Even independent operators work in conjunction with Balkan-Tourist which in Britain and the U.S.A. also acts as the national tourist office of Bulgaria.

In Britain contact: Balkan Holidays Limited, Sofia House, 19 Conduit Street, London W1R 9TD; administration telephone: (01) 491 4499, bookings telephone: (01) 493 8612; tlelx: 262923.

In the United States: Balkan Holidays/USA/Ltd., 161 East 81st Street, New York, NY 10028; tel. (212) 722-1110 or 722-7626; telex: 429767.

National Tourist Offices

Austria National Tourist Office

500 Fifth Ave.
New York, NY 10110
(212) 944-6880

500 N. Michigan Ave.
Chicago, IL 60611
(312) 644-5556

11601 Wilshire Blvd.
Los Angeles, CA 90025
(213) 477-3332

2 Bloor St. East, Suite 3330
Toronto, Canada
(416) 593-4717

30 St. George Street
London W1R 9FA
01-629-0461

Austrian snow reports in USA: From mid-December to early April, 24 hours per day: East Coast (212) 944-6917, West Coast: (213) 479-0940.

Swiss National Tourist Office

608 Fifth Ave.
New York, NY 10020
(212) 757-5944

104 S. Michigan Ave.
Chicago, IL 60603
(312) 641-0050

250 Stockton St.
San Francisco, CA 94108
(415) 362-2260

Commerce Ct. Postal Station
Suite 2015, Commerce Ct.
West
Toronto, Canada
(416) 868-0584

Swiss Center, 1 New Coventry St.
London, W1V 8EE
01-734-1921

National Tourist Office of Spain

665 Fifth Avenue
New York, NY 10022
(212) 729-8822

57 St. James's Street
London SW1A 1LD
01-499-0901

Italian Government Tourist Office (E.N.I.T.)

630 Fifth Avenue
New York, NY 10111
(212) 245-4822

360 Post St. #801
San Francisco, CA 94108
(415) 392-6206

3 Place Ville Marie
Montréal, Canada
(514) 866-7667

1 Princess Street
London W1R 7RA
01-408-1254

French Government Tourist Office

610 Fifth Avenue
New York, NY 10020
(212) 757-1125

9401 Wilshire Blvd. #840
Beverly Hills, CA 90212
(213) 271-6665

Box 8, 1 Dundas St. West
Toronto, Canada
(416) 593-4717

178 Picadilly
London W1V 0AL
01-491-7622

German National Tourist Office

747 Third Avenue
New York, NY 10017
(212) 308-3300

444 S. Flower St. #2230
Los Angeles, CA 90071
(213) 688-7332

61 Conduit Street
London W1R 0EN
01-734-2600

Balkan Holidays

161 East 86th St.
New York, NY 10028
(212) 722-1110

Sofia House, 19 Conduit St.
London W1R 9TD
01-491-4499

Yugotours

350 Fifth Ave. Suite 2901
New York, NY 10118
(212) 563-2400

3440 Wilshire Blvd. Suite 206
Los Angeles, CA 90010
(213) 383-2438

150 Regent Street
London W1R 6BB
01-734-7321

ABOUT THE AUTHORS

Charlie Leocha has lived in Europe over twenty years and has been skiing in Europe for over a decade. He is the author of *Skiing America*, an annually updated guide to America's largest resorts. He has written and edited five travel books to Europe, led tours in Europe, published a travel magazine for Americans living in Europe and written for numerous newspapers and magazines.

William Walker is a skiing journalist who has been writing and living in Germany for over fifteen years. He is coauthor of the *Escape Manual: Germany/Austria/Switzerland* and has written extensively for newspapers and magazines.